GENEALOGY AND KNOWLEDGE IN MUSLIM SOCIETIES

Exploring Muslim Contexts

Series Editor: Farouk Topan

Books in the series include

Ethnographies of Islam:
Ritual Performances and Everyday Practices
Edited by Badouin Dupret, Thomas Pierret,
Paulo Pinto *and* Kathryn Spellman-Poots

The Challenge of Pluralism:
Paradigms from Muslim Contexts
Edited by Abdou Filali-Ansary
and Sikeena Karmali Ahmed

Cosmopolitanisms in Muslim Contexts:
Perspectives from the Past
Edited by Derryl MacLean
and Sikeena Karmali Ahmed

Genealogy and Knowledge in Muslim Societies:
Understanding the Past
Edited by Sarah Bowen Savant
and Helena de Felipe

Development Models in Muslim Contexts:
Chinese, "Islamic" and Neo-liberal Alternatives
Edited by Robert Springborg

www.euppublishing.com/series/ecmc

Genealogy and Knowledge in Muslim Societies

Understanding the Past

Understanding the Past

Edited by Sarah Bowen Savant
and Helena de Felipe

EDINBURGH
University Press

IN ASSOCIATION WITH

THE AGA KHAN UNIVERSITY
INSTITUTE FOR THE STUDY OF MUSLIM CIVILISATIONS

© Editorial matter and organisation Sarah Bowen Savant
and Helena de Felipe, 2014
© The chapters, their several authors, 2014

Edinburgh University Press Ltd
The Tun – Holyrood Road
12 (2f) Jackson's Entry
Edinburgh EH8 8PJ
www.euppublishing.com

Typeset in Goudy Oldstyle by
Koinonia, Manchester and
printed and bound in Great Britain by
CPI Group (UK) Ltd, Croydon CR0 4YY

A CIP record for this book is available
from the British Library

ISBN 978 0 7486 4497 1 (hardback)
ISBN 978 0 7486 4498 8 (webready PDF)

Contents

Part Three: Genealogy as a Source for Writing History

Figures and Tables

Introduction

SARAH BOWEN SAVANT AND HELENA DE FELIPE

Genealogy has long been recognised as one of the most important and authoritative organising principles in Muslim societies. Expressions of genealogy have over the course of history taken particular forms and performed important functions in Muslim societies, so many in fact that it would be impossible to describe them comprehensively. The Prophet's family tree, including his ancestors, descendants (the *sayyids* or *sharīfs*) and adoptive clients (*mawālī*), has provided an important paradigm, underwriting dynastic arrangements, providing access to patronage and supporting power brokers and mediators. Other patterns of kinship, including tribal lineages, descent from the Companions of the Prophet or descent from Sufi saints, have conferred similar forms of opportunity and/ or prestige. Converts with family ties to other Muslims have felt a stronger sense of connection to their new faith; in the first centuries of Islam, converts even became fictively adopted into Arab tribes. Today, ideas about kinship and descent continue to shape communal and national identities in virtually every Muslim country, where they operate at the very highest levels of state and religion and where there is often a certain truth to the Arabic saying, "Nobility is genealogy. The noble in any one people shares kinship with the noble in every other people."[1]

As a result of the importance of genealogy, debates abound, the most enduring ones centring on the worthiness of particular ancestors, the legitimacy of prestige based on genealogy and the authenticity of different lineages as well as of the claims of individuals to belong to them. Several contradictory statements are attributed to the Prophet, 'Ali ibn Abi Talib and the earliest Muslims in support or denial of the social value of noble kinship, and these give a sense that during the first centuries Muslims could not agree on this question. For example, the

Prophet reportedly said, "When the noble member of a group comes to you, honour him," as well as a more circumspect remark, "A man's nobility is his piety; his manliness is his intellect; his inherited merit, his character." The family of 'Ali – the Prophet's cousin and son-in-law and, for the Shi'a, the first imam – may have become a "first family of Islam", but he, too, is remembered as devaluing pedigrees, as when he reportedly said, "There is no nobility higher than Islam." Attempts were made to balance such different values. Ibn 'Abbas (d. c. 68/687–8), another cousin of Muhammad, was cited as saying:

> [Men] differ in excellence in this world with respect to their nobility, families, ranks of authority, wealth, attractiveness, stature and eloquence. In terms of the world to come, they differ in excellence with regard to their piety and their religious conviction. For the most pious of them is the most convinced, the purest in his actions and the highest in rank.[2]

The roots of such interest may go back to the Arabian origins of Islam. In our early sources, Arabs are associated with a profound knowledge about kinship.[3] Historically, it has often been the custom in Muslim societies to identify a person by his or her genealogy through the classical *nisba*, which indicates a person's affiliations, such as to a lineage, a group, a place or a profession. Following the Arab conquests of the seventh and eighth centuries, administration of the Muslim territories required such information, most notably for the registries, or *dīwāns*, which recorded the names of those who had fought in the conquests in order to facilitate the distribution of pensions and to regulate the flow of money to and within the military settlements. Prominent families, whether among the conquerors or the conquered, often kept track of their family histories; families also grafted themselves into antique lineages, as scholars have repeatedly shown. Still, it is important to recognise that neither Arab societies nor Muslim societies more generally are unique in their fascination, nor is genealogy purely a matter of social prestige. Genealogy is, broadly speaking, a way of making sense of and shaping the past, and thus the conditions that favour a strong historical consciousness will often be favourable to an interest in genealogy. Genealogies create an aura of continuity with past times and a sense of connectivity, although an interest in them is not simply a product of a long-lived heritage and consciousness of it; rather, genealogies are often used to create a picture of continuity precisely in times of change, when a group's heritage is scattered across geography and its need to feel rooted in place and time is, as a result, most acute. As Henry James wrote of nineteenth-century New Englanders: "Only in a country where newness and brevity of tenure are the common substance of life [would] the fact of one's ancestors having lived for a hundred and seventy years in a single spot … become an element of one's morality." Or as David

Lowenthal wrote more recently as he observed the explosion of interest in gene-alogy in the United States and in Europe, "In our time, massive migration and the loss of tangible relics have stimulated interest in genealogy." During times of change, knowledge about individuals and their lineages provides concrete and convincing evidence of the endurance of social bonds as it helps to forge and affirm identities; it reaffirms and validates present attitudes and actions by affirming their connection to past ones; and it gives guidance to individuals and groups as it provides exemplars and icons of past grandeur.[4] Particularly when members of diaspora communities recall their genealogies, as often occurs, one witnesses the powerful role that representation of origins can have in holding groups together.

A link with the past provides groups not only with a place in history but also with a place in the world. Biographies focused on distinctive and exemplary indi-viduals provide paradigms of connectivity, but even more so do prosopographies, or writings about social groups such as biographical dictionaries, which feature individual members of a group and often their genealogies. Such works – that have their corollary in the "Who's Who" series of books in the English-speaking world – have a long history in Muslim contexts and offer representations of a world that is articulated around lineages and "families", including those built on blood-ties as well as those generated by shared knowledge. The oldest prosopog-raphies – often organised around professional classes, especially the 'ulama', or a geographical territory, or both – depict a dynamic cartography whose devel-opment ran parallel to the Islamic expansion. Such a world typically featured founding figures and eponyms: Companions of the Prophet, the first settlers in a territory, the earliest converts, the founders of legal schools and often legendary characters, such as the sons of Noah who populated, for example, Iranian terri-tories named for them (among them Fars, Hamadan, Isfahan and Khurasan).[5]

From the earliest of times, Muslim scholars considered knowledge about genealogy a distinct topic with its own methods. In the early 'Abbasid period, genealogists created a discipline of genealogy (*'ilm al-nasab*) and a genealogical framework meant to explain the relationships among all Arab tribes and, more broadly, the history of humanity. The *magnum opus* of Arab genealogy, the *Jamharat al-nasab*, was composed by Hisham ibn Muhammad al-Kalbi (d. 204/819 or 206/821) and cited across the Muslim world. In the eleventh century, when the Andalusi Ibn Hazm (d. 450/1058) composed his *Jamharat ansab al-'Arab*, he drew on his predecessor.[6] Members of the Prophet's family developed ways of keeping track of their numbers as well as an enforcement mechanism in the position of the *naqib al-ashraf*, the "chief of the ['Alid] nobles", whose respon-sibilities often touched on marriage and inheritance, two areas important to social cohesion. As a saying recorded in the genealogical literature goes, "Were it not for the discipline of genealogy, then judgments about inheritances would be faulty, and so too those about one's clansmen, whereas these are two pillars of the sacred law."[7] Genealogy has also been closely linked to other fields, particularly historical narrative. When in the late tenth century the bibliophile Ibn al-Nadim (d. 385/995 or 388/998) composed his *Fihrist* – one of the best records for the state of Arabic books and learning in his day – he created a separate chapter for the "*akhbārīs*, genealogists and those concerned with events".[8] In the central part of the Sahara today, the term *tawārīkh* – "histories" – refers to documents whose principal contents are genealogies, as Judith Scheele discusses in this volume (see Chapter 6).

It is not too much to say, then, that in genealogy we find a historical form of discourse linking past and present. Despite its importance, very little work has examined the field of genealogy across Muslim contexts or in different time periods, or considered what insights it may offer regarding how different societies have made sense of the past. Arab contexts and the situation of the earliest Muslims have been studied most often, but even there much work remains to be done, particularly regarding the generation, preservation and manipulation of genealogical knowledge.[9] Broadly speaking, this knowledge has taken the shape of recorded lineages, guidebooks for keepers of lineages and learned discourses about the principles of genealogical knowledge, but it is also embedded in many other forms of historical discourse, especially in the rhetorical ways that "religious" and "political" entities – among them sects, Sufi brotherhoods, dynasties and governing elites – use the past and real and imagined kinship relations to legitimise the social and political benefits they reap. Modern technology has made possible a significant commodification of this knowledge, so that what was once the preserve of specialists has become widely available and is housed in numerous works on genealogy and prosopography, in print and electronic forms. It has also facilitated the exercise of the privileges of good blood and the vetting of claims, while giving members of lineages a sense of membership in a transhistorical community that crosses national borders.

CONTENTS AND CONTEXTS

This volume originates from a 2008 international seminar organised at the Universidad de Alcalá (the University of Alcalá), Spain, by Helena de Felipe. The seminar was sponsored by the same university together with the Spanish Ministry of Science and Innovation (MICINN) (HUM2006-27941-E/FILO) and the Aga Khan University, Institute for the Study of Muslim Civilisations. Each of the nine chapters addresses a case in which genealogy has been recorded, studied, developed and formed into a resource in one or more Muslim societies. In each case, the contributor considers knowledge about kinship so as to raise questions about the past, and genealogy as a source through which the past may be contemplated and understood. Although treating a few specific contexts, the contributors aspire in three different sections to open new avenues for working with sources featuring genealogy, as well as to show the prominent place of genealogy and genealogical discourse across Muslim contexts.

The first section isolates for consideration the ways in which genealogical knowledge has been generated. From the mid- to the latter half of the ninth century CE, the Family of the Prophet (Ahl al-Bayt) developed a genealogical discipline of "*sayyid/sharīf* genealogies". As Kazuo Morimoto shows in Chapter 1, the discipline represented a development of the older study of Arab genealogies and reflected the growing dispersion of the Prophet's family. The very existence of the discipline helped to perpetuate a belief in the authenticity of genealogies; it was also put to good use by individual *sayyids* and *sharīfs*. All the same, the geographic dispersion of Muslim populations created opportunities for intruders to graft themselves onto prestigious genealogies. As Zoltán Szombathy notes in the second chapter, the more spread out a family, the better the opportunity for an impostor. Works on genealogy, such as Ibn Hazm's *Jamharat ansab al-'Arab*, could provide a resource for forgeries, as impostors, for example, could claim descent from heirless members. Chapter 3, by Zakaria Rhani, examines genealogical documents in a particular modern context – that of Morocco and specifically of the village of Zawiyat Sidi 'Abdel'aziz ben Yeffu, where a manuscript of questionable authenticity known as *al-jafriyya* has played a key role in authenticating one lineage's genealogical claims. Rhani also discusses the role of royal decrees, *ẓāhirs*, which confer and confirm economic and political privileges. These documents are paired with an "arresting mythology" that supports the image projected by members of the lineage.

The second section, "Empowering Political and Religious Elites", highlights the broader stakes of genealogies in two main contexts: al-Andalus together with the Maghrib, and the Central Sahara. In Chapter 4, Helena de Felipe examines the case of the first Almoravid amir, Yusuf ibn Tashfin (1061–1106 CE), a Sanhaja Berber, and the way that genealogy can legitimise political authority. She considers how Yusuf ibn Tashfin claimed an Arab genealogy that drew on a textual heritage shared by Muslims in the East and the West. In Chapter 5, Maribel Fierro focuses on the case of the Nasrids of Granada in late Muslim Spain. In his *al-Ihata fi akhbar Gharnata*, the Andalusi scholar Ibn al-Khatib (d. 776/1374) emphasises the genealogical links of Arab families in Granada in his day with those of ancestors dating from the conquest period. At the same time, the dynasty's genealogy connects through an ancestor to Prophetic times. These prestigious genealogical roots placed the Nasrid kingdom in a solid position to counteract its Christian and Maghribian rivals.

Chapter 6, by Judith Scheele, turns to contemporary Central Saharan *tawārīkh* and follows debates over religious legitimacy, hierarchy and status, and the embarrassment that results when contrasting worldviews meet within "family" settings that are profoundly shaped by trans-Saharan mobility. She argues that such genealogical documents are inherently hierarchical, and that all of them ultimately refer back to the qur'anic revelation whence they derive their differential moral value. As a body of texts, they carry within them the promise of universal order, with Islamic history becoming a template for the present and the future. The final section, "Genealogy as a Source for Writing History", asks: Given what we know about the generation of genealogical knowledge, how may we use genealogies for writing about the past itself? This question is addressed through two cases. The first relates to genealogies as a source for writing religious history, and particularly that of the early Muslim community in Arabia and Iran. Chapter 7, by Fred M. Donner, reads the genealogy of the Umayyad Marwan ibn al-Hakam (r. 684–5 CE) for what it may suggest of the identity of what Donner terms "the early community of Believers". He interprets Marwan's genealogy, embedded in the early Arabic tradition, as onomastic evidence and argues that Marwan's naming practices suggest a key turning point in the history of this community and the initial emergence of a Muslim identity. In Chapter 8, treating Iran, Sarah Bowen Savant finds the historian al-Mas'udi manipulating the genealogical record during the period of its islamisation in the tenth century. If Donner's genealogies suggest the religious identity of Marwan himself, Savant's show the aspirations of a student of genealogy and the presence of a new historical consciousness expressed in the genealogies of this later period. The second case involves the Family of the Prophet and the evidence that genealogies give of marriage alliances and strategies. Of particular interest is the question of endogamy, or marriage within the "family". In Chapter 9, Raffaele Mauriello finds genealogical data useful for writing the history of one branch of the Prophet's family, the al-Sadr, in today's Lebanon, Iraq and Iran. Based on works of prosopography and extensive fieldwork, he draws together sensitive data involving female members of the Family to show that this branch has followed a strategy of endogamy involving both the Family of the Prophet and non-'Alid members of what he terms "the Shi'i religious establishment".

The editors would like to thank the anonymous reviewers of the chapters, who have provided invaluable feedback. We would also like to thank Robert Jones for his translation of the chapter written by Helena de Felipe, and Hanna Siurua for copy-editing all chapters and for preparing the index. Finally, we gratefully recognise the support of our sponsors and our publishers, the Aga Khan University, Institute for the Study of Muslim Civilisations (AKU-ISMC) and Edinburgh University Press (EUP).

NOTES

1. Ibn Qutayba, *Fadl al-'Arab wa-l-tanbih 'ala 'ulumiha*, ed. W. M. Khalis, Abu Dhabi: al-Majma' al-Thaqafi, 1998, p. 35.
2. These statements derive from L. Marlow, *Hierarchy and Egalitarianism in Islamic Thought*, Cambridge: Cambridge University Press, 1997, pp. 22–30; see also Z. Szombathy, *The Roots of Arabic Genealogy: A Study in Historical Anthropology*, Piliscsaba, Hungary: The Avicenna Institute of Middle Eastern Studies, 2003.
3. The often-repeated advice attributed to the second caliph, 'Umar ibn al-Khattab, is exemplary, as he exhorted the Arabs to learn their genealogies and not to become like settled peoples who think of their origins in terms of place. Marlow, *Hierarchy and Egalitarianism*, p. 15, n. 7.
4. D. Lowenthal, *The Past is a Foreign Country*, Cambridge: Cambridge University Press, 2006 [1985], esp. pp. 37–8. Lowenthal cites Henry James, *Hawthorne*, London: Macmillan, 1879, p. 14.
5. Regarding the Iranian case, see Sarah Bowen Savant, *The New Muslims of Post-Conquest Iran: Tradition, Memory, and Conversion*, Cambridge: Cambridge University Press, 2013.
6. See especially Szombathy, *The Roots of Arabic Genealogy*, ch. 1, "The roots of 'ilm al-nasab". Also, Hisham ibn Muhammad al-Kalbi, *Ğamharat an-nasab: Das genealogische Werk des Hišām ibn Muhammad al-Kalbī*, ed. W. Caskel, Leiden: E. J. Brill, 1966.
7. Ibn Funduq, *Lubab al-ansab wa-l-alqab wa-l-a'qab*, ed. M. al-Raja'i, Qom: Maktabat al-Mar'ashi, 1989–90 [1410], p. 196.
8. Regarding this chapter within the *Fihrist*, see C. F. Robinson, *Islamic Historiography*, Cambridg: Cambridge University Press, 2003, pp. 3–8.
9. Studies include those by the authors of this volume. A few other monographs have addressed particular contexts. Of special note are A. Q. Ahmed, *The Religious Elite of the Early Islamic Hijaz: Five Prosopographical Case Studies*, Unit for Prosopographical Research, Linacre College, Oxford, 2011; T. Bernheimer, *The 'Alids: The First Family of Islam, 750–1200*, Edinburgh: Edinburgh University Press, 2013; J. Dakhlia, *L'oubli de la cité: La mémoire collective à l'épreuve du lignage dans le Jérid tunisien*, Paris: La Découverte, 1990; P. Bonte, É. Conte, C. Hamès and A. W. Ould Cheikh, *Al-Ansāb: La quête des origines; Anthropologie historique de la société tribale arabe*, Paris: Éditions de la Maison des Sciences de l'Homme, 1991; P. Bonte, É. Conte and P. Dresch, dirs, *Émirs et présidents: Figures de la parenté et du politique dans le monde arabe*, Paris: CNRS Éditions, 2001; A. Shryock, *Nationalism and the Genealogical Imagination: Oral History and Textual Authority in Tribal Jordan*, Berkeley – Los Angeles: University of California Press, 1997; E. Ho, *The Graves of Tarim: Genealogy and Mobility across the Indian Ocean*, Berkeley – Los Angeles: University of California Press, 2006; "Arab-Islamic Medieval Culture", ed. M. Marín, special issue of *Medieval Prosopography: History and Collective Biography*, vol. 23, 2002; and the series *Estudios Onomástico-Biográficos de al-Andalus*, Madrid-Granada: CSIC, 1988–.

Part One

The Generation of Genealogical Knowledge

CHAPTER 1

Keeping the Prophet's Family Alive: Profile of a Genealogical Discipline

Kazuo Morimoto

People call his [that is, 'Ali ibn Abi Talib's] descendants the People of the House (*Ahl al-Bayt*), the Family of Muhammad (*Āl Muḥammad*), the Relatives of the Prophet (*'Itrat al-Nabī*) ... and employ the titles "*sayyid*" and "*sharīf*" to address them. Because people desire to be counted among them, the discipline of genealogies (*'ilm al-ansāb*) and [its] family tree books (*kutub al-shajara*) came into being. In order to show them respect, the braids of hair [a special sign for *sayyids* and *sharīfs*] are removed from the impostors' heads.[1]

Claiming kinship relation with the Prophet Muhammad, that is, claiming an affiliation to the "People of the House" or the status of a *sayyid* or *sharīf*, has arguably been the most widespread way in Muslim societies of supporting one's moral or material objectives with genealogical credentials. Today, the ruling dynasties of Morocco and Brunei, so distant from each other, both derive legitimacy in this same way. Many a Sufi and a saint are likewise believed to have been a *sayyid* or *sharīf*. Prophetic descent can even be an asset for beggars, since they can promise their benefactors a reward from the Prophet, in addition to that from God.[2]

Respect or reverence for Prophetic descent, however, did not prevent some believers from trying to make false claims about it. Far from it: Impostors were everywhere, as suggested above by Ibn Shahrashub, an eminent Twelver Shi'i scholar from the twelfth century CE.[3] Paul Rycaut, a seventeenth-century British diplomat to the Ottomans, recounts that when a descendant of the Prophet wearing a green turban – a sign of that descent then and now – was caught drunk, the turban would respectfully be put aside and then the drunkard would be beaten severely. This was because it was widely known that Prophetic descent could easily be bought.[4]

Hence the need to check claims to descent. As we read in Ibn Shahrashub's account, the discipline specialising in the genealogy of *sayyids* and *sharīfs* (henceforth the discipline of *sayyid/sharīf* genealogies), with its family tree books, was supposed to verify claims to Prophetic descent. Those who claimed a genealogy incompatible with those already attested were to be spotted, and their twin braids – a common sign of *sayyids* and *sharīfs* before green turbans were adopted – to be systematically removed. This is the picture that Ibn Shahrashub draws.

The reality, of course, was not so straightforward. After all, how, before the emergence of modern communications and technology, could anyone constantly update and circulate such a body of knowledge? Since *sayyids* and *sharīfs* continuously reproduced themselves in different localities, how could a Baghdadi genealogist of, say, the twelfth century verify the genealogy of a man who had just arrived from Nishapur? It seems that the discipline's ability to identify impostors was not great. Still, there was a continuous need in society to safeguard the discipline's façade. Continuous production of family tree books, and periodic exposure of "impostures", kept the discipline's authority alive and thus enabled the kind of perception presented by Ibn Shahrashub. It would not be off the mark to say that the discipline contributed to keeping the Prophet's family alive not so much by effectively exposing impostures as by continuously claiming its own existence as the guardian of authenticity.[5]

The aim of this chapter is to take a closer look at this genealogical discipline, and to elucidate how it traded in its own authority. More concretely, we will survey different types of writings, and the roles that they played in building the discipline's authority as well as in lending that authority to the discipline's most important "customers", *sayyids* and *sharīfs*, in society.

As for its history, the discipline of *sayyid/sharīf* genealogies branched out from the discipline of Arab genealogies in the mid- to latter half of the ninth century. This would seem to correspond to the era when the Prophet's family dispersed widely, giving increasing opportunities to impostors. The discipline attained maturity in the tenth and eleventh centuries, with a network extending, roughly speaking, from Egypt to West Turkistan. The writings we will survey in the following pages are the products of this discipline and date, at the latest, from the fifteenth century.[6]

It is hoped that this study will add a useful dimension to our understanding of how knowledge about genealogy has kept its relevance in Muslim, and many other, societies. It is not only knowledge per se that has mattered; the ability to keep the public perception as a specialised and reliable discipline was no less important for the discipline of *sayyid/sharīf* genealogies for attaining its goal of keeping the Prophet's family alive.

COMPREHENSIVE GENEALOGIES

The standard written works of genealogists specialising in *sayyid/sharīf* genealogies trace the different lines of the Prophet's family as a whole. Such comprehensive works, compiled in book form, represent most of the discipline's written products left today, and describe genealogies either in prose, that is in *mabsūṭ* ("flattened") format, or with the use of a chart, that is in *mushajjar* ("tree") format. Let us take a look at a portion of a prose work from the early thirteenth century:

> As for ʿAbd Allah al-ʿAqiqi, the son of Husayn al-Asghar, his authentic progeny today are from Jaʿfar only. His [that is, Jaʿfar's] mother is from the Zaydi [branch of ʿAli's descendants].
>
> Jaʿfar's progeny are from the following three [sons]: Muhammad al-ʿAqiqi, whose mother is Kulthum, the daughter of ʿUbayd Allah al-Aʿraj; Ahmad al-Munqidhi and Ismaʿil al-Munqidhi.
>
> Muhammad al-ʿAqiqi had eight sons. Among them, ʿAli al-ʿAqiqi the *Raʾīs* ['chief'], who lived in Medina, and Jaʿfar, whose progeny are in Tabaristan, have authentic progeny [today]. But their number is small.
>
> As for ʿAli al-ʿAqiqi, his progeny are from five men. [First,] Ahmad, who lived in Egypt. He has progeny there, in Baghdad and in the Maghrib.[7]

Comprehensive works thus do not only record genealogy, but also prosopographical information, such as mothers' identities, positions held and/or major events in which the subjects were involved. At the same time, information about dwellings documents the migration and dispersal of the Prophet's family. All of these elements constituted the fundamental knowledge of a *sayyid/sharīf* genealogist (that is, a genealogist specialising in *sayyid/sharīf* genealogies).

A work in chart format represents the father–son relationship with a line in the shape of the prolonged Arabic word *bn* (ﺑ——————ﻦ), meaning "the son of", which connects a son to his father. Multiple sons can be represented by connecting multiple *b* characters (——————ﺑ) to one *n* character (ﻦ). By prolonging a base *bn* line horizontally all through the pages and letting the portions describing different lines branch out on appropriate pages along the way, genealogists solved the technical difficulty impeding the compilation of a multi-page book in the "tree" format (see Figure 1.1).[8]

The works' selectivity in presentation is noteworthy, and is one feature that may remain hidden behind their ostensible comprehensiveness. The phrase "his authentic progeny today" found at the beginning of the quotation above betrays a bias in favour of describing the lines continuing in the compiler's day. It would be a mistake to claim that genealogists had no pious motive when

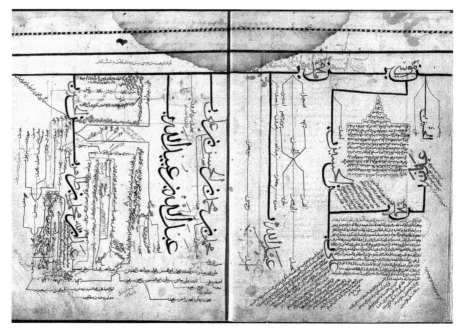

Figure 1.1 Pages of a genealogy in "tree" format.
(MS Süleymaniye Library, Bağdatlı Vehbi, 1305, fos 44ᵛ–45ʳ)

recording the genealogy of the Prophet's family. But the faithful recording of as many past ramifications as possible of the Prophetic genealogy as part of the sacred history was apparently not their priority. Rather, the contents of these comprehensive works were selected in such a way that they could – or looked as though they could – be used as practical reference works in order to verify genealogies.[9] Delicate coexistence of the two directions of interest, one "practical" in the sense that it was closely linked to genealogical verifications and the other "academic" since it had no such practical consequences, was an important feature of the discipline of *sayyid/sharīf* genealogies. We will discuss this point further in the next section.

Most probably, Ibn Shahrashub meant by "family tree books" these types of comprehensive works. The discipline, however, also gave birth to other types of writings, to which we now turn.

BUILDING THE DISCIPLINE'S AUTHORITY

The types of writings that I am now going to discuss are generally short, with only a few specimens surviving today, often merely as sections within larger books on genealogy of a compound nature. These writings are taken up here in spite of their quantitative insignificance, since their existence speaks a lot about the nature of the discipline. We will first survey the different types of these writings, and we will then discuss their functions in terms of the discipline's trade in its authority.

First, there were writings that were produced as "practical" references to be used for genealogical verification. One such text is the *Muntaqilat al-Talibiyya* (*Talibid Migrants*), a book compiled in the latter half of the eleventh century in the format of a dictionary of place names.[10] The compiler picked up personal names linked to place names found in comprehensive works (for example, 'Ali al-'Aqiqi, linked to Medina in the quotation in the previous section), and listed them, along with their genealogies, in Arabic alphabetical order according to place names. As the compiler states in the preface, this work was compiled in order to enable the verifiers to check the authenticity of genealogies, not only on the basis of the genealogies per se, but also on the basis of their homes.

Listings of those who died without leaving a son (*dārijūn*), whose progeny became extinct (*munqariḍūn*) or who were identified as impostors (*adʻiyāʼ*) can also be counted as texts with such "practical" purposes. Their professed utility was that they could be used to spot impostors who claimed descent from the people found in them.[11]

Besides these types of writings with "practical" purposes, the discipline also produced writings that catered to more "academic" interests; for example, there were glossaries of family names or *nisbas* (parts of a personal name that indicate a relationship, for example, "Husayni" to denote descent from a Husayn). The progeny of a certain individual who, for one reason or another, came to be recognised as a branching point often shared a *nisba* deriving from that individual. This *nisba* could serve as something comparable to a family name, depending on the progeny's cohesion. A dictionary of *nisbas*, or family names, clarifies from whom certain *nisbas* derived.[12]

There also existed writings concerning mothers, although no text of this type survives.[13] It can be surmised, however, that such texts gathered references to mothers from comprehensive works.[14] Although a mother's descent mattered for establishing nobility of descent, it was not among the factors affecting a genealogy's authenticity, which was instead based on paternal lines. This type of writing, useful only for assessing degrees of nobility, or clarifying marital relationships between different lines, should thus be considered to have been rather "academic" in nature.

Martyrologies (*maqātil*) could also be included among genealogical works of a compound nature. Martyrology is a common genre in early Arabic literature, with the most famous example being Abu l-Faraj al-Isfahani's (d. 356/967) text concerning members of the Prophet's family who lost their lives in tragic ways.[15] Although the subject does not appear to be directly relevant to genealogy,

Table 1.1 Excerpt from a Table on Martyrs in Ibn Funduq's *Lubab al-ansab* (compiled in 558/1163)

Name of person slain	Place of murder	Name of murderer	Location of tomb	Leader of the funeral prayer	Age at the time of murder	Reason for murder, and so forth
'Abbas, the son of [...], the son of Hasan, the son of 'Ali.	His mother was 'A'isha, the daughter of Talha al-Jud.	Died in the prison at Hashimiyya ['Abbasid capital].	Buried on the bank of the Euphrates on 23 Ramadan, 145 AH [15 Dec., 762 CE].	People of the prison carried out the funeral prayer.	He was exactly thirty-five years old when slain.	Slain because of the revolts of Ibrahim and Muhammad.

Source: Ibn Funduq (d. 565/1169–70), *Lubab al-ansab wa-l-alqab wa-l-a'qab*, in 2 pts, ed. M. al-Raja'i, Qom: Maktabat al-Mar'ashi, 1989–90 [1410], p. 408.

references to martyrdom, and murders more generally, were a staple element in comprehensive works, and thus could also be gathered separately. For example, the *Lubab al-ansab* (*Quintessence of Genealogies*), a work compiled in East Iran in the latter half of the twelfth century, includes a section presenting a table on martyrs (see Table 1.1).[16]

This entry presents a martyr who was slain by the 'Abbasids when coordinated revolts by two brothers of 'Alid descent broke out.[17] *Sayyids* and *sharifs* were deeply associated with the symbolism of oppressed justice because of the continuous sufferings of their forebears under Umayyad and 'Abbasid rule. Martyrologies like this confirm and enhance this symbolism. They were possibly meant to record the names of murderers, too. Evidently, however, genealogists could not use the martyrologies in order to verify genealogies.

Finally, the discipline produced writings visibly aimed at confirming the integrity of the discipline itself, such as lists of reputable past genealogists, sometimes featuring their achievements.[18] It is noteworthy that some such lists include names of figures from the founding period of Islam who were, however, not widely known to have been specialists in genealogy, including typically 'Ali ibn Abi Talib.[19] Such lists bolstered the authenticity of the discipline by giving it its own continuous genealogy extending back to the outset of Islamic history.

Glossaries of special signs and technical terms also contributed to the consolidation of the discipline. These glossaries were compiled, at least ostensibly, as practical references for genealogists, and they explained the meanings of technical terms and signs that were used to assess such items as the reliability of genealogies or the moral character of individuals.[20] But, if one reads them carefully, one sees that the glossaries are nothing but a heap of signs and terms that make no serious effort to clarify the system, if any, that integrates them. Here, too, one sees works, unhelpful for practical purposes, which appear to have been aimed at enhancing the status of the discipline, as can be inferred from the following passage found in a preface to one glossary:

> The discipline of genealogies is a great and sublime discipline, and the gene-alogists have used technical terms and signs comprehensible only to those who have engaged in the study of genealogies and attained the wisdom as well as the discernment of truth from falsehood. I want to explain these technical terms and signs so that students can profit from them [that is, those explanations].[21]

There is no denying that all of these writings were of some use in their respective capacities, as outlined above. We would, however, miss the forest for the trees if we failed to notice the significance that they had for the authority of the discipline of *sayyid/sharīf* genealogies itself. At the same time, they consti-tuted channels for the discipline to display its full control over genealogy and the history of the Prophet's family. A look at an entry in a treatise enumerating impostors datable to the late fourteenth century is pertinent here. X in the quotation denotes the denied father–son relationship, an "I"-shape mark cutting the word *bn* down the middle in the manuscript:

> Muhammad, the son of Muhadhdhab … the son of Husayn the impostor, [X] the son of Muhammad al-Buthani, the son of Qasim … the son of 'Ali ibn Abi Talib.
>
> 'Umari states in his book *al-Majdi* that the progeny extant today of Muhammad al-Buthani are from 'Ali, Harun, 'Isa, Musa, Qasim and Ibrahim. Thus, Muhammad did not have a son by the name of Husayn. The same is true with the book *Al al-Rasul* by the genealogist Abu l-Ghana'im … al-Dimashqi. [Reference to two other books of the same opinion follows.][22]

This treatise not only presents the genealogies claimed by impostors but cites relevant passages from earlier comprehensive works that were used as the bases for the denial; this is an obvious display of the alleged capability of the discipline to spot impostures.[23]

Even texts of an apparently "academic" nature proved that the discipline was highly specialised and could not be deceived: They were also "practical" in this indirect way. The various types of writings examined in this section served, as a whole, as deterrents against possible impostures.

AT THE INTERFACE WITH SOCIETY

Deterrence of impostures was not the only use of the authority of the discipline of *sayyid/sharīf* genealogies. Genealogists could trade in their knowledge exactly because of that very authority that they claimed to represent. The types of writings that served the interests of individual *sayyids* and *sharīfs* demonstrate how such a trade was practised.

An excellent example is a book in chart format datable to the second half of the fifteenth century, called *Ansab mushajjar* (*Charted Genealogies*), which was compiled for a family from Mosul in northern Iraq. This work, although somehow covering the whole of the Prophet's family, is nonetheless very different from the standard comprehensive works discussed above. Regard for patrons is shared by most, if not all, genealogical works. In fact, it is hard to think of a comprehensive work that fails to mention a patron's genealogy when the patron is affiliated to the Prophet's family. The case of *Ansab mushajjar*, however, is distinct in that even the structure of the work reflects the regard for its patron.

In *Ansab mushajjar*, the genealogies of the patron's family are presented in the first pages of the book, just after the introduction. They are incomparably more detailed than others in the book, and they are positioned between genealogies of two other prestigious lines: the line of the twelve imams of Twelver Shi'ism above and the line of the 'Abbasid caliphs below.[24] And so the work enhances the family's prestige by juxtaposing the family's genealogies with those of the imams and the caliphs as it asserts the authenticity of the family's descent.[25]

Another example of a work shaped by the needs of its patron is the *Lubab al-ansab*, mentioned above. The work is composed of sections on discrete topics, many of which are specimens of the different types of writings surveyed in the preceding section: for example, a listing of those who died without leaving a son and whose progeny became extinct or a glossary of *nisbas*. The intent of this seemingly incoherent compilation becomes clear in a chapter entitled "The Manners of *Naqībs*". This chapter, and the work as a whole, can reasonably be regarded as a manual for *naqībs*, those syndics of *sayyids* and *sharīfs* responsible for supervising their consanguineous wards and also, importantly, for controlling their genealogies.[26] The patron's family was gaining hegemony in the local politics of its district at the time of the *Lubab*'s compilation. Quite a few *sayyids* and *sharīfs* had immigrated to the district, seeking that patron's protection. The patron's status as a *naqīb*, however, was not in all likelihood widely recognised. Under such circumstances, the patron would benefit from such a work dedicated to him. Not surprisingly, the genealogy of the patron and the achievements of his forebears are prominently presented in this work.[27]

Not all *sayyids* or *sharīfs* could afford to have such works composed for them, but those less privileged could seek other evidence, namely written testimonies. Although I have not come across an original document bearing such a testimony from the period under study, we know what the texts of such written testimonies looked like from citations in other texts. The following citation presents three testimonies in a place:

> This genealogy is sound and there is no doubt in it. 'Abd al-Hamid ibn al-Taqi al-Husayni [d. 597/1201] wrote this.
>
> I contemplated this genealogy, and have found that this [genealogy is so elevated and lofty that it] rivals the clouds in the heavens and is equal to the stars of the Gemini. Fakhar ibn Ma'add [d. 630/1232–3] wrote this.
>
> This is a sound genealogy with no ambiguity and is as obvious as the sun. 'Abd Allah ibn Qutham al-Zaydi [sic; a clerical error for "al-Zaynabi"; fl. in the thirteenth c.] wrote this.

A later genealogist by the name of Muhammad ibn 'Abd al-Muttalib al-Husayni found these written testimonies on a family tree, presumably on a single sheet, of a family named the Zaydis, and recorded them elsewhere. It is surmised that the Zaydis, after having a genealogist (named in the source) authenticate their descent by drawing the genealogy, went on collecting testimonies from other genealogists.

What attracts our interest here is the context in which Muhammad al-Husayni recorded these written testimonies. In fact, al-Husayni was trying to refute the doubts raised by an earlier genealogist named Safi al-Din by presenting this evidence. "I was surprised at what Safi al-Din said. He is a person who is abundant in knowledge, but I do not understand the basis of this impeachment (ta'n) he made against the Zaydis," he states. After describing the original family tree, which demonstrated the full trust the drawer had in the Zaydis' genealogy, Muhammad al-Husayni mentions the three written testimonies he found on it. His verdict: "No impeachment is possible after these testimonies. God knows better."[28]

Exactly how persuasive such written testimonies were cannot be known today, and it is something that was probably not clear in their own days either. What can be said is that they functioned according to a system in which a genealogy's authenticity was enhanced gradually with the accumulation of testimonies. There was apparently no definite minimum number of testimonies that, once reached, would suddenly make the testimonies take effect. The existence of a definite number of testimonies that absolutely guaranteed the authenticity of a genealogy is likewise unlikely, in spite of the impression that Muhammad al-Husayni's declaration may give. This means that there would always be a demand for genealogists' testimonies.

Thus, besides building its own authority and protecting the Prophet's family, generally speaking, the discipline of *sayyid/sharīf* genealogies also created writings that lent authority to particular *sayyid* and *sharīf* families.

Conclusion

It is hoped that this brief survey of types of writings produced by *sayyid/sharīf* genealogists has been able to show how they contributed to the functioning of a discipline of *sayyid/sharīf* genealogies as a social device. The writings included those of an "academic" nature, with no direct consequence for genealogical verification. Even those writings, however, enhanced the discipline's authority, as did more "practical" reference works and the types visibly aimed at the consolidation of the discipline. The authority thus attained and maintained – and accepted by Ibn Shahrashub in the opening quotation of this chapter – helped perpetuate belief in the authenticity of *sayyid/sharīf* genealogies in general. People could persuade themselves that *sayyid/sharīf* genealogies were generally authentic, and put aside doubts, because an authoritative discipline was constantly monitoring genealogies.

But that was not all. The authority was also put to use by individual *sayyids* and *sharīfs* for the purpose of authenticating their own status. The two types of writings presented in the last section exemplify this aspect of the genealogical discipline, and differ from the types mentioned earlier, in that they were tailored for the consumption of authority rather than for its production. And only with the smooth functioning of writings in both areas – "production" and "marketing" – could this discipline fulfil its role as the guardian of authenticity.

Notes

1. Ibn Shahrashub, *Manaqib Al Abi Talib*, vol. 2, ed. Y. al-Biqa'i, Beirut: Dar al-Adwa', 1991 [1412], pp. 222–3.
2. See C. van Arendonk; W. A. Graham (rev.), "Sharīf", in P. Bearman, Th. Bianquis, C. E. Bosworth, E. van Donzel, and W. P. Heinrichs (eds), *Encyclopaedia of Islam*, 12 vols, 2nd edn. Leiden: E. J. Brill, 1960–2004, online edition, for further details about *sayyids* and *sharīfs*. "Prophetic descent", as used in this chapter, is meant to be both direct and collateral, meaning "descent closely linked to the Prophet". Many of 'Ali ibn Abi Talib's descendants, the subject of the opening quotation, were direct descendants of the Prophet because of their issuance from Fatima, the Prophet's beloved daughter who married 'Ali, himself a paternal cousin of the Prophet. But 'Ali's descendants from other wives as well as the descendants of his brothers, and for that matter even of his paternal uncles, have also been considered as belonging to the "People of the House" because of their paternal filiation, as a rule in the past and as a less common practice today.
3. Ibn Shahrashub, an Iranian scholar who migrated to and died in Aleppo, was a

representative of the moderate strand of Shi'ism prevalent in his time. The bulk of the materials collected in his *Manaqib Al Abi Talib* concern the biographies and virtues of the twelve imams.

4. Paul Rycaut, *The History of the Present State of the Ottoman Empire*, 6th edn, London: R. Clavell, 1686, p. 211. Cited previously in H. L. Bodman, *Political Factions of Aleppo, 1760–1826*, Chapel Hill: University of North Carolina Press, 1963, p. 96.

5. In actuality, it was the popular voice of the people expressed through formal testimonies that, as a rule, had the strongest impact on whether the Prophetic descent of a claimant would be accepted. See, for example, my "The Formation and Development of the Science of Talibid Genealogies in the 10th & 11th Century Middle East", in B. Scarcia Amoretti and L. Bottini (eds), "The Role of the *Sādāt/Ašrāf* in Muslim History and Civilization: Proceedings of the International Colloquium (Rome, 2–4 March 1998)", special issue, *Oriente Moderno*, n.s., vol. 18 (79), no. 2, 1999, pp. 541–70.

6. This chapter draws heavily on the findings in my unpublished doctoral dissertation in Japanese, "*Sayyids*, Genealogists, *Naqibs*: A Study of the Genealogical Literature on *Sayyid/Sharīfs* from the Late 10th Early 15th Centuries", University of Tokyo, Tokyo, 2004, the preparation of a revised English version of which is still on the way. See, for the time being, my "Formation and Development" for a study on the emergence of the discipline of *sayyid/sharīf* genealogies.

7. Al-Marwazi al-Azwarqani (d. after 614/1217–18), *al-Fakhri fi ansab al-Talibiyyin*, ed. M. al-Raja'i, Qom: Maktabat al-Mar'ashi, 1988–9 [1409], p. 71.

8. For an excellent example of a book in chart format with the mentioned features, see Muhammad ibn Ahmad ibn 'Amid al-Din al-Husayni al-Najafi (fl. in the fifteenth c.), *Bahr al-ansab al-musamma bi-l-Mushajjar al-kashshaf li-usul al-sada al-ashraf*, facsimile edn, ed. A. Y. al-Kutubi al-Hasani, Medina: Dar al-Mujtaba, 1999 [1419].

9. The way that the pieces of genealogical information were collected by the genealogists also contributed to this bias. They collected fragmental pieces of information from contemporary *sayyids* and *sharīfs*. So, the bulk of the information that they gathered naturally concerned the lines that were extant.

10. Abu Isma'il al-Tabataba'i (d. after 482/1089), *Muntaqilat al-Talibiyya*, ed. M. M. H. al-Khursan, Najaf: al-Matba'a al-Haydariyya, 1968 [1388].

11. See Ibn Funduq (d. 565/1169–70), *Lubab al-ansab wa-l-alqab wa-l-a'qab*, in 2 pts, ed. M. al-Raja'i, Qom: Maktabat al-Mar'ashi, 1989–90 [1410], p. 723; see also p. 338.

12. Abu Isma'il al-Tabataba'i, *Manqul min kitab Ghayat al-mu'qibin fi ansab al-Talin* [sic], MS Kitabkhanih-i Malik, 3532, fos 28ᵛ–39ʳ is an excellent example of this type. Ibn Funduq's *Lubab al-ansab* and al-Marwazi's *al-Fakhri* also each contain a section written in this style (*Lubab*, pp. 223–317; *al-Fakhri*, pp. 195–217).

13. Abu Talib al-Harawi's late tenth–early eleventh-century book on the "*asāmī al-ummahāt*" (the names of the mothers), mentioned in Ibn Funduq, *Lubab al-ansab*, p. 720, is not known to be extant.

14. See the quotation in the preceding section. For a study of women's names appearing in the comprehensive works, see Scarcia Amoretti, "Women's Names in Early Islamic Pro-Shi'ite Texts on the Genealogy of the *Talibiyyin*", in M. Marín (ed.), "Arab-Islamic Medieval Culture", special issue, *Medieval Prosopography*, vol. 23, 2002, pp. 141–65.

15. See S. Günther, "*Maqâtil* Literature in Medieval Islam", *Journal of Arabic Literature*, vol. 25, 1994, pp. 192–212.

16. Ibn Funduq, *Lubab al-ansab*, pp. 396–431. The table, however, occupies only up to p. 409, and the rest of the section is in plain text. The excerpt shown is from p. 408.

17. The discrepancy between the column titles and the contents is present in the original. The revolts in question are of course those of al-Nafs al-Zakiyya and his brother Ibrahim.

18. 'Izz al-Milla wa-l-Niqaba wa-l-Din Ishaq (fl. later than the early fifteenth century), *Asami al-nassabin*, MS Kitabkhanih-i Malik, 3532, fos 11ᵛ–13ᵛ, and Anonymous, *Asami al-nassabin*, appended to Ibn Muhanna al-'Ubaydili (d. 682/1283), *Tadhkirat al-ansab*, MS Astan-i Quds, 3626, fo. 163ʳ, perhaps different recensions of originally the same work, can be named as lists that were compiled as independent, albeit quite short, works. Quite a few books on *sayyid/sharif* genealogy contain a section(s) in this style, especially in their introductions.

19. 'Ali's name appears in Anonymous, *Asami al-nassabin*. Although of questionable prestige, Abu Talib's name is also recorded in one such list. Of course, the names of those who were indeed famous for their knowledge of genealogies, for example, Abu Bakr and 'Aqil ibn Abi Talib, are mentioned far more frequently.

20. Two representative glossaries are Baha' al-Din 'Ali ibn 'Abd al-Hamid (fl. about the turn of the fourteenth–fifteenth centuries), *Risala fi istilahat al-nassabin* and Ibn al-Tiqtaqa's (d. 709/1309–10) glossary appended to his *al-Asili fi ansab al-Talibiyyin* (the latter is not included in the Qom edition of *al-Asili*). Both were appended to Ibn 'Inaba's famous *'Umdat al-talib fi ansab Al Abi Talib* (the "Wusta" or "Jalaliyya" version of the three different versions or works with the same title), and are thus accessible, although in much deteriorated forms, in several of its published editions. My unpublished doctoral dissertation (see n. 6) includes the edited texts of both glossaries (pp. 453–98).

21. From Baha' al-Din's glossary found in the version appended to *'Umdat al-talib* (the preface is most probably not Baha' al-Din's own); Ibn 'Inaba, *'Umdat al-talib*, 2nd edn, ed. M. H. Al al-Taliqani, Najaf: al-Maktaba al-Haydariyya, 1961 [1380], p. 371.

22. Ibn Katila al-Husayni, *Bayan al-ad'iya'*, MS British Library, Or. 1406, fo. 20ʳ. My doctoral dissertation includes the edited text of this intriguing treatise (pp. 521–63). For details on this manuscript, see my "The Notebook of a *Sayyid/Sharif* Genealogist: MS. British Library Or. 1406", in D. Bredi et al. (eds), *Scritti in onore di Biancamaria Scarcia Amoretti*, Rome: Dipartimento di Studi Orientali, Sapienza Università di Roma and Edizioni Q, 2008, vol. 3, pp. 823–36.

23. I have to note here, not quite kindly to the genealogists, that the unanimity among the genealogical works found in the above quotation could not have been so usual. For a case in which a reputed genealogist finds himself at a loss in the face of the different opinions expressed in the works he draws upon for genealogical verification, see my "Formation and Development", p. 567. The predicament was solved when the genealogist confirmed the general acceptance of the claimant's lineage by the people around him, expressed through formal testimonies.

24. Remember that the base *bn* line in a book in chart format pierces the pages horizontally. Here, there are three quasi-base lines from which different derivative lines of the three lines (that is, those of the imams, the patron's family and the caliphs) branch out.

25. Ghiyath al-Din Mansur Dashtaki (attr.), *Ansab mushajjar* [*sic*], MS Astan-i Quds, 3624. The mentioned format of the book is taken over by Rukn al-Din al-Husayni al-Mawsili (fl. c. seventeenth century), *Bahr al-ansab*, facsimile edn, ed. M. al-Husayni al-Mar'ashi, Tehran: Ufsit-i Islamiyyih, 1965–6 [1385], dedicated to the same family.

26. For a definition, albeit rather idealised, of the *naqibs'* duties by a near-contemporary Muslim scholar, see al-Mawardi (d. 450/1058), *The Ordinances of Government*, trans. W. H. Wahba, Reading: Garnet, 1996, pp. 107–11.

27. For a detailed study on this work, see my "Putting the *Lubāb al-ansāb* in Context: *Sayyids* and *Naqībs* in Late Saljuq Khurasan", *Studia Iranica*, vol. 36, no. 2, 2007, pp. 163–83.

28. Muhammad al-Husayni's transcription of the written testimonies as well as his comments are copied in al-'Ubaydili, *Tadhkirat al-ansab*, fo. 92^r.

CHAPTER 2

Motives and Techniques of Genealogical Forgery in Pre-modern Muslim Societies

ZOLTÁN SZOMBATHY

In a society that attributes great significance to descent, genealogical forgeries will abound. Such phenomena were ubiquitous in pre-modern Muslim societies, where the dominant ideology considered descent to be a paramount factor in deciding a person's character, prestige, status and political legitimacy, despite the contrary teachings of the Qur'an and hadith.

In an important recent article, Ella Landau-Tasseron analyses the issue of falsifying descent. Her focus, however, is on adoption and the acknowledgement of paternity, not on forged genealogies, which, as she notes, tend to be glued to ancestors "already dead and buried".[1] She hardly treats such brazen forgeries and the techniques of producing them, largely confining herself to cases of disputable paternity. By contrast, this chapter's goal is to explore the practical methods of manufacturing false genealogies. I will discuss descent, not paternity, and my concern here is with down-to-earth issues: techniques and tricks, not theoretical dilemmas.[2] As this chapter will illustrate, passing for someone else is not easy, even if sources tend to mention such cases as if they were common. Before turning to this subject, however, it will be necessary to explore another problem, namely the motives behind genealogical forgeries. Given the difficulties described below of having a forged genealogy accepted, there is certainly the need to explain why so many people were willing to undertake the considerable risk and trouble involved. As I argue in the following section, the potential spoils were worth the effort.

CORPORATE INTERESTS

It is important to realise just how far genealogy was from a merely academic question. High-status groups had materially much to lose through the successful intrusion of unworthy outsiders, and thus the injury to their honour was more than symbolic when a lowly outsider dared to claim to be their equal. Above all, it meant that they would have to share their privileges, a consideration that tends to motivate people more than any ideology does. Intruding on a genealogy is not a scholarly hobby – it has to pay dividends to make it worthwhile.[3] Those dividends were especially enticing in the case of the Prophet's descendants. In fact, in referring to "high-status" or "elite" groups, I have chiefly the 'Alids in mind, partly because of the relative wealth of source material about them and my heavy reliance on such works.

In many, if not most, parts of the Islamic world, 'Alid lineages derived enormous benefits, both tangible and symbolic. This does not imply that all such groups were necessarily rich and powerful; indeed, some were poor nomads, and some quite destitute.[4] Apart from such obvious advantages as virtually guaranteed respectability and prestige, there were more benefits, some even convertible into hard cash (directly or through political influence). *Sharīf* men (that is, putative descendants of the Prophet) could marry women of any other social group while their own women were reserved for them.[5] For instance, the celebrated Buyid vizier al-Sahib ibn 'Abbad (d. 385/995), for all his political influence and learning, considered it an immense honour to give his daughter in marriage to a member of the Prophet's lineage, and to have a grandchild belonging to that noblest of lineages.[6] An extreme extension of this principle, widespread in the popular culture of some Muslim lands, was the attribution of *baraka* (divine blessing) to all members of the Prophet's lineage,[7] which in some communities even spawned a sort of *ius primae noctis* accorded to young *sharīf* men to transfer their blessing through the sexual act. This custom, which is totally alien to Islamic law, was practised, for instance, in Lamu (Kenya) and in parts of Morocco.[8] In some special cases – Hadramawt in Yemen being one of them – a veritable social stratification based on descent emerged, a system in which the Prophet's descendants occupied the highest level.[9] Even where social stratification was not strictly based on genealogy, the political claims of the 'Alids were widely regarded as having legitimacy, a view taken to its logical extreme by the Shi'a with their insistence on the 'Alid descent of the imam. 'Alid descent would thus be a natural boost to political pretensions, hence the ubiquitous (and nasty) controversies concerning the descent of some dynasties and political leaders. The Fatimids of Egypt, the Idrisids of Morocco and the leader of the Zanj slaves' rebellion in Iraq are all good examples of this tendency. The 'Abbasids twice (402/1011–12 and 444/1052–3) resorted to recruiting the most eminent 'Alids of Baghdad, as well as jurisprudents, judges and notaries, in order to produce a document to question the descent of their rivals the Fatimids, which they distributed in several copies as widely as possible.[10]

Whether politically dominant or not, many 'Alids also derived monetary and legal privileges from their origins. Their corporate interests were efficaciously defended by the system of appointing some from among their number as naqībs (leaders, high representatives), whose task it was to oversee their affairs, smooth away legal problems among them, and represent their interests vis-à-vis other groups and the state.[11] In some periods and regions, sharīf individuals would be treated more leniently than other people in cases of acts of criminal behaviour.[12] In one legal source, it is recommended that an ordinary believer should renounce, as a way to please God, anything that is owed to him by an 'Alid, as well as refrain from hurting or harming him in any way whatsoever.[13] Furthermore, royal monetary awards, often in quite substantial amounts, were regularly distributed among the Prophet's descendants. In the medieval period, this custom actually drew 'Alids to such places as the Fatimid court in Egypt, the Buyid court in al-Rayy and the sultanate of Kilwa on the East African coast.[14] In al-Sahib ibn 'Abbad's court, the 'Alids would receive gifts of luxurious silk garments by virtue of their descent, gifts that jurisprudents, scholars and poets could earn only by their efforts and services.[15] It was noted as a gross iniquity when a governor in Mecca, 'Umar al-Rukhkhaji (mid-3rd/9th c.), banned the solicitation of gifts by the 'Alids and the giving of such gifts to them, a loss of income that soon impoverished many. The next caliph, al-Muntasir (r. 247–8/861–2), renounced the ban and distributed lavish gifts to the Meccan shurafā'.[16] Some Marinid rulers in Morocco are described as having been extraordinarily generous towards the 'Alids, to the point of providing a grossly inflated allowance of one golden dinar every day to some shurafā' of Fez.[17] In the popular culture of the Shi'a tribes of southern Iraq, the privileges of the 'Alids went even further. In addition to incredible tolerance for bad behaviour on their part, tantamount to impunity, the shurafā' also received a regular tithe, a one-fifth share in harvests and agricultural products, which they called ḥaqq jaddī (my grandfather's right).[18]

As the last example indicates, it was not only from rulers that members of the 'Alid lineage received regular gifts and awards, but also from people lower on the social ladder. In late third/ninth-century Egypt, a wealthy man called Yusuf ibn Ibrahim kept a register of the regular stipends (daftar jirāyāt) that he distributed to the local 'Alids, one of whom alone would receive from him no less than two hundred dinars and one hundred irdabb (nearly 20,000 litres) of wheat annually.[19] No wonder, then, that a fatwa by al-Suyuti (d. 911/1505) entitled al-'Ajaja al-zarnabiyya fī al-sulala al-Zaynabiyya (The Sweet-smelling Billow of Incense: Zaynab's Lineage) bears witness to the material motivations – notably the proceeds from certain *waqf* endowments and bequests made to the *shurafā'* – behind ostensibly academic genealogical controversies.[20] The attempts of a group in tenth-/sixteenth-century Medina to gain acceptance as descendants of the Prophet, which they were not, are described in a near-contemporary source as having stemmed from a desire to have a share in the stipends intended for the *shurafā'* (*ṭam'an fī al-ṣadaqāt*).[21] The following text likewise leaves no doubt regarding the real motives behind genealogical pretensions:

> The reason [a number of lineages in Medina] claimed Ansari ancestry is that [in the year 1155/1742–3] a pious gift (*ṣadaqa*) was sent by the Moroccan ruler to the Ansar, consisting of a hundred dinars. We [members of the Ansar family] were absent from Medina at the time … having been exiled from there. So these aforementioned people determined to grab [the royal gift], and some others, unjustly and mendaciously (*ẓulman wa-zūran*), helped their cause. They ended up sharing [the money] with us by lying and cheating, without proof or evidence.[22]

Methods of Intrusion

Given the jealous guarding of the genealogies of elite groups against intruders, and given the awareness that such a threat existed, claiming membership in a group would necessitate considerable cunning and audacity. Once the great edifice of medieval Arabic genealogical science – contained in such standard reference manuals as Ibn Hazm's *Jamharat ansab al-'Arab* – had been created, it served as the stump from which all offshoots would grow and on to which all foreign branches and twigs would be grafted. The existence of widely circulated manuals made it advisable for an impostor to study the available genealogies before making a claim. Al-Jahiz thus tells of the instant exposure of a false claim of descent from the Kinda tribe because the man made his allegation "before looking into any of the Kinda genealogies (*qabla an yanẓura fī shay' min nasab Kinda*)".[23] Similarly, efforts by the Bayt al-Awghani lineage of Medina (twelfth/eighteenth century) to forge an Arab ancestry extending back to Khalid ibn al-Walid were readily exposed as ridiculous by the Medinan 'Abd al-Rahman al-Ansari on the grounds that, as Ibn Qutayba points out in his *Kitab al-Ma'arif*, Khalid's offspring had already been extinct in the third/ninth century.[24]

The great Arab conquests of the seventh century and the early eighth and all of the subsequent population movements within the Muslim lands had momentous consequences for Arabic genealogy. Given the vast geographical distances over which many groups were scattered, the sudden or gradual loss of any effective relations between two groups sharing a common ethnic or tribal origin was inevitable, even if this quite natural process was slowed by the spread of literacy and written documentation. Lacking modern communications tech-nologies, even the highest-status elite groups had no practical means of keeping track of the internal relationships of a related but geographically distant clan or lineage. For instance, of the hundreds of medieval Talibid families (that is, those regarded as descended from the Prophet's uncle Abu Talib), that of Ja'far al-Multani had subgroups in India and Sind, Khurasan, Transoxania, Northern Iran, Fars, Iraq, Diyar Bakr, Syria and Yemen; and that of Abu Nami in the Hijaz, Yemen, Iraq and Khurasan.[25]

The genealogy of a distant group, known to be related to one's own but otherwise completely unknown, is termed *nasab al-qaṭ'* (severed genealogy) in some of the remarkably meticulous genealogical manuals of the *sharīf* groups of Iraq and Iran. Other works had no special term to describe the phenomenon. Here is the definition of the term by Ibn 'Inaba (d. 828/1424):

> If no information has reached us on a community in a given region, and genealogists have no knowledge concerning its affairs, they will say: "They are in a severed genealogy (*hum fī nasab al-qaṭ'*)", meaning that their gene-alogies are barred from reaching us, even though they used to be well-known in the past.[26]

This genealogical disconnect between any two areas' inhabitants appears to have been exploited in forgeries, and thus had a great impact on the evolution of Arabic genealogical traditions. The same (Iranian) source states this about the Idrisid dynasty of Morocco: "The offspring of Idris are numerous. They [fall into the category of] *nasab al-qaṭ'*, so whoever traces his descent to them must produce unusually strong proofs, as they live far from us and we know little of their situation." One finds similar observations about an 'Alid lineage that ruled the city of Multan in the Punjab.[27]

It is in fact little wonder that geographical distance all but invited forgery, given the difficulties of intruding into the well-kept internal genealogical records of a local branch of a high-status group. One's own kin may also prove to be a liability in one's homeland, because if they did not make the same genea-logical claim, the result would be ludicrous. That someone should make the foolish attempt to falsify a genealogy without agreeing with his own immediate kinsmen beforehand is difficult to believe, yet various sources testify that such attempts occurred, even if they were predictably unsuccessful. A fatwa given by the great Shafi'i jurist Ibn al-Salah al-Shahrazuri (sixth–seventh/twelfth–thir-teenth century) was occasioned by the case of a man in Hama who claimed 'Alid descent (from the imam Musa al-Kazim [d. 183/799], no less) despite the fact that his own father had always claimed to be, and was generally known as, an 'Abbasid descendant.[28] A story about the famous philologist al-Asma'i

(d. 213/828) describes in an anecdotal manner the difficulties of claiming an untrue genealogy while one's own kin are still around. It has little relevance here whether the story has any basis in factual truth. Al-Asma'i's former professor took some disciples outside Basra to see al-Asma'i's father, a lowly shepherd, to make sure "he should not claim tomorrow to be a member of the Hashimite family" (*hādhā Abū l-Aṣma'ī, lā yaqūlu ghadan annahu min Banī Hāshim*).[29]

It was obviously far safer to make a claim away from one's own home community. More precisely, one had to claim membership in a distant branch of a high-status group, in the hope that it would be next to impossible for the claim's audience to verify or reject it. For instance, it is a telling detail that the first member of the Medinan al-Tamtam lineage to profess to be descended from the Ansar of Medina did so when abroad on a journey to Constantinople.[30] In view of the tendency to falsify genealogies away from one's homeland, it should not be surprising that the Banu Shishdiw, a family of 'Alids described as widely scattered, were the object of strong suspicions (*ghamz*).[31] A particularly audacious bluff – and apparently a quite successful one at that – is the case of a man who, settling in the region of Kerman and Yazd, claimed to be a member of the lineage of the governors of Mecca, the Al Abi Nami, more specifically the son of someone in their genealogies who happened to have died as an infant (and, to be sure, childless).[32] A poetaster called Abu Tahir settled in Nishapur, where, at a safe distance from Basra, he claimed to be the son of the famous Basran poet al-Khubzaruzzi (d. 327/938-9). Although the vast distance between the two towns impeded instant discovery of the fact that the alleged father was in fact notorious as a homosexual and known to have never had any children, the information did transpire at last and the forgery was exposed.[33] An influential man in Oman known as Ibn al-Khabbaz (early fifth/eleventh century) claimed descent from the imam Musa al-Kazim through a great-great-grandson whose name did not appear in the official genealogies of the lineage, a claim that would probably not have succeeded in Iraq, where descendants of the imam lived in great numbers. What makes the account truly bizarre is the fact that this man, suspected as he was of a genealogical fraud among Iraqi genealogists, was actually head and official representative (*naqīb*) of the 'Alid lineages in Oman.[34]

Some of the above examples already illustrate the use of another method of intrusion: One may attach one's pedigree to a man who died childless or whose offspring were extinct. In the absence of living close kin, there would logically be less risk of opposition and exposure. In Bedouin society, individuals without living offspring were removed from the genealogical record because their names lost ongoing sociological significance.[35] Such was certainly not the practice among literate, high-status, urban groups, which gave a ready opportunity for forgery, as a childless and long-dead name was an easier point of intrusion than an ancestor whose descendants were alive with interests to guard. The data suggest that this method was used fairly frequently. In fact, medieval Muslim genealogists were quite awake to the possibility of such forgery, as evidenced by the occasional warning along the lines of, "Such-and-such a person has no living progeny, so anyone who claims to be his descendant must be a liar."[36] The nature of the issue means that we are typically unable today to decide such cases either way, but the existence of many controversies over such points in genealogies is suggestive of the use of this trick. Consider the following account about a son of the Sharif (governor) of Mecca in the fourth/tenth century:

> ['Abd Allah] al-Qawad died childless (*inqaraḍa*), so he has no living offspring, yet a man in Egypt claimed to be descended from him (*idda'ā ilayhi*), saying: "I am 'Alyan ibn Jama'a ibn Musa ibn Mus'ab ibn Dahi ibn Nu'man ibn 'Asim ibn 'Abd Allah al-Qawad." His genealogy (*nasab*) has not been verified. He has descendants in Egypt. The *naqīb* of Egypt, who is known as Ibn al-Jawani al-Nassaba, rejected (*dafa'a*) [the claims of] 'Alyan and declared his genealogy forged (*abṭala nasabahu*), yet later it was entered into the genealogical registers (*jarā'id*) of the Talibids of Egypt by wrongful and coercive means (*ẓulman wa-'udwānan*).[37]

Rather than an isolated irregularity, this can be said to be a fairly typical account if one consults genealogical manuals.[38]

Another ruse was the addition of a very common male name to the list of a distant ancestor's children. Even with some genuine descendants somewhere, such a trick still had some chance of passing undetected.[39] That is because of the pervasive problem of the recurrence of common personal names (and sequences of such names) in the genealogical chains of various groups, which proved to be a standing invitation to "mistake", say, one 'Ali ibn Ibrahim ibn Muhammad for another who was unrelated to him and to thus transfer someone to a more prestigious lineage. Here is Yaqut al-Hamawi expressing uncertainty about the ancestry of a greatly respected friend:

> I asked him: "Who is this Hamdun appearing in your genealogy (*man huwa Ḥamdūn alladhī tunsabūna ilayhi*)? Does he happen to be the Hamdun who was the boon-companion of the caliph al-Mutawakkil and his successors?" He said: "No. We belong to the lineage of [the ruler of Aleppo] Sayf al-Dawla ibn Hamdan ibn Hamdun, from the Banu Taghlib [tribe]." This is the way he explained it.[40]

The confusion regarding the genealogical identity of many names is noted by a sixth-/twelfth-century author who complains that the descendants [of the old tribal groups] alive today would often find it difficult to distinguish their own ancestors, let alone other people's, having little interest in keeping precise genealogies; there is many a man who claims to be an 'Adawi, but when asked which 'Adi he is descended from, he would be unable to respond.[41]

The *nisba* al-'Alawi could refer not only to the descendants of 'Ali ibn Abi Talib but also to less celebrated 'Alis, and the potential for mix-up (whether purposeful or not I am unable to decide) did lead to confusion.[42] Even an honorary title may help in obfuscation of a genealogy. In the year 1080/1669–70, a Moroccan called Muhammad al-Mawhub arrived in Medina and settled there. Bearing the honorific *al-sayyid* (master) on account of his high social position in Morocco, he would later be identified by his offspring living in Medina as a descendant of the Prophet, as this title was reserved for the *shurafā'* in the Eastern Islamic lands. Even though Moroccans used the title *mawlāy* instead of *sayyid* in this sense, members of the Mawhub family would continue to claim *sharīf* status on the basis of this "misunderstanding" (*min hādhā al-tawahhum*).[43]

The problem of confusing identical names is present even in the standard corpus of early Arabian *ansāb* (genealogies), hence the various manuals elucidating the differences between groups with similar names (*mukhtalif al-qabā'il wa-mu'talifuhā*). The phenomenon of confusing the identities of people who had similar names was known as *jam' wa-tafrīq* in Hadith scholarship, where the problem was common and acute enough to give rise to separate manuals for clarifying the confusing mass of names.[44]

Conclusion

The genealogist Abu Nasr al-Bukhari (fourth/tenth century) notes that the pedigree of a relatively small and compact group is not amenable to genealogical forgeries; by implication, manipulations tend to thrive in more confusing genealogies.[45] While that is a very perceptive observation, I have argued in this chapter that a number of additional factors could also be exploited by those who would forge a new, more prestigious descent for themselves. In summary, we can now observe that sheer geographical distance, the extinction of certain branches of a lineage and the ubiquity of many male names would often conspire to facilitate the work of impostors.

NOTES

1. E. Landau-Tasseron, "Adoption, Acknowledgement of Paternity and False Genealogical Claims in Arabian and Islamic Societies", *BSOAS*, vol. 66, 2003, p. 184.

2. Neither do I study here changes in tribal affiliation made with the full consent of the receiving group, which may be referred to by the verb *dakhala fi*, "he entered such-and-such a tribe". On this phenomenon, see Abu l-'Abbas Ahmad al-Qalqashandi, *Nihayat al-arab fi ma'rifat ansab al-'Arab*, Beirut: Dar al-Kutub al-'Ilmiyya, n.d., p. 30. On the difference between false genealogical claims, the adoption of someone else's son and the acknowledgement of disputed paternity, phenomena all too often confused, see Landau-Tasseron, "Adoption", p. 169. Also, as regards source material, Landau-Tasseron's apparent focus is on early cases of disputed paternity – roughly from the pre-Islamic to the late Umayyad period or to the early 'Abbasid period – while I will rely on source material relating to later periods, starting approximately from the Buyid era (320–454/932–1062).

3. In an interesting case, a Qur'an reader from Abiward, Iran, who was an expert genealogist and who was author of several genealogical works, fabricated a *nasab* linking him to Mu'awiya ibn Abi Sufyan with the aim of dispelling the 'Abbasid caliph's suspicions of his secret allegiance to the Egyptian Fatimids (to whom Mu'awiya's very name would be an anathema). The man would later stick to his forged pedigree, which not only served him well but was a respectable one in its own right. See Yaqut al-Hamawi, *Mu'jam al-udaba'*, ed. I. 'Abbas, Beirut: Dar al-Gharb al-Islami, 1993, vol. 5, pp. 2,360–1 (and vol. 5, pp. 2,364–5 for a list of al-Abiwardi's works, including some on genealogy).

4. Some poor and nomadic Talibid lineages are reported to have lent little attention to the preservation of their genealogies; see Ibn 'Inaba al-Dawudi al-Hasani, *'Umdat al-talib fi ansab Al Abi Talib*, Beirut: Dar Maktabat al-Hayat, n.d., p. 77; Ibn Shadqam al-Hasani al-Madani, *Nukhbat al-zahra al-thamina fi nasab ashraf al-Madina*, published in one volume with al-Hazimi's *'Ujalat al-mubtadi*, eds M. Z. M. 'Azb, 'A. al-Tihami and M. al-Sharqawi, Beirut: Maktabat Madbuli, n.d., p. 214. In Lamu town (Kenya), there were two major *sharif* groups, the Mahdali and the Huseini, whose respective status, prestige and genealogical credentials showed a sharp contrast. The former did not speak Arabic at all, had no genealogical documents proving their descent from the Prophet and were thought to be of suspect origins and consequently of lower status than the latter, who usually knew some Arabic (even though speaking Swahili as their mother tongue) and possessed some records of their pedigree. See A. H. el Zein, *The Sacred Meadows: A Structural Analysis of Religious Symbolism in an East African Town*, Evanston, IL: Northwestern University Press, 1974, pp. 41, 106.

5. The Shafi'i school insisted on this rule with special rigour. See al-Qalqashandi, *Nihaya*, p. 14.

6. Yaqut, *Mu'jam*, vol. 2, pp. 707–8; Ibn 'Inaba, *'Umda*, p. 100. The Shafi'i jurist al-Mawardi regards it as one of the duties of the supervisor of markets and public morals (*muhtasib*) to ensure that a widowed woman should only be given in a new marriage to a *kufu'* (equal in social standing); see his *al-Ahkam al-sultaniyya wa-l-wilayat al-diniyya*, ed. K. R. al-Jumayli, Baghdad: al-Maktaba al-'Alamiyya, 1989 [1409], p. 371.

7. For instance, an early tenth-/sixteenth-century king of the Songhay state in West Africa, while on his pilgrimage, asked the Sharif of Mecca to send some relative of his to settle in Songhay, with the express aim of benefiting from the *baraka* of the Prophet's lineage (*li-yatabarrakū bihi*). See Mahmud Ka'ti al-Tinbukti al-Wa'kori, *Ta'rikh al-fattash fi akhbar al-buldan wa-l-juyush wa-akabir al-nas*, eds O. Houdas and M. Delafosse, Paris: Librairie d'Amérique et d'Orient, Maisonneuve, 1981, p. 16.

8. I thank Abdessamad Belhaj for the information on Morocco. On the custom's prevalence in Lamu, see el Zein, *Sacred Meadows*, p. 156. For examples in Moroccan popular Sufism of the transfer of *baraka* through sexual intercourse as well as through saliva and even vomit, see F. R. Mediano, "Santos arrebatados: Algunos ejemplos de *maẓdūb* en la *Salwat al-anfās* de Muḥammad al-Kattānī", *Al-Qanṭara*, vol. 13, 1992, pp. 242–4.

9. A. S. Bujra, *The Politics of Stratification: A Study of Political Change in a South Arabian Town*, Oxford: Clarendon Press, 1971, pp. 13–14.

10. 'Izz al-Din ibn al-Athir, *al-Kamil fi al-ta'rikh*, Leiden: E. J. Brill, 1851–71, vol. 9, p. 591 (and vol. 9, p. 236); and on the controversies concerning the descent of the Fatimids, Idrisids and the leader of the Zanj, see *Muqaddimat Ibn Khaldun*, ed. 'A. 'A. W. Wafi, Cairo: Dar Nahdat Misr, n.d., vol. 1, pp. 309–17; Ibn 'Inaba, *'Umda*, pp. 265 and 322–3; Ibn Hazm al-Andalusi, *Jamharat ansab al-'Arab*, Beirut: Dar al-Kutub al-'Ilmiyya, 1998 [1418], pp. 56–7; Ibn Taymiyya, *al-Fatawa al-kubra*, vol. 3, ed. Muhammad 'Abd al-Qadir 'Ata and Mustafa 'Abd al-Qadir 'Ata, Beirut: Dar al-Kutub al-'Ilmiyya, 2002 [1422], pp. 487–503 (esp. pp. 493–5); Abu Sa'd 'Abd al-Karim al-Sam'ani, *Kitab al-ansab*, vol. 4, ed. 'A. A. 'U. al-Barudi, Beirut: Dar al-Jinan, 1988 [1408], pp. 458–9; Shams al-Din Muhammad al-Sakhawi, *al-I'lan bi-l-tawbikh li-man dhamma al-ta'rikh*, ed. F. Rosenthal, Beirut: Dar al-Kutub al-'Ilmiyya, n.d., pp. 20, 177; and for a modern summary of the Fatimid question, see 'A. H. 'Uways, *Qadiyyat nasab al-Fatimiyyin amam manhaj al-naqd al-ta'rikhi*, Cairo: Dar al-Sahwa, 1985 [1406], pp. 3–24, 30–1. The Shafi'i school regarded proximity of genealogical relations to the Hashimite family as a decisive factor in assessing the legitimacy of a contender to the imamate; see al-Qalqashandi, *Nihaya*, p. 14. It was not only ruling dynasties that could become the targets of vicious genealogical controversies. Sometimes whole treatises were composed and circulated locally with the aim of discrediting the legitimacy of a given group's pedigree. See, for instance, the case of the booklet *al-Qawl al-mu'talif fi nisbat al-khamsa al-buyut al-mansubin* [sic] *ila al-sharaf* (On the falsity of the purported origins of the al-Bukhari family of Medina) in 'Abd al-Rahman al-Ansari, *Tuhfat al-muhibbin wa-l-ashab fi ma'rifat ma li-l-Madaniyyin min al-ansab*, ed. M. 'A. al-Mitwi, Tunis: al-Maktaba al-'Atiqa, 1970 [1390], p. 109.

11. On the duties of the *naqīb*, including the protection of his group's material interests and the prevention of marriages with non-equal outsiders, see al-Mawardi, *Ahkam*, pp. 154–5.

12. Such was the custom around Mecca under the rule of Shihab al-Din Abu Sulayman Ahmad, where a *sharīf* would be banished from the region for the crime of theft but the general punishment was the cutting off of a hand or even execution. See Ibn 'Inaba, *'Umda*, p. 175. While theft should theoretically be treated as a crime subject to a non-negotiable, fixed *ḥadd* punishment, such differentiation was recognised as

perfectly licit in the case of ta'zīr (discretionary) punishments; see M. Fierro, "Idra'u l-hudud bi-l-shubuhat: When Lawful Violence Meets Doubt", Hawwa, vol. 5, 2007, p. 235.

13. Ahmad ibn al-Bashir al-Shinqiti, Mawarid al-najah wa-masadir al-falah 'ala Risalat Ibn Abi Zayd al-Qayrawani, Abu Dhabi: al-Majma' al-Thaqafi, 2003 [1424], vol. 1, p. 120. Some Hadiths, no doubt forged, went as far as claiming for the Prophet's descendants unconditional exemption from hell; see ibid., vol. 1, pp. 120–2.

14. In the Fatimid era, the shurafā' of the Hijaz would apparently make regular visits to Cairo to collect royal gifts and awards. See Yaqut, Mu'jam, vol. 3, p. 1,104. In the early eighth/fourteenth century, the sultan of the Muslim African state of Kilwa had a separate treasury whose contents he regularly distributed among the shurafā' visiting him from the Arabian Peninsula (esp. the Hijaz and Yemen) for that purpose. See Rihlat Ibn Battuta, Beirut: Dar Sadir, 2001, p. 150.

15. See, for instance, Yaqut, Mu'jam, vol. 2, p. 701. In a revealing passage, a poet of the Hamdanid Sayf al-Dawla's (r. 333–56/945–67) court, known as Ibn al-Abyad, is offered a royal award simply because of his being an 'Alid ("a'tihi shay'an fa-innahu 'Alawī"), on which the poet indignantly comments in verse that he should rather receive that gift on account of his personal achievements, notably his poetry. See Abu l-Hasan Muhammad Shaykh al-Sharaf al-'Ubaydili, Tahdhib al-ansab wa-nihayat al-a'qab, ed. M. K. al-Mahmudi, Qom: Maktabat al-Mar'ashi, 1413 AH, pp. 255–6.

16. Abu l-Faraj al-Isfahani, Maqatil al-Talibiyyin, 2nd edn, ed. A. Saqr, Beirut: Mu'assasat al-A'lami li-l-Matbu'at, 1987 [1408], p. 479.

17. 'Abd al-Salam ibn al-Tayyib al-Qadiri, Matla' al-ishraq fi nasab al-shurafa' al-waridin min al-'Iraq, ed. A. al-'Iraqi, Fez: Imprimerie Info-Print, 2006, pp. 62–3.

18. 'Ali al-Wardi, Dirasa fi tabi'at al-mujtama' al-'iraqi, Baghdad: Matba'at al-'Ani, 1965, pp. 246–7.

19. Incidentally, this pious habit proved prescient later, when the ruler Ahmad ibn Tulun (254–70/868–4) decided to confiscate the family's property but had to accept the intercession made on their behalf by a grateful 'Alid courtier. See the story in Yaqut, Mu'jam, vol. 2, p. 559.

20. Jalal al-Din 'Abd al-Rahman al-Suyuti, al-Hawi li-l-fatawi, vol. 2, ed. 'A. L. H. 'Abd al-Rahman, Beirut: Dar al-Kutub al-'Ilmiyya, 2000 [1421], pp. 32–3. The discussion of these aspects of the issue follows a rather tortured argumentation for the exclusion of Zaynab bint 'Ali's descendants from the nasab of the Prophet on the grounds that two uterine links to the Prophet, namely through Fatima and Zaynab, are one too many in order to qualify as proper descent.

21. Ibn Shadqam, Nukhba, p. 220.

22. Al-Ansari, Tuhfa, p. 206. While the Hashimites were legally entitled to a part of the zakāt (obligatory alms), some of them apparently made attempts to go even further and get a share in the kaffārāt (expiatory monies or alms) as well, to which they had no lawful claim. See Ibn al-Salah al-Shahrazuri, Fatawa wa-masa'il Ibn al-Salah fi al-tafsir wa-l-hadith wa-l-usul wa-l-fiqh, vol. 2, ed. 'A. M. A. Qal'aji, Beirut: Dar al-Ma'rifa, 1986 [1406], p. 645.

23. Abu 'Uthman al-Jahiz, Kitab al-Hayawan, vol. 1, ed. Y. al-Shami, Beirut: Dar wa-Maktabat al-Hilal, 1986), p. 366. Also, if one's genealogical pretensions came to be known as false, a new claim would likely bring still more ridicule upon the

claimant; see al-Raghib al-Isfahani, *Muhadarat al-udaba' wa-muhawarat al-shu'ara' wa-l-bulagha'*, vol. 1, ed. R. 'A. H. Murad, Beirut: Dar Sadir, 2004 [1425], p. 745. Sporadically, attempts may be made to produce fake documents in order to support otherwise preposterous genealogical claims. An interesting passage in Miskawayh's chronicle tells of an impostor called al-Daniyali, who, during the reign of al-Muqtadir (r. 295–320/908–32), faked, with great skill, a number of "ancient" writings that he attributed mostly to the prophet Daniel. Among others, he produced a document "proving" that the commander Muflih was a descendant of Ja'far ibn Abi Talib, which earned him huge rewards and favours from the military leader. See Abu 'Ali Miskawayh, *Tajarib al-umam*, vol. 1, ed. H. F. Amedroz, Baghdad: Maktabat al-Muthanna, 1914 [1332], pp. 215–16.

24. Al-Ansari, *Tuhfa*, p. 73.

25. Al-'Ubaydili, *Tahdhib*, p. 298; Ibn 'Inaba, *'Umda*, pp. 169–70. Members of the Al Abi Nami, another Talibid offshoot, could apparently be encountered in various towns of East Africa, too; see Ibn Battuta, *Rihla*, p. 150.

26. Ibn 'Inaba, *'Umda*, p. 22.

27. Ibn 'Inaba, *'Umda*, pp. 186, 405–6. For some similar cases, see ibid., pp. 180, 181, 199, 263, 264; and Abu Nasr Sahl al-Bukhari, *Sirr al-silsila al-nabawiyya*, ed. M. S. Bahr al-'Ulum, Najaf: al-Maktaba al-Haydariyya, 1963 [1382], pp. 52, 98. About the important Banu l-Ukhaydir lineage of al-Yamama, similarly unknown ("*lam taqa' ilaynā ansābuhum*"), see al-Isfahani, *Maqatil*, pp. 551–2. In the genealogical tradition of the Talibids of Iraq and Iran, groups living in North Africa were the *par excellence* cases of *nasab al-qat'*; see, for instance, al-'Ubaydili, *Tahdhib*, pp. 59, 61, 62, 96, 99, 172, 173, 190, 200, 285, 329, 347–8.

28. Ibn al-Salah, *Fatawa*, vol. 2, p. 536; compare Yaqut, *Mu'jam*, vol. 2, p. 560 (the case of al-Qifti and his brother); Ibn Bassam al-Shantarini, *al-Dhakhira fi mahasin ahl al-Jazira*, vol. 1, ed. S. M. al-Badri, Beirut: Dar al-Kutub al-'Ilmiyya, 1998 [1419], pp. 104–5 (the family of Ibn Hazm).

29. Yaqut, *Mu'jam*, vol. 4, pp. 1,622–3. On al-Asma'i's tribal background, see al-Wazir al-Maghribi, *al-Inas fi 'ilm al-ansab*, ed. A. al-Jasir, Riyadh: al-Nadi al-Adabi fi al-Riyad, 1980 [1400], pp. 74–5; Abu Bakr Muhammad ibn Musa al-Hazimi, *'Ujalat al-mubtadi wa-fudalat al-muntahi fi al-nasab*, eds M. Z. M. 'Azb, 'A. al-Tihami and M. al-Sharqawi, Beirut: Maktabat Madbuli, n.d., pp. 29–30.

30. Al-Ansari, *Tuhfa*, pp. 133–4.

31. Ibn 'Inaba, *'Umda*, p. 95; al-'Ubaydili, *Tahdhib*, p. 118. Similar doubts surrounded a lineage living in the borderland between Palestine and the Sinai desert, whose members claimed to be descended from the imam Musa al-Kazim; in all probability, distance and a remote locality combined to thwart any attempts at settling the matter. See Ibn 'Inaba, *'Umda*, p. 250. On other suspect genealogical claims made by various groups living in Tabaristan, Iraq, Hijaz, Shiraz, al-Ahwaz, Khurasan, Balkh and Morocco, and rejected by some genealogists, see Ibn 'Inaba, *'Umda*, pp. 128, 211, 391, 403. Unsurprisingly, a comprehensive modern *fiqh* manual on ascertaining genealogies contends that the idea of someone's genealogy being "widely known", and therefore not requiring positive proof, should only be allowed in a person's birthplace, and not in a place where he settled subsequently. See 'A. M. Y. al-Muhammadi, *Ahkam al-nasab fi al-shari'a al-islamiyya: Turuq ithbatihi wa-nafyihi*,

Doha: Dar Qatari ibn al-Faja'a, 1994 [1414], p. 301.

32. Ibn 'Inaba, *'Umda*, p. 174.
33. Abu Mansur 'Abd al-Malik al-Tha'alibi, *Yatimat al-dahr fi mahasin ahl al-'asr*, vol. 2, Beirut: Dar al-Kutub al-'Ilmiyya, 1979 [1399], p. 366.
34. Ibn 'Inaba, *'Umda*, p. 256.
35. E. Peters, "The Proliferation of Segments in the Lineage of the Bedouin of Cyrenaica", *Journal of the Royal Anthropological Institute*, vol. 90, 1960, p. 36.
36. For example, al-Bukhari, *Sirr*, pp. 2, 3, 4, 9, 27, 33, 34, 43, 44, 73, 78, 85, 92, 94; Ibn 'Inaba, *'Umda*, pp. 160, 231. Such cautionary locutions are especially common in Abu Nasr al-Bukhari's work.
37. Ibn 'Inaba, *'Umda*, p. 157.
38. By way of further example, two cases from the *'Umdat al-talib*. First, despite a lineage of rich and influential 'Alids in Abarquh claiming to be descendants of Mahdi al-Jawhari, it seemed probable to many respected genealogists that the latter actually had no living offspring, and especially not any living offspring who lived outside of Bukhara. Second, in about 670/1271–2, a group of pilgrims who came to visit 'Ali ibn Abi Talib's tomb identified themselves there as the descendants of a certain 'Ali ibn Muhammad ibn Ahmad ibn Muhammad ibn Ahmad from the lineage of Zayd ibn Zayn al-'Abidin, a man who genealogists knew for a fact had no surviving offspring. See these and other cases in Ibn 'Inaba, *'Umda*, pp. 56–7, 113–15, 126, 230, 244, 251–3, 294, 402; al-Bukhari, *Sirr*, pp. 8, 20, 27, 37, 38; and Muhammad Murtada ibn Muhammad al-Zabidi, *Jadhwat al-iqtibas fi nasab Bani al-'Abbas*, ed. Y. M. ibn Junayd, Beirut: al-Dar al-'Arabiyya li-l-Mawsu'at, 2005 [1426], pp. 30, 37.
39. See, for instance, Ibn 'Inaba, *'Umda*, pp. 132, 243, 251.
40. Yaqut, *Mu'jam*, vol. 3, p. 1,013. For similar cases of (no doubt, often deliberate) genealogical mistakes, see al-Bukhari, *Sirr*, pp. 12, 42, 63, 71, 93 and Ibn 'Inaba, *'Umda*, pp. 182, 354. The commonality of names as a principal source of genealogical confusion is also noted in Fayiz ibn Musa al-Badrani al-Harbi, "al-Ta'lif fi al-ansab: al-Zahira wa-l-asbab", *Hadith al-Dar*, vol. 26, Kuwait: Mathaf al-Kuwayt al-Watani, 2008, p. 52.
41. Al-Hazimi, *'Ujala*, p. 10.
42. For example, al-Sam'ani, *Ansab*, vol. 4, p. 229; see also ibid., vol. 4, p. 340 on the *nisba* al-Fatimi. Similarly, such well-known eponymous figures as Umayya, Asad, Khazraj, Ghatafan and Mazin actually appear in a host of tribal subgroups, a potential source for confusion. See al-Maghribi, *Inas*, pp. 75, 77, 138, 230 and al-Hazimi, *'Ujala*, pp. 23–6, 185.
43. Al-Ansari, *Tuhfa*, pp. 451–2; also see pp. 453, 569–70.
44. For more on *jam' wa-tafriq*, see my book *The Roots of Arabic Genealogy: A Study in Historical Anthropology*, Piliscsaba, Hungary: The Avicenna Institute of Middle Eastern Studies, 2003, pp. 150–60.
45. Al-Bukhari, *Sirr*, pp. 49, 86.

CHAPTER 3

The Genealogy of Power and the Power of Genealogy in Morocco: History, Imaginary and Politics

Zakaria Rhani

In his incisive criticism of Ibn Rushd's views of nobility (*sharaf*), Ibn Khaldun addressed the significant role of politics and social solidarity in genealogical affiliation (*nasab*). While for Ibn Rushd nobility belongs to a people or a house (*bayt*) consisting of ancient settlers in a town and depends exclusively on the number of ancestors and their prominent origins, for Ibn Khaldun nobility refers to a sense of "group feeling" (*'aṣabiyya*) and its associated political power and social authority – as "influence among men". Since nobility is the result of personal qualities and group solidarity, only those "who share in a group feeling" can possess it, while others have it only in a metaphorical and figurative sense, and, hence, the assumption that they are noble is a "specious claim". Therefore, on every occasion that the group feeling is effaced or even simply weakened, the genealogical nobility loses its socio-political significance and becomes a "delusion".[1]

Through his argument, Ibn Khaldun tries to elucidate how effective and symbolic aspects of genealogies are entangled with their socio-political dimensions. For him, *nasab* does not necessarily refer to a historical reality (although it may), and its authority lies in its social, economic and political effectiveness. In fact, Ibn Khaldun's conception of Maghribian and Islamic kinship systems is a part of his thesis concerning *taghallub* – domination in its broad political, economic and military significance – and *'aṣabiyya* (solidarity). The ties of descent appear as a necessary, yet insufficient, condition for the emergence of *'aṣabiyya*; while *taghallub*, on the other hand, reinforces genealogical claims. For this reason, origins and pedigrees are constantly reconsidered and even reconstructed by groups and houses according to their fortunes and socio-political ambitions.[2]

SHARAF PERSONIFIED: PROPHETIC DESCENT

Ibn Khaldun was undoubtedly an ardent supporter of the Prophet's Family, the Ahl al-Bayt (literally, "the People of the House"), which he considered the supreme "house" within which political authority must reside. This probably explains why he peculiarly excludes prophetic lineages from such reconstructions. Yet, as we shall see, Ibn Khaldun's remarks could just as well be applied to the sharifian pedigree, and conceivably more intensely, given the political and economic issues involved. It was probably Mulay Idris I (d. 791), also known as Idris al-Akbar – a great-grandson of Fatima and 'Ali, through their eldest son al-Hasan – who first brought the idea of the Ahl al-Bayt to Morocco. Mulay Idris I contested the right of the 'Abbasid caliphs to take power, since in his view they could not be counted among the Ahl al-Bayt. When he fought them, he was defeated near Mecca, but he managed to escape to Morocco where he founded the first Muslim dynasty. He also initiated the largest line of descendants of the Prophet (shurfa), the Idrisids.[3] Yet sharifism was not definitively established as a metaphysical and socio-political principle until the ascension, in the seventeenth century, of another sharifian dynasty, the 'Alawites, the ruling family of Morocco today. Like the Idrisids, the 'Alawites are Hasanids who trace back

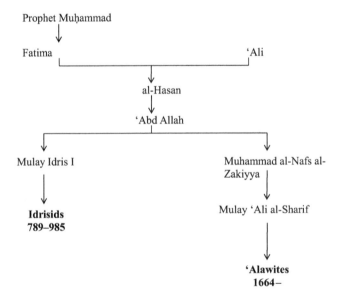

Figure 3.1 Idrisids vs 'Alawites

their genealogical tree to al-Hasan through other founding ancestors, namely Muhammad al-Nafs al-Zakiyya (d. 762) and, then, Mulay 'Ali al-Sharif (d. 1659), who is considered to be the actual founder of the dynasty (see Figure 3.1).

It was, in fact, during the sixteenth century that sharifian ideology witnessed a strong re-emergence, helped by the turmoil that characterised the epoch – that is, a major socio-economic crisis, an Ottoman threat, the expulsion of the Moriscos from Spain, the Iberian invasions, and the rise of tribalism. The impotence of the last Marinids (1215–49) to face the crises, and especially to resist Iberian assaults, precipitated the collapse of their political authority.[4] This period also witnessed an enormous expansion of popular piety around mystical groups (al-tawā'if), among them one known as al-tā'ifa al-jazūliyya, which called for "true successors of the Prophet" to guide Muslims and to lead them in battle against the Christian conquerors. It was in these particular circumstances that the shurfa of Morocco began to promote themselves as the "right imams" and as combatants against the conquerors, that is, as "mujāhidīn".[5] While the Idrisids could not take advantage of this new growing veneration for the Prophet's descendants – as they were symbolically and politically weakened by their complicity with the Marinids – the Zaydis or Sa'adian shurfa, whose emergence was closely related to the jazūliyya movement, experienced a stunning ascension. It is true that their reign was brief (1524–1660), but they prepared the way for the 'Alawite shurfa, who established permanently the sharifian genealogy as the foundation of political power and religious authority, especially after the consolidation of the dynasty by Sultan Mulay Isma'il (r. 1672–1727).

This historical overview is primarily intended to illustrate the seminal significance of prophetic descent in Moroccan political and religious practice and belief. There are, certainly, many other historical details and analyses that may elucidate it. But my method here is not only historical; it is rather an ethno-historical one, which consists of reading and questioning history from an anthropological perspective. Such an approach has the advantage of showing how, and to some extent why, these significant symbols (that is, Ahl al-Bayt, sharaf, nasab, walāya, baraka, and so on) and historical individuals ('Ali, Idris, al-Jazuli, Ben Mshish, and so on) are presented and represented on the ground today. In view of that interest, and relying on my ethnographic research on Moroccan cults of saints, syād (sg. sayed), I will try to elucidate how genealogical representations are anchored in the Moroccan imagination and in everyday practice and attempt to show how, in turn, these imaginary and symbolic representations (mythology, rituals, and manuscript documentation) have somehow "commented upon" and "rearranged" sharifian genealogies, mainly for political and socio-economic reasons.

The Cult of Saints: Fusing the Mystical and the Genealogical

One of the major consequences of the socio-political turmoil of the sixteenth century was a broad proliferation of the cults of saints, whose political and religious expressions reached an unprecedented intensity. An extensive search for *baraka*, led by "charismatic" men – that is, *awliyā'*, *shyūkh*, *shurfa*, *murābiṭūn* and tribal leaders – animated Moroccan society.[6] The dissemination of such "exemplary" individuals across the country contributed significantly to the reconstruction of disintegrated societies, since many lineages, groups and tribes adopted them – for religious, ecological, territorial and political reasons – through eponymous ancestors, to whom they generally assigned sanctity, supernatural powers and sharifian pedigrees. The descendants of these adopted saints were venerated as the legitimate heirs on account of their nobility, sacredness and, hence, their "cosmic" authority. Likewise, the current descendants of a saint today, *wlād sayed*, are considered to be the contemporary guardians of their holy ancestor's shrine and the masters of the cult surrounding him. Their ritual functions consist of mobilising the *baraka* embodied in the saint, in his tomb and in nearby locales, mostly for therapeutic and cathartic purposes.[7]

The village where I did my fieldwork is named after the saint Sidi 'Abdel'aziz ben Yeffu, and is called Zawiyat 'Abdel'aziz ben Yeffu.[8] Four lineages (*fakhdhat*, sg. *fakhdha*) claim direct descent from the saint and four others from his brother Sidi 'Ali, with the eight lines regarded jointly as the "wlad ben Yeffu". These lineages are Timgret, Dhahja, Tyur, wlad Sidi Hmed, l-A'rawat, l-Hsasna, wlad Sidi 'Ali and l-Ghlamat latter, also known as the l-Baghli family. This last lineage has been the subject of unremitting controversies and has even been excluded from the wider family by critics. Many *shurfa* from the other lineages have believed that the l-Baghli family acquired its status as *sharaf* and the decrees that attest to it through close ties with Morocco's sultans, particularly Sultan Mulay al-Hasan I (r. 1873–94). In fact, this socio-political closeness is attested by several decrees of honour and respect (*ẓahīrs*) from the 'Alawite sovereign addressed to 'Ali l-Baghli. Influential members of the family, including the latter, were the official leaders of Ben Yeffu's sanctuary (*mqadmīn*, sg. *mqadem*) until the 1990s.[9] However, for their part, the Baghlis vigorously affirm the authenticity of their nobility and throw doubts on that of other lineages, as, according to them, the *ẓahīrs* they hold are irrefutable confirmation of their genealogical claims. It is difficult to confirm any allegations, as it is hard to certify the historical reality of the saint himself; there is no independent historical documentation about him and there is therefore no way to trace these lineages back to him. In fact, all of these genealogical rivalries underpin a permanent conflict, regarding not only spiritual and political leadership, but also economic issues – that is, gift and income distribution.

As just mentioned, there is not any undisputed historical data that could attest to the historicity of the saint and therefore to the authenticity of his own or his descendants' membership in the prophetic lineage. Nevertheless, some of the wlad ben Yeffu possess a handwritten document that in their view "authenticates" such a claim. This document, signed in 1971 (1369 AH), is itself copied from another manuscript, named *al-jafriyya*, which was written in the eighteenth century (1116 AH). While acknowledging its obvious anachronisms, I do not intend to discuss the authenticity of this document here but rather to analyse its semantic and political connotations. First, it should be noted that the word *al-jafriyya* is rather curious, since it presumably refers to *al-jafr*, widely known in Shi'i mythology as a parchment (or container) made of animal skin and inherited from 'Ali and Fatima, who had themselves inherited it from the Prophet, and from which the imams drew their secret knowledge.[10] Thus, this reference to *al-jafr* by wlad ben Yeffu probably aims to stress the strong genealogical and mystical ties that bind them to the Prophet's family core. The document places Ben Yeffu in a double affiliation: first, a genealogical one that links Ben Yeffu to other eponymous saints, principally Mulay 'Abdeslam ben Mshish (d. 1228) and Mulay Idris; and, second, a mystical one, in which Ben Yeffu is related to famous saints and scholars, namely Abu Madyan (d. 1198) and al-Ghazali (d. 1111). Both lines are traced back to the Prophet through 'Ali, but given that Abu Madyan was also Ben Mshish's spiritual master, the two lines intersect already before reaching the Prophet's son-in-law (see Figure 3.2).

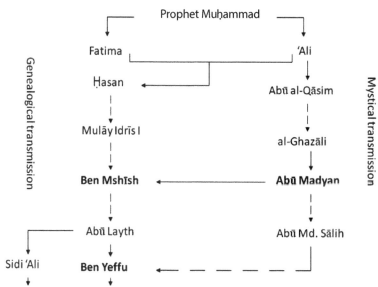

Figure 3.2 Ben Yeffu's mystical and genealogical transmission lines
as indicated in *al-jafriyya* document

Ben Mshish is, in several respects, a "legendary" saint whose genuine history is unknown even though he is a great celebrity. He neither initiated a mystical path nor, *a fortiori*, did he found a brotherhood.[11] His actual influence was chiefly felt in the fifteenth century thanks to another very prominent saint, al-Jazuli (d. 1465 or 1470).[12] As his name suggests, al-Jazuli was originally from Jazula, a member of a Berber tribe, yet he had always considered himself a *sharif*: "I am *sharif* in lineage," he claimed. "My ancestor is the Messenger of God."[13] In addition to his energetic promotion of sharifism, his doctrine of *al-ṭarīqa al-Muḥammadiyya* (Muhammadian path) – that also emphasises that social consciousness and political activism are part of the very essence of Sufism – fostered the socio-political and, hence, the genealogical aspirations of Moroccan saints and their descendants. Thus, notions of sharifism and of sainthood, which prior to al-Jazuli were largely separate, merged and initiated the emergence of massive sharifian claims. Likewise, thanks to al-Jazuli, Moroccan Sufism was "nationalised" through the discovery and promotion of local figures, especially Ben Mshish, who has become the "pole" of Moroccan mysticism and the symbol of Idrisid sharifism.[14]

In this sense, the *al-jafriyya* manuscript should be considered an eloquent commentary on that significant turning point in Moroccan history. The document illustrates clearly the fusion that occurred since the fifteenth century between mystical transmission and patrilineal descent, as spiritual and genealogical affiliations with Ben Mshish reach back to the Ahl al-Bayt in its Idrisid version. Accordingly, wlad ben Yeffu are not only the biological descendants of the saint Ben Yeffu, but they have inherited his mystical knowledge and power. In this particular case, "spiritual" power/knowledge is expressed in terms of uncanny powers and an authority over the world of spirits (*'ālam al-jinn or jnūn*).[15] Since the saint was known for his power over *jnūn*, his descendants have inherited his *baraka* to cure spirit possession and related diseases. The healing ritual is very simple and no initiation is required, given that everything revolves around the saint and his authority over the supernatural world. The space where wlad ben Yeffu perform the ritual is called the *maḥkama*. The term "*maḥkama*", literally meaning "court", points to the judicial dimension of the ceremony in which the possessing spirit and his victim are tried before a tribunal. Thanks to the *baraka* of their ancestor, known as *sulṭān al-jinn*, the *shurfa* are capable of controlling supernatural beings and resolving conflicts between spirits and humans.[16] On the other hand, this mystical authority – the ability to heal diseases caused by the attacks of spirits – underlines a political one, as it is the significant proof that the saint's descendants are authentic *shurfa*.

The identity of the wlad ben Yeffu lineages is contained, so to speak, in this fused chain of genealogical descent and mystical transmission, that is, *al-jafriyya*. The *jafriyya* is considered a "symbolic encapsulation"[17] of the family's authentic history. As many anthropologists who have worked in Morocco have convincingly argued, genealogies can usefully be employed when reconstructing historical times and history as locally understood. That is, sacred genealogies, punctuated by "meta-saints" (such as Ben Mshish and Mulay Idris) and terminating in the most prestigious origin (the Prophet's Bayt), are actually the validation of the saintly status of a given lineage existing at the present time.[18] Genealogical information is thus conceived as the written memory of charisma, and, in return, is solicited to confirm that nobility and prestige presuppose continuity of descent.[19] Accordingly, the document that could authenticate such succession is viewed as legitimising authority; this is why the al-jafriyya manuscript should be considered less as a *nasab*, in a purely genealogical sense, and more as a "factual" history, *ta'rīkh* (or, in Moroccan, *tārīkh*).

Yet, to designate the history of their ancestor, members of the wlad ben Yeffu do not use the word *tārīkh*, but rather the terms *ḥkāya* (that is, *ḥikāya*) and *qaṣṣa* (that is, *qiṣṣa*). While these two words denote etymologically "tale" and "story", they are meant to express the idea of history. However, this history recounts less the different stages of the saint's life and more the noteworthy "miracles" (*karāmāt*) that he accomplished.[20] By evoking exemplary men, heroes, supernatural beings and celestial geographies, the "story", so to speak, describes the origin of social life and explains the birth of culture. It is indeed a founding *voice*. But it is a voice chosen by history, since, as Roland Barthes convincingly put it, the mythological account cannot arise from the "nature of things"; it must have historical bases.[21]

HISTORY AND COUNTER-NARRATIVE STORIES: THE GENEALOGY IMAGINED

While this oral story certainly contains many inaccuracies and anachronisms, it also expresses historical messages that are probably more significant than as are expressed in written history itself. And as paradoxical as it may seem, it is the absence of written history – especially when it is politically very charged – that may preserve history in its semantic "limpidness". In addition, if such stories, with their historical deficiencies, do not inform us about a people's true histories (that is, the history of wlad ben Yeffu), they, nevertheless, narrate the cultural symbols that have truly influenced their identities. Accordingly, instead of trying to comprehend the events and their diachronic succession, we should, rather, analyse and interpret the semantic scope of the absence of history (of the saint) – or the ahistoricity of his story – as it is in these obscure absences that anthropology penetrates to examine the intimate entanglement between history and imaginary.

Ben Yeffu's tale recounts a decisive encounter between the saint himself and Sultan l-Khel, the Black Sultan. The story relates that when the Black

Sultan learned that a saint performing miracles had arrived in his region, that is, al-Madina al-Gharbiyya (an antique city in the region of Dukkala), he assembled his army and rode out to meet him. The Black Sultan demanded that Ben Yeffu leave his territory, but the saint, comforted by the presence of a supernatural army of spirits, namely, *jnūn*, refused. Ben Yeffu's stubbornness enraged the sultan, who ordered his army to attack him. The saint gave a sign to his *jnūn* to counter-attack, and the soldiers started flying away with their horses. Defeated and humiliated, the Black Sultan implored Ben Yeffu's forgiveness; the saint took this opportunity to ask for a signed document stating clearly that he was a *shrīf*. The sultan agreed. The saint then ordered his *jnūn* not to harm the sultan and his army. The Black Sultan accordingly signed the decree of *sharaf* and, before leaving, solemnly declared, while pointing to Ben Yeffu: "I am a sultan and you are a sultan."

The meanings that the saint's descendants give to the term "sultan" evoke not only his spiritual authority and his supernatural powers, but also his temporal sovereignty. According to some of them, Ben Yeffu was a veritable monarch, just as the current king Mohamed VI is. Since he combines the two forms of *baraka*, the spiritual and the genealogical, it is he and not the king who ideally deserves the title of "sultan". To explain the difference between the authority of the saint and that of the sultan, one of the descendants of Ben Yeffu powerfully expresses the nature of this tension: "Sovereignty (*mulk*) in Morocco has two faces: one is apparent and visible (*ẓāhir*), which is represented by Mohamed VI and his 'Alawite family, whereas the other is hidden and unseen (*bāṭin*), represented by Ben Yeffu and the Idrisids." As in the Sufi distinction, the hidden kingship is more significant, more authentic and hence more powerful than the external one, which is, by contrast, superficial, peripheral and thus less authoritative. Yet Ben Yeffu's narratives should not be considered an "explicit" discourse, but rather they should be considered a "counter-discourse", for they do not tell a real history but rather an ideal story in which it is the saint who dominates the sultan and not the contrary.[22]

Notwithstanding many historical details that relate the mysterious Black Sultan to the Almohads or to Marinid kings, he rather symbolises the 'Alawite Mulay Isma'il in the imaginations of wlad ben Yeffu and many other Moroccans.[23] As mentioned earlier, it was during the reign of this sovereign that sharifism had to find a new cultural, political and symbolic authority, which it has maintained until today. Therefore, the myth of Ben Yeffu can be considered a subversive commentary on that crucial moment in Moroccan history when the 'Alawite sultan had monopolised power and, using forces and favours, had subdued saints and scholars.

Indeed, Mulay Isma'il was deeply involved in legitimising centralised authority. Seriously challenged by *zāwiyas* and influential charismatic men, he put to work an ingenious idea – most likely borrowed from the Ottomans. He assembled a new army that was allied not to any specific social group but to the sovereign himself. This army was made up of slaves of the country who were required to give an oath of loyalty on the *Sahih* of al-Bukhari, considered by Sunnis to be the most authentic collection of hadith. Hence, this army was given the name *'Abīd al-Bukhārī*, that is, "the slaves of al-Bukhari". First, Mulay Isma'il assembled the slaves that Ahmad al-Mansur had brought from Sudan after his 1591 campaign. As their number was insufficient, he enlisted all slaves, including those who belonged to individuals, whereas their children were taken to the capital, Meknes, to be regimented later.[24]

Certainly this was not the only strategy employed to support centralisation; rather, it was part of a wider plan that involved political and religious justification. The control of sharifian genealogies simultaneously with the promotion of sharifism served as a means to thwart the political and spiritual ambitions of all those who would find in sharifian descent a way to strengthen their political claims and separatist tendencies – that is, saints, scholars and *zāwiya* leaders.[25] Mulay Isma'il also established a policy of sharifian tax exemptions and royal donations, so that being a member of the sharifian genealogy became the ultimate route to social mobility. Thus, those who were not *shurfa* aimed to be so, while those who were real *shurfa* wanted to be *shurfa* even more fervently than the others. Historians are indeed in unanimous agreement on the fact that the number of *shurfa* increased considerably after these policies were established.[26] As they could enhance people's wealth and their social and symbolic status, royal decrees confirming sharifian titles have since then played an important role in social and economic transactions. The 'Alawite sultans have often granted such recognition to important lineages in order to acquire their political support. As Henry Munson Jr has noted:

> The powerful and the wealthy, especially descendants of saints venerated by ordinary Moroccans, were also the most likely to be useful to sultans; they were also able to afford the sums of money that often had to be paid to obtain royal decrees. Just as nineteenth-century European businessmen were able to buy titles of nobility, so too have many prominent Moroccan descendants of saints been able to purchase titles attesting to their descent from the Prophet. Such descent was much more than a source of political legitimacy, it was the paradigmatic source of status (or "symbolic capital") in Morocco from the eighth century to the colonial period (1912–56). It remains important today.[27]

Another version of Ben Yeffu's account clearly illustrates this socio-historical reality, for the certificate that the Black Sultan gave to the saint includes permission to exploit the land extending from Marrakesh to the Atlantic Ocean.[28] Combined, these two versions of the myth give an idea of the nature of favours assigned by the royal decrees.

In fact, the wlad ben Yeffu possess several *zahīrs* decreed by 'Alawite sovereigns – that is, Muhammad ben 'Abderrahman (r. 1859–73), Mulay al-Hasan I (r. 1873–94), Mulay 'Abdel'aziz (r. 1894–1908), Mulay 'Abdelhafid (r. 1908–12) and Sidi Muhammad ben Yusef, or Mohamed V (r. 1927–61), Mohamed VI's grandfather. Each sovereign renews his predecessors' decrees, confirming the respect and reverence (*tawqīr wa-ihtirām*) that have been promised to the saint's descendants ('*ūhida lahum*) and reiterating all economic and political privileges that they have been granted. Mohamed V's *zahīr*, for example, stipulates: "With respect to the preceding *zahīrs* decreed by our magnanimous ancestors, we grant the descendants of the virtuous saint, Sidi 'Abdel'aziz ben Yeffu ... respect, generosity and assistance." Other *zahīrs* solemnly specify the nature of these favours; the one decreed by Mulay al-Hasan I in 1886 (1304 AH) affirms that 'Ali l-Baghli – wlad ben Yeffu's *mqadem* at that time – was to be exempt from taxes, while a subsequent decree signed by Mulay 'Abdel'aziz in 1895 (1313 AH) authorises the same 'Ali to exploit the suq, or market, of the region (in the town of Thnin l-Gharbiya) and to benefit from its income.[29]

Thus, to establish the authenticity of their sharifian origin, the wlad ben Yeffu mobilise different kinds of documents (such as *al-jafriyya* and *zahīr*) and an arresting mythology. Yet none of these can be taken as evidence for their prophetic descent: The myth is just a myth; the manuscript is just a manuscript; and the royal decree itself does not prove anything, except perhaps the intimate relationships that have related some of the saint's descendants with some sultans. However, my purpose here is not to examine the genuineness of their nobility but to illustrate how these socio-political representations reflect, in many respects, a well-attested socio-historical reality. The myths recounting the lives of Moroccan saints and the documents that can attest to them have often been emptied of their mythological thickness and their historical and epistemological depth. Their potential socio-political and semantic dimensions are usually reduced to "hole-filler narratives" and regarded as supplements, always suspect, which could in the final resort be used to compensate for historical absences and deficiencies. In addition to obscuring our understanding of the myth itself, such reductionism prevents us from grasping the distorted, repressed and silenced histories.

In their quest to distinguish between a *sharīf* and a *mutasharrif* (that is, a suspicious *sharīf*), Moroccan genealogists, especially during the first stage of the 'Alawites' reign, used numerous documents and family archives. Examples include marriage certificates, inheritance or transaction records, validated pedigrees and, of course, royal *zahīrs*. Likewise, oral testimonies, collective memory, premonitory dreams (ru'ā), miracles (karāmāt) and myths were accepted by genealogists as proof of the authenticity of sharifian descent. Given that the miracle (karāma) – the dream (ru'yā) is considered a kind of miracle – is a derivative sign of prophecy and hence a means of accessing transcendent realities, it is embodied, lived and socialised as a gracious gift that God gives to individuals that He has elected. Therefore, if a saint was honoured by such a divine gift, also viewed as an achievement of his spirituality, he and/or his descendants also tend to perpetuate it through biological and/or spiritual transmission.[30] Such transmission is often "routinised" through ritual practices, jinn eviction and healing rituals, among other ways.

We can easily foresee the socio-political permissiveness of this elastic system of verification, especially if we consider that 1) the claimed shurfa are treated according to their position in the scale of wealth and power; 2) the desirability of prestige and nobility takes precedence over morality and honesty; and 3) the myths, dreams and miracles tend to become a genealogical "memory" and an "imaginary" archive. It is for that reason that genealogical rearrangements, whether done consciously or unconsciously, were very common practices.[31] As it implies enormous socio-political and economic considerations, the sharifian policy promoted by Mulay Isma'il had probably stimulated genealogical inquests and hence genealogical fiction – a fiction that has been notably taken up and reproduced by mythology.

CONCLUSION

It is in the above sense that one could understand Ibn Khaldun's assertion that genealogy is an illusion/fiction: "al-nasabu amrun wahmiyyun".[32] In his view, pedigree is something "imaginary", something that is "devoid of reality". Ibn Khaldun believes that the idea of pedigree is useful only in so far as it implies solidarity that is a consequence of biological ties: "Anything beyond that is superfluous."[33] Apart from its socio-political effects, nasab refers more to a "mental construction" than to tangible descent; it is a social and cultural representation of a historical reality. Therefore, genealogical nobility is not "mechanically determined", but it is rather constantly rearranged, if not fabricated, according to the social status of groups and lineages. That is to say that a non-sharifian descent of yesterday may become noble today if it is politically, economically and/or militarily advantageous.[34]

NOTES

1. Ibn Khaldun, *The Muqaddimah: An Introduction to History*, trans. F. Rosenthal, Princeton: Princeton University Press, 2005, p. 103. Ibn Khaldun wrote:

Abu l-Walid b. Rushd (Averroës) erred in this respect. He mentioned prestige in the *Rhetoric*. "Prestige", he states, "belongs to people who are ancient settlers in a town." He did not consider the things we have just mentioned [that a "house" possesses an original nobility through group feeling and personal qualities]. I should like to know how long residence in a group can help (anyone to gain prestige), if he does not belong to a group that makes him feared and causes others to obey him. Averroes considers prestige as depending exclusively on the number of forefathers. Yet, rhetoric means to sway the opinions of those whose opinion count, that is, the men in command. It takes no notice of those who have no power. They cannot sway anyone's opinions, and their own opinions are not sought. The sedentary inhabitants of cities fall into that category. It is true that Averroes grew up in a generation and a place where people had no experience of group feeling and were not familiar with the conditions governing it. Therefore, he did not progress beyond his well-known (definition of) "house" and prestige as something depending merely on the number of one's ancestors, and did not refer to the reality of group feeling and its influence among men.

2. C. Hamès, "La filiation généalogique (*nasab*) dans la société d'Ibn Khaldūn", *L'Homme*, vol. 27, no. 102, 1987, pp. 99–118.

3. In Morocco the descendants of the Prophet are designated by the term *shurfa* (sg. *shrīf*). The Arabic word *sharaf* signifies nobility and honour. It refers to a biological affiliation to the Prophet Muhammad through his daughter Fatima and his cousin and son-in-law 'Ali. In Morocco, the descendants of the Prophet are designated by the term *shurfa* (sg. *shrīf*). Accordingly, I use the terms as expressed on the ground, not as uttered in classical Arabic, that is, *shurafā'* (sg. *sharīf*), although the distinction between the two will be made when necessary.

4. Unlike their predecessors – the two visionary and puritanical movements of the Almoravids (r. eleventh–twelfth century) and Almohads (r. twelfth–thirteenth century) – the Berber dynasty of the Marinids (r. thirteenth–sixteenth century) did not grow out of a revivalist movement, and therefore lacked such ideological bases and religious authority. This is why their sultans undertook several sharifian policies in order to surmount such a handicap. Likewise, the discovery of the tomb of Idris II – Idris I's son and successor – in Fez, their capital, contributed to reinforcing their religious legitimacy. Mulay Idris II thus became the greatest saint, and Fez, a city that he himself had founded, one of the most venerated religious centres in Morocco. In fact, by making their capital a prestigious spiritual city, the Marinids tried to centralise authority and thwart the growing power of *zāwiyas* and mystical movements, but they also contributed to resurrecting and upholding an ideology of sharifism that helped to precipitate their fall. M. Kably, *Société, pouvoir et religion au Maroc à la fin du Moyen-Âge XIVᵉ–XVᵉ siècle*, Paris: Maisonneuve et Larose, 1986; A. Sebti, "Au Maroc: Sharifisme citadin, charisme et historiographie", *Annales, Économies, Sociétés, Civilisations*, vol. 2, 1986, pp. 433–57.

5. M. García-Arenal, "Mahdī, Murābit, Sharīf: L'avènement de la dynastie sa'dienne", *Studia Islamica*, vol. 71, 1990, pp. 77–114; V. J. Cornell, *Realm of the Saint: Power and Authority in Moroccan Sufism*, Austin: University of Texas Press, 1998, p. 240.

6. In short, the *walī* (pl. *awliyā'*) is a man very close to God, since He chose him and granted him His *baraka*. In addition to the word *walī*, the terms *sayed* (master),

ṣaliḥ (virtuous) and *fqīr* (poor, in the sense of mystical poverty) also designate the Moroccan saint. They are used everywhere in Morocco with variations from one region to another. The notion of *baraka* features the idea of the manifestation of the divine in this world in the form of gifts given to some individuals (or some animals and things). Only the *wali*, however, has this gift in its exemplary forms. For a recent discussion of these notions, see Rhani, "Le chérif et la possédée: Sainteté, rituel et pouvoir au Maroc", *L'Homme*, vol. 190, 2009, pp. 27–50.

7. E. Dermenghem, *Le culte des saints dans l'Islam maghrébin*, Paris: Gallimard, 1954; C. Geertz, *Islam Observed: Religious Development in Morocco and Indonesia*, Chicago: University of Chicago Press, 1968; E. Gellner, *Saints of the Atlas*, Chicago: University of Chicago Press, 1969; S. Andezian, "L'Algérie, le Maroc, la Tunisie", in A. Popovic and G. Veinstein (eds), *Les Voies d'Allah: Les ordres mystiques dans le monde musulman des origines à aujourd'hui*, Paris: Fayard, 1996, pp. 389–408.

8. The village belongs to the region of Dukkala, in mid-west Morocco. It is located between two villages: Oualidia (c. 20 km) and Thnin al-Gharbiya (c. 12 km).

9. The latest *mqadem* was Muhammad l-Baghli who was forced to resign in the 1990s due to a conflict within the leadership of the group. All information about wlad ben Yeffu and their history comes from repeated interviews and from documents held by some of wlad ben Yeffu, namely *ẓahīrs* and handwritten genealogies (such as *al-jafriyya*); see below.

10. 'Ali ibn Abi Talib, *Kitab al-jafr al-jami' wa-l-nur al-lami'*, Beirut: Dar Maktabat al-Tarbiya, 1987.

11. Ben Mshish nevertheless had a distinguished disciple, Abu l-Hasan al-Shadhili, whose influence on Moroccan religious history has been considerable. Most Moroccan brotherhoods trace back their mystical tradition to him, through another influential saint, al-Jazuli. Ben Mshish left also a text, *al-Salat al-Mashishiyya* – a prayer for the Prophet Muhammad and his family – that is still recited in Morocco today.

12. D. Gril, "Le saint fondateur", in Popovic and Veinstein (eds), *Les Voies d'Allah*, pp. 104–20.

13. García-Arenal, "Mahdī, Murābit, Sharīf", p. 84; Cornell, *Realm of the Saint*, p. 186.

14. Cornell, *Realm of the Saint*; Andezian, "L'Algérie, le Maroc, la Tunisie".

15. The *jnūn* (sg. *jinn*) are ambivalent spirits, so they could be benevolent and/or malevolent. When attacking humans, they cause various mental and physical illnesses. For a typology of *jnūn* and their modes of action, see V. Crapanzano, *The Ḥamadsha: A Study in Moroccan Ethnopsychiatry*, Berkeley – Los Angeles: University of California Press, 1973; and A. Aouattah, *Ethnopsychiatrie maghrébine: Représentations et thérapies traditionnelles de la maladie mentale au Maroc*, Paris: L'Harmattan, 1993.

16. Rhani, 'Le chérif et la possédée'.

17. D. F. Eickelman, *Moroccan Islam: Tradition and Society in a Pilgrimage Center*, Austin: University of Texas Press, 1976, p. 186. Speaking about the family of the Sherqawa, the descendants of the saint Sidi Mhammed Sherqi, and the way that they represent their sacred genealogy and history, Eickelman wrote: "The ideological core of Sherqawi identity and its internal differentiation is contained in genealogies and chains of mystical descent. These are regarded by the Sherqawi and others as symbolic encapsulations of Sherqawi histories." The author uses the plural

since there are many ways in which the genealogies are constructed, understood and related to one another. Each history, says Eickelman, is constructed in terms of the social reality as seen by certain elements of society, and these conceptions of the past shape that reality. In principle, the Sherqawa maintain registers of descendants of Sidi Mhammed Sherqi, just as registers of descendants of the Prophet are supposed to be kept. These registers are largely inaccessible, and many Sherqawa correctly maintain that they are incomplete and out of date. For all but certain highly educated Sherqawa, these genealogies are accepted in their entirety as being historically valid. They unquestionably are, in the sense that for many they constitute history as locally understood.

18. Gellner, *Saints of the Atlas*; Eickelman, *Moroccan Islam*; D. M. Hart, *The Aith Waryaghar of the Moroccan Rif: An Ethnography and History*, Tucson: University of Arizona Press, 1976; D. M. Hart, *Tribe and Society in Rural Morocco*, London: Frank Cass, 2000.
19. Sebti, "Au Maroc".
20. *Karāma* for the *walī* is what *mu'jiza* is for the Prophet. This semantic distinction is in fact an informal one, since both terms refer to the idea of miracle.
21. R. Barthes, *Mythologies*, Paris: Seuil, 1957.
22. Many other tales I collected in different shrines – Mulay Brahim, Sidi Rahhal, Sidi Mas'ud ben Hsein and Mul l-Bargui – confirm this hypothesis. See also Rhani, "Saints et rois: La genèse du politique au Maroc", *Anthropologica*, vol. 50, no. 2, 2008, pp. 375–88.
23. For an exhaustive discussion of the symbolic association between Mulay Isma'il and the Black Sultan, see Rhani, "Saints et rois". For similar encounters between saints and Mulay Isma'il/Black Sultan, see Geertz, *Islam Observed*; Gellner, *Saints of the Atlas*; Crapanzano, *The Ḥamadsha*; R. Jamous, *Honneur et Baraka*, Paris: MSH, 1981; A. Mana, *Les Regraga: La fiancée de l'eau et les gens de la caverne*, Casablanca: Eddif, 1988; K. Naamouni, *Le culte de Bouya Omar*, Casablanca: Eddif, 1993; M. Maarouf, *Jinn Eviction as a Discourse of Power: A Multidisciplinary Approach to Moroccan Magical Beliefs and Practices*, Leiden: E. J. Brill, 2007.
24. A. Laroui, *L'histoire du Maghreb: Un essai de synthèse*, Casablanca: Centre Culturel Arabe, 1995.
25. Sebti, "Au Maroc"; Laroui, *L'histoire du Maghreb*.
26. Laroui, *Les origines sociales et culturelles du nationalisme marocain (1830–1912)*, Paris: Maspero, 1977.
27. H. Munson, *Religion and Power in Morocco*, New Haven: Yale University Press, 1993, pp. 21–2.
28. Maarouf, *Jinn Eviction*.
29. These fiscal exemptions are often associated with a system of royal donations. This policy is still practised today. The wlad ben Yeffu, for example, receive 60,000 DH annually (approximately £4,500).
30. Sebti, "Au Maroc".
31. For Moroccan genealogists' work of verification, see Sebti, "Au Maroc". See also Hart, *Tribe and Society*, pp. 148–51. In his analysis of a genealogical document that attests to the fact that the Imjjat lineage – located both in Aith Waryaghar and in Igzinnayen – is an Idrisid one, Hart notes that this document, although it may not

actually "prove" the Idrisid *shurfa*-hood of the lineage,

> sheds some light on the time-honoured practice of genealogical rearrangement, telescoping and foreshortening, in which the past is generally rearranged to suit the present: for between Mawlay 'Abd al-Salam bin Mashish and ... the ancestor of the Imjjat ... there is a time gap of over six centuries! ... It seems possible, therefore, that the attempt in this particular *shajara* [genealogical document] to establish the *bona fide* Idrisid *shurfa'*-hood of the Imjjat lineage may be a complete fabrication through interstitial planting, an attempt to graft a new line or element onto a pre-existing genealogy.

Hart draws similar conclusions about the Imbrabdhen of the Aith Waryaghar who claim to be Idrisid *shurfa* and trace their descent back to the Prophet's daughter, Fatima, through Ben Mshish. Hart, *The Aith Waryaghar*, pp. 256–60, 481–97.

32. Ibn Khaldun, *Muqaddimat al-'allama Ibn Khaldun*, Damascus: Dar al-Fikr, n.d., p. 129.
33. Ibn Khaldun, *The Muqaddimah*, p. 99.
34. Hamès, "La filiation généalogique (*nasab*) dans la société d'Ibn Khaldun".

PART TWO

Empowering Political and Religious Elites

CHAPTER 4

Berber Leadership and Genealogical Legitimacy: The Almoravid Case

HELENA DE FELIPE[*]

They only knew the desert and had never seen a city. Neither did they know of wheat, barley or flour. They ate dairy products and, occasionally, meat. They rode camels and were brave and bold.[1] That was how Ibn Hawqal, the famous tenth-century Muslim geographer, described the tribes living between Aoudaghost and Sijilmasa in the south of the Maghrib. Several of these tribes, including the Sanhaja, were part of the Almoravid movement and, within a short time, made the transition from the arid African sands and the lifestyle mentioned above to a structure with a political-military leader, Yusuf ibn Tashfin (r. 1061–1106), whose forces fought against the Castilian King Alfonso VI (r. 1072–1109) and who ruled over a vast territory in the Islamic West.

The Almoravids played a key role in the expansion and defence of Islam in the Islamic West, and they controlled a territory, West Africa, where this religion was disseminated, as well as another region, al-Andalus, where it was necessary to defend the religion against the advances of the Christian kings from the north. The development of the Almoravid movement from the union of the tribes within it to the establishment of a power structure based on a dynastic order took place over about a century (from the mid-eleventh century to the mid-twelfth) and, among other important events, brought about the founding of the city of Marrakesh.[2]

The names given in the Arabic sources to those involved describe these events: al-Ṣanhājïyyūn refers to the tribal group that included other tribes, such as the Lamtuna, the Massufa and the Judala, among others; al-Mulaththamūn (the veiled ones) mentions this group's most striking distinguishing feature, as the men covered their heads and faces, which surprised their contemporaries from other regions. Finally, al-Murābiṭūn, the origin of the term "Almoravid" used today, refers to the group's religious origins, which originally coalesced around the charismatic figure of 'Abd Allah ibn Yasin.

The Almoravids were Maliki Sunnis who opposed other groups, such as the Bargawata, which had settled along the Atlantic coast of the Maghrib. They ended up becoming rulers not only of the Maghrib but also of al-Andalus, where, shortly before, the fall of the Umayyad caliphate of Cordoba and its division into multiple kingdoms, called the Taifa kingdoms, had taken place. In this context, the Almoravid Yusuf ibn Tashfin succeeded in imposing a unified government in the two territories by adopting the titles of *amīr al-muslimīn* ("prince of the Muslims") and *nāṣir al-dīn* ("supporter of the religion"). Given the above, we must consider the extent to which his status as a Sanhaji and a Lamtuni affected his leadership in the context of Islam. These tribal links were very far removed from the Arab genealogical links that Muslim political leaders should have had according to Islamic political theory and which the Umayyads of al-Andalus had been able to claim.

This chapter will analyse the leadership of Yusuf ibn Tashfin from the genealogical standpoint. As mentioned above, he was a Lamtuna Sanhaja Berber, although the sources sometimes refer to him and his tribe as being of Himyari origin, from the branch of the southern Arabs. The reasons for this discursive justification are related to the non-Arab rulers' need for legitimacy in the Islamic world and to a textual tradition that originated in the East and moved westwards and that was used in specific contexts. As we shall see, the decisive factor in this case was the Almoravid conquest of al-Andalus.

THE COMPLEXITY OF THE SPACE OF AL-ANDALUS

Even if you were to convince them [the infidels] with some of these proofs, those of them who profess to be well-versed and sound in learning would reply by saying: "Surely he was a Messenger to the Arabs!" You can thus see that this is self-contradictory and how, by saying this, they acknowledge the Prophet's message. If such a person acknowledges the Prophet's message, he must believe in all that the Prophet said or did. Moreover, God says: *And we have not sent thee save as a bearer of good tidings and a warner unto all mankind* (Qur'an 34:28). The Prophet said: "I have been sent to the black, the white, the free and the slave." Such people therefore cannot deny completely nor yet can they believe in one thing and disbelieve in another.[3]

The above comments were made by 'Abd Allah ibn Buluggin, the last king of Zirid Granada (d. 1093), in a very specific textual context: his memoirs, in which he reminisces about al-Andalus during the time of the Taifa kingdoms (before the arrival of the Almoravids), which was a very complex situation from the point of view of ethnic identities and political and religious legitimacy. The issues on which 'Abd Allah is reflecting are connected with the universal nature of Islam and the recipients of its message. 'Abd Allah was not an Arab himself, but instead a Sanhaji Berber who experienced pressure from the Christians in the north. Along with other Andalusi leaders, he was forced to react in various ways in order to meet the challenge. In the end, the rulers of al-Andalus, faced with the unstoppable progress of the Christian forces, requested help from the Almoravids, who by then had already occupied a significant proportion of the Maghrib.

As a Sanhaji, 'Abd Allah was nominally related to the Almoravids, who like him were Sanhajis; hence, as he acknowledges in his memoirs, he assumed that his position was safe when they reached al-Andalus.[4] However, this relationship (qarāba in the text), which the king of Granada hoped would lead to him being treated differently from the other Taifa kings, did not yield the expected results, and the Zirid king was eventually deposed, as were the other rulers of al-Andalus.[5]

Once they had obtained power, the Almoravids recognised the 'Abbasid caliphate and considered themselves to be its representatives in the West. At the same time, they developed a complex relationship with the 'ulama' (scholars) – at that time, mostly Andalusis – with regard to the latter's use of religious discourse as a means of achieving legitimacy.[6] Unlike the Almohads (r. twelfth century–thirteenth century) after them, the Almoravids had no aspirations to the caliph's title of amīr al-mu'minīn and merely called themselves amīr al-muslimīn – "prince of the Muslims". The background to this choice of title can be found in the accounts of al-Bayan al-mughrib by Ibn 'Idhari (d. 1312) and in al-Hulal al-mawshiyya (dating from the fourteenth century), where it is accounted for the fact that the shaykhs of the tribes met and told Yusuf ibn Tashfin that he was the khalīfat Allāh[7] in the Maghrib and was entitled to call himself something more than a mere amir; he should take the title amīr al-mu'minīn ("prince of the believers"). Yusuf ibn Tashfin refused to take the title and advocated the legitimacy of the 'Abbasid caliphate, of which he considered himself the guardian in the Maghrib. Finally, faced with the shaykhs' opinion that he needed to use a title that gave him distinction, Yusuf ibn Tashfin decided to call himself amīr al-muslimīn and nāṣir al-dīn.[8]

Paradoxically, this tale, in which Yusuf ibn Tashfin and his courtiers discuss what form his title should take, unequivocally emphasises his leadership by placing him in a position of arguing and almost selecting the title that expressed it. His reluctance to aspire to be the khalīfat Allāh, that is, a political-religious authority directly linked to God, to some extent "freed" the Almoravids from having to create a discourse based on genealogical justification in order to create a connection to the tribe of the Prophet, because the caliph – in principle – had to be a member of the Quraysh.[9]

Some well-known and controversial texts are particularly relevant in the context of the issue of Yusuf ibn Tashfin's legitimacy. These texts are letters from the Andalusi scholar Abu Muhammad 'Abd Allah ibn 'Umar ibn al-'Arabi (d. 1099) that, according to the sources, date from the latter's journey with his son to the East from 1092 to 1098. The purpose of these letters was to gather various forms of support for the Almoravids' legitimacy, as represented by Yusuf ibn Tashfin, from both the 'Abbasid caliph al-Mustazhir bi-llah and the leading scholars of the day. The latter included the eminent thinker and scholar al-Ghazali (d. 1111)[10] – a key figure in reshaping the political and religious doctrine of the era – and the Andalusi al-Turtushi (d. 1126),[11] who was also at the time in the East, where he met the Banu l-'Arabi.

Researchers who have dealt with these texts have debated their authenticity, their intentions and the context in which they should be analysed.[12] For the present purposes, the letter in which Ibn al-'Arabi requests from al-Ghazali a fatwa in favour of Yusuf ibn Tashfin's intervention in al-Andalus is particularly relevant to the subject at hand. The letter perfectly illustrates the situation of the Muslims in al-Andalus, the details of Yusuf ibn Tashfin's position and, more importantly, the weaknesses of that position. Ibn al-'Arabi draws a vivid profile of the political and religious anarchy prevailing in al-Andalus since the *fitna* (1009–10),[13] the various self-proclaimed rulers, the alliances of the Taifa kings with the Christians, and so on, and lists the difficulties faced by Yusuf ibn Tashfin:

> They were then summoned by the amir of the Muslims to Holy War and to obey him, as everyone was (*bay'at al-jumhūr*), to which they responded: "We will accompany nobody to the Holy War but an imam of Quraysh, which you are not, or the representative of such an imam, which you also are not." He replied: "I serve the 'Abbasid imam." They answered: "Then show us how you have been given priority over us (*taqdīm*)." To which he then replied: "Are not prayers said in his name throughout my territory?" They answered: "That is a ruse", and they acted furtively against him.[14]

Given this attitude of the Andalusis, what the Almoravid amir was asking for was the 'Abbasid caliph's recognition that Yusuf ibn Tashfin was his representative, thereby sanctioning his position at the head of a community – that of al-Andalus – that was unwilling to accept his leadership on genealogical grounds. It should be remembered that during the Umayyad caliphate, al-Andalus had witnessed the arrival of Berber troops recruited by the caliphs of Cordoba to swell the ranks of their armies, and, moreover, that the riots associated with the fall of the Umayyads of al-Andalus, mentioned above, were referred to as "al-fitna al-barbariyya".

The argument attributed to the kings of al-Andalus in the letter by Abu Muhammad ibn al-'Arabi clearly shows that the Almoravids' problem of legitimacy, as it could best be expressed in the Andalusi context, was based on genealogy.[15] For this reason, Ibn al-'Arabi also seeks to bolster Yusuf ibn Tashfin's legitimacy by adding genealogically based arguments to religious ones in his letter to al-Ghazali. Thus, on the one hand, the text presents Yusuf ibn Tashfin's virtues by extolling him as a champion of Islam, the "amir of the two Wests", whose tribe (qabīla) is dedicated to jihād. On the other hand, Ibn al-'Arabi also points out that the Almoravid leader has a Himyari lineage.[16]

It should be noted that despite the mention of Himyar, at no point do the replies from the East refer to the Almoravid amir's genealogical link. Rather, they speak exclusively of his role as a defender of Islam, but one who hails from the Maghrib.[17] However, the mention of a link with the Arab tribe of Himyar by the Andalusi Abu Muhammad Ibn al-'Arabi was important in the context of the Islamic West because it was linked to traditions that can be documented in previous eras and that were now being used to legitimise a new dynasty – the Almoravids.

THE HIMYARI ORIGINS OF THE SANHAJA

There is a considerable Arab historiographical heritage concerning the origins of the Berbers. The question of Himyar and its relationship with some Berber tribes must be placed within this corpus of classical traditions that advocate the Berbers' oriental origin,[18] with a significant portion focusing on Yemen as the place of origin of the population of North Africa and linking the latter to the southern Arab tribes.[19] This material was analysed by Harry T. Norris, who, discussing the "Himyari myth" and its relationship to the origin of the Almoravids, showed the link between the tales on the subject preserved in Arabic sources and older traditions, in which even Alexander the Great plays an important role.[20]

Traditions linking the Berbers with Yemen were already present in the work of Wahb ibn Munabbih (d. 728 or 732),[21] a Yemeni of Persian origin, whose work has been preserved in Ibn Hisham's (d. 833)[22] Kitab al-Tijan fi muluk Himyar.[23] This book refers to several episodes and figures related to the Berbers, further discussed in later literature. These include the idea of the barbar as the Canaanite populations that were expelled from Palestine. The figure of the Himyari king Ifriqis appears in the same book. He is assumed to be responsible for the transfer of the Berber populations from the East to the Maghrib and to be the man after whom the region of Ifriqiya was named.[24] This famous character, Ifriqis, is repeatedly mentioned by Arab sources when referring to the origin of the Berbers, not only with regard to the place name of Ifriqiya, but also as the first to have called the barbar by that name.

There are numerous and varied references in later Arab sources to the Yemeni ancestry of some Berber tribes (that is, the Hawwara of the tribe of 'Amila, the Zawila of the Jurhum, and so forth).[25] I will not dwell on the casuistry and the legends arising from this textual material, which has already been studied,[26] because I aim to focus here on the links between the Sanhaja and the Himyar tribes, which were the grounds for the legitimation of Yusuf ibn Tashfin.

The famous genealogist Ibn al-Kalbi (d. 819–21),[27] in his book *Nasab Ma'add wa-l-Yaman al-kabir*, and specifically in the chapter on the descendants of Himyar ibn Saba', refers to Ifriqis ibn Qays ibn Sayfi, setting out the aforementioned arguments, as the originator of the Berbers' name in the form of *barbar* because of their way of speaking (*al-barbara* signifies a mixture of sounds without meaning).[28] The most important point about this reference is that it mentions the Sanhaja and the Kutama as Yemenis belonging to the tribe of Himyar and as sons of al-Sur ibn Sa'id ibn Jabir ibn Sa'id ibn Qays ibn Sayfi. According to the text, both tribes had settled among the Berbers "until today".[29] The author wants to emphasise that at the time of his writing, those people had not returned to the Yemen and remained in the Maghrib.

As regards this subject, it is also important to take into account the *Kitab al-Iklil* by al-Hasan ibn Ahmad ibn Ya'qub al-Hamdani (d. 945),[30] as it is specifically mentioned as proof of the Himyari origin of the Sanhaja in western Islamic sources, as we shall see below. Indeed, in the part that focuses on the descendants of the Himyari Murra ibn 'Abd Shams ibn Wa'il, the *Kitab al-Iklil* says that these include the Sanhaja and the Kutama, as well as the Uhama, the Lawata and the Zanata. The author is well aware that these are Berber tribes, as he explains that the *ru'asā' al-barbar* (leaders of the Berbers) were transferred to Ifriqiya by Ifriqis.[31]

Later Eastern authors echoed previous traditions, as in the case of the Yemeni Nashwan ibn Sa'id al-Himyari (d. 1178), who used al-Hamdani as a source. In his *Muluk Himyar wa-aqyal al-Yaman*, he relates the ancient stories about the journeys of the Himyari king Abraha and his son Ifriqis. The latter travelled as far as Tangiers, ordered the city of Ifriqiya to be built, and settled several Himyari tribes of his *qawm* ("people") there, namely the Kutama, Uhama, Zanata, Lawata and Sanhaja, who remained in the Maghrib.[32]

Ibn al-Athir (d. 1233), when discussing the origin of the Berbers and quoting Ibn al-Kalbi, mentions that the Sanhaja and Kutama are both *banū* ("sons of") Ifriqis ibn Sayfi ibn Saba' and that both are tribes of Himyar that remained in the Maghrib among the Berbers.[33] Yaqut al-Hamawi (d. 1229), an author who compiled sources of various origins, also quotes Ibn al-Kalbi and says that the Sanhaja and the Kutama – unlike the rest of the Berbers – were sons of Ifriqis. They stayed on as governors of the Maghrib when their father returned to Yemen.[34]

We do not know exactly when these traditions reached al-Andalus, but interesting information on this subject is provided by Sa'id al-Andalusi (d. 1069), who, in his work *Tabaqat al-umam*, refers to the kings of Himyar, their travels and their extensive knowledge of other peoples.[35] Although his work is not a treatise on genealogy but instead focuses on the development of science and knowledge among various peoples, his use of the *Iklil* by al-Hamdani, a work he cites as a source when referring to the kings of Himyar among other topics, is very relevant. The Andalusi author discusses this work and its constituent parts at length and says that he has read details on the death of al-Hamdani in prison in San'a in 834 written in the handwriting of al-Hakam II, the second Umayyad caliph of al-Andalus.[36] It therefore seems clear that the copy that Sa'id read was part of the extensive library of that Andalusi caliph[37] who also was very interested in genealogies. Here we have a meeting between the "école orientale" and the "école ibérique", to use the terms of Maya Shatzmiller.[38]

Sa'id also uses the work of Ibn al-Kalbi, although he makes no mention of the tradition regarding the Yemeni ancestry of the Sanhaja and the Kutama, which is not particularly surprising given the subject of his book. This author is almost a contemporary of Ibn Hazm (d. 1058), the most important reference for genealogies in al-Andalus, whose *Jamharat ansab al-'Arab* was a fundamental source for later authors. The *Jamharat ansab al-'Arab* contains various traditions, some of which refer to the Yemeni origin of the Berbers. However, from the beginning of the section devoted to them, Ibn Hazm declares himself completely opposed to the idea, saying that such links are only to be found in the lies of Yemeni historians.[39] Ibn Hazm's way of expressing himself may be related to his strong partisanship in defence of the Arabs, especially the northern Arabs and the Umayyads.[40]

Data from authors of the eleventh century also show that the thesis concerning the Himyari origin of the Sanhaja was well known in al-Andalus. Ibn 'Abd al-Barr (d. 1071) refers to the Sanhaja and the Kutama as sons of Ifriqis, although he also includes testimonies that cast doubt on this lineage,[41] and al-Bakri (d. 1094) refers to Abraha Dhu l-Manar (al-Himyari) and his troops who remained in the Maghrib.[42] Some of this information is mentioned in much later works, such as the texts of the *Kitab al-'Ibar* by Ibn Khaldun (d. 1406) and the *Kitab al-Ansab* by Ibn 'Abd al-Halim (fourteenth century).[43]

These traditions were debated in various testimonies and questioned by genealogists including Ibn Hazm,[44] although it seems clear that in the medieval Islamic West there was a deep and lasting knowledge of them that linked not only the Berbers in general with Yemen, but the Kutama and the Sanhaja with the Yemeni tribe of Himyar in particular.

YUSUF IBN TASHFIN AL-HIMYARI

Yusuf ibn Tashfin was not the only Sanhaji figure whose links to the tribe of Himyar are mentioned. The Sanhaji Zirids of the eastern Maghrib also had their own texts and traditions on the subject;[45] Yusuf Buluggin ibn Ziri ibn Manad al-Sanhaji, for example, also carried the *nisba* (here, tribal name) of al-Himyari.[46] Abu 'Umar Maymun Ibn Khattab, the mufti and hadith expert of the Banu Khattab of Sanhaja, as stated in *Mafakhir al-barbar*, also claimed a Himyari lineage as well as a Qahtani lineage due to being Sanhaji.[47]

In the case of Yusuf ibn Tashfin, the above-mentioned text by Ibn al-'Arabi is particularly important for several reasons. First, because it is a contemporary text; second, because it is part of a discourse that seeks legitimacy; and finally, because it shows us how genealogical knowledge is used in a given context.

Later authors and texts refer to this link between the Almoravid amir and the tribe of Himyar. Ibn 'Idhari includes the *nasab* Yusuf ibn Tashfin ibn Turjut[48] ibn Wartantin ibn Mansur ibn Masala ibn Amina ibn Wanmali al-Sanhaji, and adds: "Al-Hamdani mentioned in his book *al-Iklil* that Sanhaj was one of the descendants of 'Abd Shams ibn Wa'il ibn Himyar, and the stories that say Sanhaja is from Himyar agree."[49] In this case, the Maghribi author selects only this information to accompany the biography of Yusuf ibn Tashfin, ignoring the rest of the tradition, which as we have seen also includes the Kutama. This is a good example of the use of genealogical history and its adaptation to a specific context.

The work *al-Hulal al-mawshiyya* includes the departure of the *Mulaththamūn* from Yemen, the reasons why they wore the veil and how they arrived in the Maghrib and intermarried with the Berbers.[50] Furthermore, when it discusses the origins of the Sanhaja Lamtuna, it states that they are related to the Berbers only through their kinship with their Berber wives and adds that the Sanhaja trace their genealogy to Himyar who came from the Yemen, went to the desert and settled in the Maghrib. Later, the part of this work dedicated to Yusuf ibn Tashfin, which includes detailed descriptions of his career in the Maghrib and al-Andalus, contains his *nasab*, which differs from that in Ibn 'Idhari's text. *Al-Hulal al-mawshiyya* gives the Almoravid amir the *nisba* al-Himyari[51] but provides no relevant explanations for this, having already done so in the preceding pages. Ibn Abi Zar' (d. 1326) also mentions the Eastern authors al-Hamdani and Ibn al-Kalbi and compiles all of this genealogical information on the Sanhaja and the Almoravids.[52]

Returning to the sources of al-Andalus, Ibn al-Khatib (d. 1374) mentions Yusuf ibn Tashfin in his *A'mal al-a'lam*, calling him al-Himyari as well as al-Lamtuni and al-Sanhaji.[53] This is particularly interesting since it is only this Almoravid amir who receives the *nisba* al-Himyari; neither his son, Ali ibn

Yusuf, nor his father, Tashfin ibn 'Ali, both amirs themselves, are deemed worthy of this attribute.[54]

In his biography of the Almoravid amir, the Eastern author Ibn Khallikan (d. 1282) says that Yusuf ibn Tashfin's people (*qawm*) descended from Himyar ibn Saba' and quotes some verses that explain that the reason why the *Mulaththamūn* wore the veil was the modesty they felt about the honour of being Himyarite.[55]

Other well-known verses include those by the Andalusi Ibn Wahbun, celebrating the victory of Zallaqa, where the Almoravids inflicted a decisive defeat on the Christians of the Iberian Peninsula in a prelude to the Almoravids' occupation of al-Andalus. Ibn Wahbun mentions Yusuf's membership in the tribe of Himyar, making him a relation of the king of Seville, al-Mu'tamid ibn 'Abbad – one of the most powerful Taifa kings who was among those who had sought help from Yusuf ibn Tashfin against the Christians. The 'Abbadids of Seville were Lakhmids and southern Arabs, like the Qahtani branch.[56] Other verses dedicated to the glory of Himyar and specifically linked to the Almoravids and Yusuf ibn Tashfin are those of Abu Faris al-Malzuzi (d. 1297), in which he explains that the Sanhaja are descended from Himyar and that the lineage of the *Mulaththamūn* goes back to Himyar (and the southern Arabs) and is a long way from Mudar (northern Arabs).[57]

Apart from names, we have seen how the sources mention other related aspects, such as the questions of why these Himyari men wore the veil and why Yusuf ibn Tashfin, despite being from Himyar, only spoke Berber, *al-lugha al-murābiṭiyya* ("the Almoravids' language"). The author of *al-Hulal* attempts to answer this linguistic question by explaining that although they came from Yemen, the tribes had become Berbers due to their contacts and kinship with the Berber people among whom they lived when they settled in the Maghrib. The fact that the author of *al-Hulal* attempts to explain the circumstances through which the Sanhaja came to speak Berber rather than Arabic demonstrates that this was not a trivial matter: If the Almoravids did not speak Arabic, their Arab origin and therefore their legitimacy as rulers could be questioned.[58]

The Almoravids were not the only Berbers to use genealogical traditions as a means to reinforce their legitimacy. According to Norris, the propagation of these myths of origin has a great deal to do with the need of the society that used them to address social, political or religious changes.[59]

In this respect, the case of the Almohads (r. twelfth–thirteenth centuries), who succeeded the Almoravids, is very significant, because the proclamation of the Berber Zanata 'Abd al-Mu'min (d. 1163) as caliph and his consequent rise to the highest possible level of political and religious leadership created a historiographical context that encouraged the appearance of genealogies linking him to Qays 'Aylan, a prominent northern Arab tribe.[60] This genealogical connection was necessary to establish the Almohads' link with the caliphate, precisely the position rejected by Yusuf ibn Tashfin when he decided to assume the lesser title of *amīr al-muslimīn*.

Among the successors to the Almohads, the Marinids (r. thirteenth–fourteenth centuries) – who were Zanata Berbers – also did not claim the caliphate but used other instruments to reinforce their legitimacy. Shatzmiller has already pointed out the alleged similarities that some historians have attempted to find between the Almoravids and the Marinids, despite their membership in different tribal groups (the Almoravids being Sanhaja and the Marinids Zanata).[61] These similarities include their roots in the desert, the charisma of the figures of Yusuf ibn Tashfin and 'Abd al-Haqq, the ancestor of the Marinids, and both men's lack of knowledge of the Arabic language. Shatzmiller suggests that the Marinids also sought an Arab genealogy. Marinid historiography presented them as descendants of the tribes that settled in the Maghrib led by Hasan ibn Nu'man, one of the most famous figures of the first century of Islam who participated in the conquest of North Africa. Shatzmiller adds that the origins of this historiography lie in the complex context of al-Andalus.

CONCLUSION

It is reasonable to assume that Yusuf ibn Tashfin's problems related to political and religious legitimacy led not only to the letters discussed above, but to the recovery of a genealogical background produced in the East but known to experts in the West and at some point in time placed at the disposal of the Almoravid amir. His Almoravid predecessors did not have to deal with the problems of legitimacy that Yusuf ibn Tashfin faced, and it appears that the fundamental difference in this respect, besides the differences in the careers of the Almoravid leaders, should be sought in al-Andalus. Clearly, being an Arab did not have the same connotations as being a Berber for a religious-political leader in al-Andalus. Al-Andalus was the origin of the text by Abu Muhammad Ibn al-'Arabi, and it was where the search for support for legitimacy from the East took place. The fact that the claim of descent from Himyar is mentioned in the text is therefore revealing of a historical context that accords with the argument of Shatzmiller:

> The Berbers' drive to identify themselves in historical terms ... was clearly linked to the historical experience of al-Andalus, coming either as a reaction to an anti-berber feeling, or as a reflection of an Andalusian concept of racial separatism which was alive and invigorated during the eleventh century.[62]

It is therefore not surprising that fourteenth-century historiography, dating from the Marinid era, places the greatest emphasis on the links between Yusuf ibn Tashfin and the tribe of Himyar. As we know, historians in the Marinid context, when seeking legitimacy for the dynasty, would foster the dissemination of these genealogical links,[63] especially given the alleged parallels, mentioned above, between the dynasty's key figure and Yusuf ibn Tashfin. However, the traditions used to support this relationship did not come from al-Andalus, but rather from the East, from historians and genealogists in Yemen and elsewhere. It is a heritage of traditions that had reached al-Andalus and was well known to scholars there. A good example of this is the fact that al-Hakam II himself knew of and annotated the *Kitab al-Iklil* by the Yemeni al-Hamdani as well as the works of other, subsequent authors.

The genealogical discourses of the three Maghribian dynasties – the Almoravids, the Almohads and the Marinids – are striking testimony to the value of genealogy as a factor in political and religious legitimacy. The Berbers were thus part of the Eastern Arab genealogical framework, using ancient traditions that sustained their leadership. This genealogical knowledge was part of an extensive textual corpus circulating from East to West, which remained dormant until its use was required for the purposes of legitimation. It was, therefore, a dynamic genealogical discourse. Over time, the same historiographical resource could be returned to again and again and adapted according to political needs. A good example of this is the survival of the "Himyari legend" in the heritage of the Sahara, as shown by Norris.[64]

Genealogy is, in short, a corpus of knowledge that moves within a specific cultural universe among elite experts who have their own distinctive space and for whom neither geographical space nor chronological borders are a determinant factor. How many centuries and kilometres were there between the Yemeni al-Hamdani and the Maghribi Ibn 'Idhari? The details are almost irrelevant because they both inhabit the same intellectual abode of a shared textual heritage.

NOTES

* This study has been carried out within the framework of the "Ramón y Cajal" research programme of the Spanish Ministry of Education, "History of Maghreb and al-Andalus: History of the Berbers", and the research project "Geographical and Social Mobility of the Muslim Population in the Iberian Peninsula (XI–XIII centuries)" (HUM-08644). I would like to thank M. Fierro and M. Marín for their careful reading of this chapter. Translated from Spanish by Robert Jones.

1. Ibn Hawqal, *Kitab Surat al-ard*, vol. 1, 2nd edn, ed. J. H. Kramers, Leiden: E. J. Brill, 1938, p. 101.
2. On the Almoravids, see J. Bosch Vilá, *Los Almorávides*, Tetuan: Editora Marroquí, 1956, re-ed. with study by E. Molina, Granada: Universidad de Granada, 1990; V. Lagardère, *Les Almoravides, jusqu'au règne de Yūsuf b. Tāšfīn (1039–1106)*, Paris: L'Harmattan, 1989; I. Dandash, *Dawr al-murabitin fi nashr al-islam fi gharb Ifriqiyya*

430–515 h./1038–1121 m. ma'a nashr wa-tahqiq Rasa'il Abi Bakr Ibn al-'Arabi, Beirut: Dar al-Gharb al-Islami, 1988; H. T. Norris, *The Berbers in Arabic Literature*, Norfolk: Longman House – Librairie du Liban, 1982 and *Saharan Myth and Saga*, Oxford: Oxford University Press, 1972; P. Chalmeta, "al-Murābiṭūn", in P. Bearman, Th. Bianquis, C. E. Bosworth, E. van Donzel, and W. P. Heinrichs (eds), *Encyclopaedia of Islam*, vol. 7, 2nd edn. Leiden: E. J. Brill, 1979–2004, pp. 583–91; and R. El Hour, *La administración judicial Almorávide en al-Andalus: Élites, negociaciones y enfrentamientos*, Helsinki: Academia Scientiarum Fennica, 2006.

3. 'Abd Allah ibn Buluggin, *al-Tibyan 'an al-haditha al-ka'ina bi-dawlat Bani Ziri fi Gharnata*, ed. E. Lévi-Provençal, Cairo: Editions Al-Maaref, 1955, p. 5; *The Tibyān: Memoirs of 'Abd Allāh b. Buluggīn, Last Zīrid Amīr of Granada*, trans. A. T. Tibi, Leiden: E. J. Brill, 1986, p. 36. emphasis in original.

4. 'Abd Allah ibn Buluggin, *al-Tibyan*, p. 104; *The Tibyān*, trans. Tibi, p. 115.

5. On the limited role played by *'aṣabiyya* (tribal or clan solidarity) in al-Andalus during this period, see M. Benaboud, "'Aṣabiyya and social relations in Al-Andalus during the period of the Taifa states (11th century A.D./5th century A.H.)", *Hespéris-Tamuda*, vol. 19, 1980–1, pp. 5–45, and F. Clément, *Pouvoir et légitimité en Espagne musulmane à l'époque des Taifas (Veᵉ/XIeᵉ siècle): L'imam fictif*, Paris: L'Harmattan, 1997, p. 15.

6. On the Almoravids' legitimacy, see Levi-Provençal, "Le titre souverain des Almoravides et sa légitimation par le Califat 'Abbaside", *Arabica*, vol. 2, 1955, pp. 265–80; M. Fierro, "Entre el Magreb y al-Andalus: La autoridad política y religiosa en época almorávide", in F. Sabaté (ed.), *Balaguer, 1105: Cruïlla de civilitzacions*, Lleida: Pagès editors, 2007, pp. 99–120; D. Serrano, "¿Por qué llamaron los almohades antropomorfistas a los almorávides?", in P. Cressier, Fierro and L. Molina (eds), *Los Almohades: Problemas y perspectivas*, vol. 2 Madrid: CSIC, 2005, pp. 815–52; M. Vega and S. Peña, "Alternancias epigráficas en las monedas almorávides", *Al-Andalus–Magreb*, vol. 10, 2002–3, pp. 293–314.

7. On this term and its difference from *khalīfat rasūl Allāh*, see P. Crone and M. Hinds, *God's Caliph: Religious Authority in the First Centuries of Islam*, Cambridge: Cambridge University Press, 2003.

8. Anonymous, *Al-Hulal al-mawshiyya fi dhikr al-akhbar al-marrakushiyya*, eds S. Zakkar and 'A. Q. Zamama, Casablanca: Dar al-Rashad al-Haditha, 1979 [1399], p. 29; Ibn 'Idhari, *al-Bayan al-Mughrib*, vol. 4, ed. I. 'Abbas, Beirut: Dar al-Thaqafa, 1980, pp. 27–8; *al-Bayan al-Mughrib*, trans. A. Huici Miranda, Valencia: Gráficas Bautista, 1963, p. 58. Norris mentions that the 'Abbasid caliph honoured Yusuf ibn Tashfin as *amīr al-muslimīn* (*The Berbers*, p. 152). The same author points out that Ibn Yasin appointed Yahya ibn 'Umar and Abu Bakr ibn 'Umar, Yusuf's predecessors, *amīr al-muslimīn* (*The Berbers*, pp. 119, 129). However, I do not find in Norris's work the sources upon which he bases this statement.

9. On this issue and minority positions on it, see Crone, *Medieval Islamic Political Thought*, Edinburgh: Edinburgh University Press, 2004.

10. The bibliography on this well-known scholar and his political thought is extensive. See esp. Crone, *Medieval Islamic Political Thought*, pp. 237–55.

11. On this scholar, see the study by Fierro in al-Turtushi, *Kitab al-hawadith wa-l-bida'*, Madrid: CSIC, 1993, pp. 17–107.

12. On the Banu l-'Arabi, these texts, the debate regarding them and Almoravid legit-imacy, see the study by M. Ya'la in *Tres textos árabes sobre beréberes en el occidente islámico*, Madrid: CSIC and AECI, 1996, pp. 30–63, 91–4, and Clément, *Pouvoir et légitimité*, pp. 94–8.

13. The so-called *al-fitna al-barbariyya*, literally "the Berber revolt", is traditionally considered the starting point of a period of political instability in al-Andalus that brought about the end of the Umayyad caliphate. On this subject, see Clément, *Pouvoir et légitimité*.

14. *Kitab Shawahid al-jilla*, ed. Ya'la, in Ya'la, *Tres textos árabes*, p. 301; trans. to English from Spanish translation by Mª J. Viguera, "Las cartas de al-Gazali y al-Turtusi al soberano almorávid Yusuf b. Tasufin", *Al-Andalus*, vol. 42, 1977, p. 352.

15. The kings of al-Andalus had their own legitimacy problems. See Clément, *Pouvoir et légitimité*, pp. 83–202.

16. *Kitab Shawahid al-jilla*, ed. Ya'la, pp. 299–300 and Viguera, "Las cartas", p. 351.

17. See, for example, the hadith from *Sahih Muslim* that al-Turtushi "gave" to Yusuf ibn Tashfin: "There will always be a group of Maghribian people that will support the Truth, while God so decides." [Al-Turtushi] then explains:

> God knows whether by this the Messenger of God, God bless him and save him, is referring to the confederation (*ma'shara*) of the Almoravids or all the people of the Maghrib, and their obligation to accept the Sunna and Jama'a and to remain free of heresies (*bida'*) and innovations in religion, following the path of the good ancestors, God be pleased with them. I ask God for you to be one of those that still prevents corruption on the earth.

See *Kitab Shawahid al-jilla*, ed. Ya'la, pp. 330–1, trans. to English from Spanish trans-lation by Viguera, "Las cartas", p. 372. On the hadith, see *Kitab Shawahid al-jilla*, p. 331, n. 1, 979. This hadith is also in *Kitab Shawahid al-jilla*, p. 297.

18. Regarding Arab legends about the origin of the Berbers, see Norris, *The Berbers*, pp. 32–43; M. Shatzmiller, "Le mythe d'origine berbère: Aspects historiographiques et sociaux", *Revue de l'Occident Musulman et de la Méditerranée*, vol. 35, 1983, pp. 145–56; H. de Felipe, "Leyendas árabes sobre el origen de los beréberes", *Al-Qanṭara*, vol. 11, 1990, pp. 379–96.

19. Regarding the Yemeni origins of the Berbers, see Norris, *The Berbers*, pp. 35–9. The author makes an interesting comparison between these legends and those concerning Queen Dido and the foundation of Carthage as well as Procopius's narrative on the Vandal War, p. 36.

20. Norris, *Saharan Myth*, pp. 26–73. On the relations between Alexander and the Yemen, see also M. Marin, "Legends on Alexander the Great in Moslem Spain", *Graeco-Arabica* (Athens), vol. 4, 1991, pp. 71–90.

21. For more about this author, see R. G. Khoury, "Wahb b. Munabbih", *Encyclopaedia of Islam*, vol. 11, 2nd edn, pp. 34–6.

22. W. M. Watt, "Ibn Hishām", *Encyclopaedia of Islam*, vol. 3, 2nd edn, pp. 800–1.

23. Ibn Hisham, *Kitab al-Tijan fi muluk Himyar*, Hyderabad: Matba'at Majlis Da'irat al-Ma'arif al-'Uthmaniyya, 1347 AH.

24. Ibn Hisham, *Kitab al-Tijan*, pp. 321–2.

25. Many sources can be cited in this regard; see, for example, Ibn Khaldun, *Kitab*

al-'Ibar, vol. 6, Beirut: Dar al-Kutub al-'Ilmiyya, 2003, p. 114 on the Himyarite origins of other Berber tribes and of the Kutama and the Sanhaja.

26. See above, n. 18.
27. On Ibn al-Kalbi and his work, see the classic study by W. Caskel, *Ğamharat an-nasab*, Leiden: E. J. Brill, 1966.
28. Ibn Khaldun, *Kitab al-'Ibar*, vol. 6, p. 104.
29. *Nasab Ma'add wa-l-Yaman al-kabir*, vol. 2, ed. N. Hasan, Beirut: Maktabat al-Nahda al-'Arabiyya, 1988, pp. 548–9. It is noteworthy that Ibn al-Kalbi provides this information, as his father is one of the sources mentioned in the *Kitab al-Tijan*; see, for example, p. 132.
30. O. Löfgren, "al-Hamdānī", *Encyclopaedia of Islam*, vol. 3, 2nd edn, p. 124.
31. *Kitab al-Iklil*, vol. 2, 3rd edn, ed. M. ibn 'Ali al-Akwa, Beirut: Manshurat al-Madina, 1986, p. 115.
32. *Muluk Himyar wa-aqyal al-Yaman, qasidat Nashwan ibn Sa'id al-Himyari wa-sharhuha al-musamma Khulasat al-sira al-jami'a li-'aja'ib akhbar al-muluk al-tababi'a*, eds I. ibn Ahmad al-Jarafi and 'A. ibn Ismail al-Mu'ayyad, Beirut – San'a': Dar al-'Awda and Dar al-Kalima, 1978, pp. 71–2. On the influence of the work of this Yemeni author on Mauritanian scholars, see Norris, *Saharan Myth*, pp. 46-47.
33. *Al-Kamil fi al-ta'rikh*, vol. 1, ed. U. ibn 'A. S. Tadmuri, Beirut: Dar al-Kitab al-'Arabi, 2006, pp. 74, 176.
34. Yaqut al-Hamawi, *Mu'jam al-buldan*, vol. 1, Beirut: Dar Sadir, 1977, pp. 368–9.
35. Sa'id al-Andalusi, *Tabaqat al-umam*, ed. H. Bu'alwan, Beirut: Dar al-Tali'a li-l-Tiba'a wa-l-Nashr, 1985, pp. 113–15, 120; *Libro de las categorías de las naciones*, trans. F. Maíllo, Madrid: Akal, 1999, pp. 90–1, 94.
36. Sa'id al-Andalusi, *Tabaqat*, pp. 147–9 and *Libro de las categorías*, trans. Maíllo, pp. 113–14.
37. On the library of al-Hakam II, see D. Wasserstein, "The Library of al-Hakam II al-Mustansir and the Culture of Islamic Spain", *Manuscripts of the Middle East*, vol. 5, 1990–1, pp. 99–105.
38. Shatzmiller, "Le mythe", p. 146.
39. Ibn Hazm, *Jamharat ansab al-'Arab*, ed. A. M. Harun, Cairo: Dar al-Ma'arif, 1962, pp. 495, 497, 498.
40. Clément, *Pouvoir et légitimité*, p. 61, n. 2.
41. Ibn 'Abd al-Barr, *al-Qasd wa-l-aman*, Beirut: Dar al-Kitab al-'Arabi, 1985, p. 36.
42. Al-Bakri, *Kitab al-Masalik wa-l-mamalik*, vol. 1, eds A. Ferré and A. P. Van Leeuwen, Tunis: al-Dar al-'Arabiyya li-l-Kitab, 1992, p. 329.
43. Ibn Khaldun, *Kitab al-'Ibar*, vol. 1, pp. 11–12, vol. 2, pp. 59–60 and vol. 6, pp. 105, 107, 113; Ibn 'Abd al-Halim, *Kitab al-Ansab*, ed. Ya'la, in Ya'la, *Tres textos árabes*, p. 41.
44. On the issue of the authenticity given to these traditions in the work of Ibn Khaldun by Berber genealogists, see Norris, *Saharan Myth*, p. 26.
45. Norris, *The Berbers*, pp. 37–8. On this link between Zirids and Himyarites, see also Shatzmiller, "The Legacy of Andalusian Berbers in the 14th Century Maghreb: Its Role in the Formation of Maghrebi Historical Identity and Historiography", in M. García-Arenal and Viguera (eds), *Relaciones de la Península Ibérica con el Maghreb (siglos XIII–XVI)*, Madrid: CSIC and ICMA, 1988, p. 213, p. 233, n. 29, where

it is mentioned that the Aftasids of al-Andalus also claimed a Himyarite origin. According to Shatzmiller, this historiographical "école Ifriqi", linked to the Zirids, was the most fruitful for the Himyarite origin of the Sanhaja; see "Le mythe", p. 150.

46. Ibn al-Athir, al-Kamil fi al-ta'rikh, vol. 7, p. 306.

47. Kitab Mafakhir al-barbar, ed. M. Ya'la, in Ya'la, Tres textos árabes, p. 209.

48. An interesting analysis of this particular name in the context of this nasab can be found in Norris, The Berbers, pp. 108–9.

49. Ibn 'Idhari, al-Bayan al-mughrib, vol. 4, pp. 46–7 and al-Bayan al-mughrib, trans. Huici, pp. 110–11.

50. Al-Hulal al-mawshiyya, pp. 17–19. On the issue of matriliny among these Berber groups, see Norris, Saharan Myth, pp. 37–9; The Berbers, pp. 40–3; and C. Hamés, "Le pouvoir dynastique almohade entre parenté berbère, arabe et islamique", in Cressier, Fierro and Molina (eds), Los Almohades: Problemas y perspectivas, vol. 2, pp. 425–50, especially 425–31.

51. The text includes a nasab for Yusuf ibn Tashfin, with some variations on the above, to which he adds the aforementioned nisba "al-Himyari"; al-Hulal al-mawshiyya, p. 24.

52. Al-Anis al-mutrib bi-rawd al-qirtas, ed. 'A. W. ibn Mansur, Rabat: Dar al-Mansur, 1972, p. 119; El Cartás, trans. A. Huici Miranda, Valencia: Imp. Hijos de F. Vives, 1918, pp. 119–20. Norris refers to this text, saying that these traditions were repeated ad nauseam in later Eastern and Maghribi literature; Norris, Saharan Myth, p. 35.

53. A'mal al-a'lam, eds A. M. al-'Abbadi and M. I. al-Kattani, Casablanca: Dar al-Kitab, 1964, pp. 233–4. Interestingly, however, the same author, Ibn al-Khatib, in al-Ihata, does not include in the biography of Yusuf the nisba "al-Himyari", or any information about this link. Al-Ihata fi akhbar Gharnata, vol. 4, ed. M. 'A. A. 'Inan, Cairo: Maktabat al-Khanji, 1973–7, pp. 347–54.

54. Ibn al-Khatib, A'mal al-a'lam, pp. 253, 256.

55. Ibn Khallikan, Wafayat al-a'yan, vol. 7, ed. I. 'Abbas, Beirut: Dar al-Thaqafa, 1968–72, pp. 112–30, and specifically p. 128. On traditions related to the use of the veil by the Almoravids, see Norris, Saharan Myth, pp. 39–44.

56. Norris, Saharan Myth, p. 35 and Clément, Pouvoir et légitimité, pp. 154–5, both of them quoting H. Pérès, Esplendor de al-Andalus, Madrid: Hiperión, 1953, p. 106; Ibn Bassam, Dhakhira, vol. 2, ed. I. 'Abbas, Beirut: Dar al-Thaqafa, 1979, p. 245.

57. Abu Faris al-Malzuzi, Nazm al-suluk fi al-anbiya' wa-l-julafa' wa-l-muluk, ed. 'A. W. ibn Mansur, Rabat: Matbu'at al-Qasr al-Malaki, 1963, p. 48. The same verses are also found in al-Hulal al-mawshiyya, p. 183. On this author and his work, see Shatzmiller, L'historiographie mérinide: Ibn Khaldun et ses contemporains, Leiden: E. J. Brill, 1982, pp. 11–13. For an English translation of the first verses, see Norris, Saharan Myth, p. 26.

58. On the use of Arabic and Berber by Yusuf ibn Tashfin, see Norris, The Berbers, pp. 139–41; and de Felipe, "Medieval Linguistic Contacts: Berber Language through Arab Eyes", eds M. Lafkioui and V. Brugnatelli, Berber Studies, vol. 22, 2008, pp. 19–37, especially pp. 23, pp. 25–7, the latter on the Berber language and genealogical debate. Norris states that the three main characteristics of the Sahara Sanhaja, that is, their Yemeni origin, the men's use of the veil and some degree of matriliny in their social structure, are evidenced in the text of al-Hulal al-mawshiyya.

Saharan Myth, pp. 37–9.

59. *Saharan Myth*, p. 28.
60. Besides Qays 'Aylan, links were also made to other Arab tribes. On 'Abd al-Mu'min's genealogies, see Fierro, "Las genealogías de 'Abd al-Mu'min, primer califa almohade", *Al-Qanṭara*, vol. 24, 2003, pp. 77–107 and C. Hamés, "Le pouvoir dynastique".
61. Shatzmiller, *L'historiographie*, pp. 117–18. On the Marinids' legitimacy, see also M. A. Manzano, "Onomástica Benimerín: El problema de la legitimidad", in Mª L. Ávila (ed.), *Estudios onomástico-biográficos de al-Andalus II*, Granada: CSIC, 1989, pp. 119–36.
62. Shatzmiller, "Legacy", p. 230.
63. Shatzmiller, *L'Historiographie*, p. 131.
64. On the sagas of the Lamtuna Almoravids, see Norris, *Saharan Myth*, ch. 4.

CHAPTER 5

Ways of Connecting with the Past: Genealogies in Nasrid Granada

MARIBEL FIERRO

COULD AL-ANDALUS BE SAVED FROM THE CHRISTIANS? FEAR AND HOPE IN ESCHATOLOGICAL TRADITIONS

The Malagan jurist al-Fakhkhar (d. 723/1323) compiled a number of eschato-logical traditions that addressed the dangers that Muslims had to face in al-Andalus. His was an age – the Nasrid period (seventh/thirteenth–ninth/fifteenth centuries) – when Muslim rule was reduced to a small area around the city of Granada, after the loss of a major part of the territory where formerly the Arabic language and Islam had predominated. Al-Fakhkhar's eschatological traditions could be understood as having been fabricated ad hoc to help the Andalusis face their predicament. However, they can be proven to be old tradi-tions, some of which had been circulating since very early times.

> A man among the enemies of the Muslims of al-Andalus, called *dhū l-'urf*, will gather a big group from among the tribes of polytheism. The Muslims living in al-Andalus will realise that their strength would not be sufficient to stop them [the polytheists, that is, the Christians], and for this reason the Muslims of al-Andalus will be obliged to escape. The strong among them will arrive in ships to Tangiers, while the weak among them will stay [in al-Andalus], together with a group [from among the strong] who will not have ships to cross [the sea]. … God will send them an eminent man (*wa'l*) for whom God will open a path in the sea for him to cross. The people will understand and follow that man, crossing in his steps. Then, the sea will return to its former shape. The enemies will cross in ships in order to persecute the Muslims.

This tradition could easily be interpreted as a prediction *post eventum*, fabricated some time after the beginning of significant territorial losses – the fall of Toledo had taken place in 478/1085, and in the first half of the seventh/thirteenth century major towns such as Cordoba, Murcia, Jaén and Seville had been lost by the Muslims – and after migration of the Andalusis to North Africa. Al-Fakhkhar, however, took the tradition from Abu 'Amr al-Dani (d. 444/1053), and, moreover, it was already circulating in Egypt towards the end of the second/eighth century, having been included by Nu'aym ibn Hammad (d. 228/842) in his *Kitab al-fitan*.[1]

In spite of the antiquity of the material he collected, al-Fakhkhar was obviously concerned with its present significance. Abu l-Hasan 'Ali al-Bunnahi (d. 794/1391) – formerly referred to as al-Nubahi[2] – also quoted eschatological traditions, such as one in which six signals of the Last Hour are listed: the Prophet's death, the conquest of Jerusalem, a great plague, a surplus of wealth, a period of unrest and civil wars (*fitna*) and "a truce between you and the Banu l-Asfar [that is, the Christians] that they will betray. They will go against you under eighty banners, and with each of them twelve thousand men will march." In al-Bunnahi's times, the plague of the year 750/1349 was interpreted as the third signal.[3] By then, al-Andalus was commonly referred to as an island, surrounded both by the sea and by the Christians, in which its inhabitants led a life of both religious devotion and military struggle that earned them a precious reward, as they would be witnesses to the Truth until the end of times.[4] Al-Andalus may have been doomed, but salvation in the afterlife was ensured for those who stayed there.

After the fall of Granada into Christian hands, when Muslims had to face not only military defeat and political submission but also the possibility of losing their language, culture and religion under Christian rule, some eschatological traditions still gave hope that a reversal of fortune was possible.[5] Hernando de Válor, the leader of the Morisco rebellion that erupted in 1568, proclaimed himself to be an Umayyad and adopted the name of Muley Muhammad aben Humeya.[6] As one of the predictions then circulating stated, the saviour will arrive from Syria,[7] and Syria implied a clear reference to Umayyad rule. Al-Andalus had been gained for the Truth when an Umayyad caliph ruled over the Islamic world, and an eschatological tradition promised that Umayyad rule would last until the appearance of the Dajjal (Antichrist).[8] During the last centuries of Muslim presence in the Iberian Peninsula, therefore, the beginnings that had made possible such a presence were being closely linked to the end. Another way in which this connection was accomplished was through the adoption of very specific Arab genealogies by some of the most important scholars of Nasrid Granada.

THE BANU L-ZUBAYR AL-'ASIMI: A NASRID FAMILY CLAIMING AN ARAB CONQUEROR AS AN ANCESTOR

One such scholar was Ibn al-Zubayr (d. 708/1308), who is best known for a biographical dictionary devoted to the scholars of the Islamic West.[9] Ibn al-Zubayr was a member of an influential family, the Banu l-Zubayr, which claimed as its ancestor a man called 'Asim ibn Muslim ibn Ka'b, who belonged to the Banu 'Adi ibn Murra ibn 'Awf ibn Thaqif (a tribe of Mudar, that is, northern Arabs). This 'Asim was presented by some sources as a descendant of 'Urwa ibn Mas'ud al-Thaqafi, a loyal servant of the Umayyads linked by marriage with the famous governor al-Hajjaj ibn Yusuf (d. 95/714), also a member of the tribe of Thaqif. 'Asim played an important role in the early history of al-Andalus as one of the Umayyad clients who joined the Umayyad 'Abd al-Rahman – later to become 'Abd al-Rahman I (r. 138–72/756–88) – when the latter disembarked in the Iberian Peninsula and started gathering an army to fight the then-governor Yusuf al-Fihri. In the battle that took place on the day of 'Arafa of the year 138/756 and that brought 'Abd al-Rahman I to power, 'Asim commanded both the infantry and the Berbers loyal to the Umayyads. 'Asim gained then the appellation "al-'Uryan", the "naked", because he undressed himself in order to cross the river Guadalquivir that separated 'Abd al-Rahman I's army from that of his enemies.[10]

Ibn Harith al-Khushani (d. 361/971) records that in spite of their noble Thaqafi lineage, 'Asim's descendants stressed their ties with the Umayyads because of the rank they had achieved with them and their service to them, and in fact two members of 'Asim's family are mentioned as Umayyad *mawālī* (that is, clients). In the fourth/tenth century, those descendants claimed to have in their possession a document written by 'Abd al-Rahman I in which he ordered one of his governors not to cause problems for his *muwālī* (client) 'Asim al-'Uryan.[11] Seventeen descendants of 'Asim are known, the last ones living in the first half of the fifth/eleventh century. Many became scholars, mostly grammarians and poets, and served the Umayyad amirs in different capacities, such as as inspector of the market, judge, chief of police or inspector of the official textiles (in charge of the manufacture of *tiraz* textiles). Their fortunes started to decline under the 'Amirids, who controlled the Umayyad caliphate in the last decades of the tenth/fourth century. After the collapse of the Umayyad caliphate and with the ensuing political fragmentation, a member of 'Asim's family seems to have moved to the Taifa kingdom of Almería, and one of his descendants (d. c. 540/1145) was a scholar active in the eastern part of al-Andalus under the Almoravids.[12] Two centuries later, 'Asim al-'Uryan's memory was still kept alive. The famous Nasrid scholar Ibn al-Khatib (d. 776/1374) devoted an entry to Ibn al-Zubayr in his biographical dictionary of scholars of al-Andalus connected with Granada, and in that entry he mentioned 'Asim al-'Uryan as Ibn al-Zubayr's ancestor.[13] Ibn al-Khatib seems to know more than earlier sources about 'Asim. He says that 'Asim entered al-Andalus with the troops of the Umayyad commander Balj ibn Bishr in the year 123/741, a point not mentioned in previous extant writings and one that explains how 'Asim had settled in al-Andalus in the first place. In the year 121/739, a Berber rebellion had broken out in North Africa. The Umayyad caliph in Damascus sent a powerful army to put an end to it, but the resistance of the Berbers was strong. The Syrian troops were defeated by the Berbers in 123/741. With what was left of the army, Balj ibn Bishr al-Qushayri took refuge in Ceuta, a town a short distance away but separated from the Iberian Peninsula by the sea. After some hesitation, the military governor of al-Andalus sent ships to help the Syrians cross the Straits of Gibraltar. In exchange, Balj helped the governor by fighting those Berbers who had followed the rebellion of their North African tribesmen and who were causing trouble for the Arabs in the Iberian Peninsula. Cooperation between the two Arabs did not last long, with Balj eventually displacing the former governor. The Arabic sources refer to Balj's troops as the "second wave" of Muslim conquerors who settled in the Iberian Peninsula. 'Asim al-'Uryan would then, according to Ibn al-Khatib, have been part of that "second wave". 'Asim entered al-Andalus as a member of the regiment (jund) of Qinnasrin, which was eventually settled by the governor Abu l-Khattar (r. 125–7/743–5) in the province of Jaén.

Jaén was the place of origin of Ibn al-Zubayr's father. Ibrahim ibn al-Zubayr ibn Muhammad ibn Ibrahim al-Thaqafi abandoned his native town in 643/1245, shortly before it was conquered by the Christians. He settled in Granada, where his son 'Abd Allah was born. His other son, Abu Ja'far Ahmad – the famous Nasrid scholar Ibn al-Zubayr – had been born in Jaén in 627/1230, and he died in Granada in 708/1308. Another three members of his family are known, the last dying in 765/1363.[14]

If we accept the genealogy recorded by Ibn al-Khatib, this means that in eighth-/fourteenth-century Granada, there was a family that had managed to preserve the memory of an ancestry six centuries old. In other words, six centuries after 'Asim's arrival in the Iberian Peninsula, his descendants still remembered their origins. And this despite the fact that from the first half of the fifth/eleventh century – when we still have trustworthy information about the descendants of 'Asim al-'Uryan[15] – until the appearance of scholars claiming him as their ancestor in the first half of the seventh/thirteenth century, nothing is known about the Banu 'Asim al-Thaqafi.

NASRID ELITES IN GRANADA AND THEIR ARAB ANCESTORS
AMONG THE CONQUERORS, ACCORDING TO IBN AL-KHATIB

As indicated, the information regarding the ancient origins of Ibn al-Zubayr's family is found in Ibn al-Khatib's biographical dictionary devoted to Granada. Earlier biographers do not record this ancestry of Ibn al-Zubayr.[16] There are eleven other occasions on which Ibn al-Khatib points to the fact that the ancestors of some notable families from both the region and the city of Granada could be counted among the first Arab settlers – and conquerors – of the Iberian Peninsula,[17] thus connecting present days with the founding moment of al-Andalus.

1. Banu l-Hakim. The Banu 'Abbad al-Lakhmi (Yemeni or southern Arabs) – rulers of the Taifa kingdom of Seville in the fifth/eleventh century – had as an ancestor 'Itaf ibn Balj ibn Bishr, the son of the previously mentioned military commander who had entered al-Andalus in 123/741. The family's relatives, the Banu l-Hakim, moved to Ronda, and one of them became so famous as a doctor or *ḥakīm* that they became known by this name (al-Hakim).[18] Two family members, who lived in the seventh/thirteenth century, devoted themselves to agriculture in the lands they owned in the area of Ronda. The youngest, Abu 'Abd Allah – after travelling to the East where he obtained many scholarly licences (*ijāzas*) and books – in 686/1286 entered the service of the Nasrid sultan Muhammad II. His two brothers became independent rulers in Ronda, where they acknowledged Marinid rule (the Marinids ruled over the Maghrib and tried to extend their kingdom to the Iberian Peninsula). Eventually, the Banu l-Hakim submitted to the Nasrids who named them viziers. In 701/1302, the blind Nasrid sultan, Muhammad III, left actual rule in the hands of Abu 'Abd Allah, who was eventually killed in a conspiracy in 708/1309.[19]

2. Banu Adha al-Hamdhani (Yemen).[20] The Granadan 'Ali ibn 'Umar ibn Muhammad al-Hamdhani (d. 540/1145)[21] was a descendant of the first Yemeni born in al-Andalus, al-Gharib ibn Yazid.[22] Members of the family living during the Umayyad period behaved as independent lords in the area of Granada during the second half of the third/ninth century, until they submitted to 'Abd al-Rahman III. Nothing else is known about them until we reach 'Ali's father, 'Umar (active in the second half of the fifth/eleventh century–beginning of the sixth/twelfth century), to whom Ibn al-Zubayr and Ibn 'Abd al-Malik al-Marrakushi devoted a biography. 'Umar's son 'Ali – who has an entry in Ibn al-Khatib's biographical dictionary – was a judge in Almería and Granada under the Almoravids, and after the assassination of the Almoravid amir in 539/1145, he took power in Granada for a brief period. Not much is known about the family until Ibn al-Khatib's father married a daughter of the vizier Abu l-Ula Adha ibn Adha al-Hamdhani.

3. Banu l-'Amiri/Banu Mas'ada al-'Amiri (Qays).[23] The family's ancestor was Bakr ibn Bakkar ibn al-Badr ibn Sa'id ibn 'Abd Allah, who entered al-Andalus among the conquerors in the year 94/712. He settled in the area of Granada (Tígnar) and is credited with transmission of Prophetic traditions (aḥādīth),[24] although the standard narrative about the introduction of the Prophet's tradition in al-Andalus does not mention him.[25] This Bakr ibn Bakkar was a descendant of Maymuna ibn al-Harith, one of the Prophet's wives. The most famous among his descendants – of whom some names and biographies have been preserved – was Ahmad ibn Muhammad ibn Ahmad ibn 'Abd al-Rahman ibn 'Ali ibn Muhammad ibn Sa'd ibn Sa'id ibn Mas'ada ibn Rabi'a ibn Sakhr ibn Sharahil ibn 'Amir ibn al-Fadl ibn Bakr ibn Bakkar ibn al-Badr ibn Sa'id ibn 'Abd Allah (d. 699/1299), a judge in the early Nasrid period and author of a lost history about his family (ta'rīkh qawmihi wa-qarābatihi), which seems to be the source of the information about his own ancestors.[26] Another member of the family (d. 603/1206), who served the Almohads, wrote a refutation of Ibn Garsiya's epistle against the Arabs.[27]

4. Banu 'Atiyya al-Muharibi (Qays).[28] The family's ancestor was 'Atiyya ibn Khalid ibn Khifaf, who entered al-Andalus during the conquest and settled in Qashtala (la Zubia), a village in the area of Granada. 'Atiyya's descendants were prominent especially under the Almoravids and the Almohads. The most famous member of the family is 'Abd al-Haqq ibn Ghalib ibn 'Abd al-Rahman (d. 541/1147), author of a Fahrasa and a commentary on the Qur'an.[29]

5. Banu l-Balafiqi al-Sulami (Qays).[30] The family's ancestor was 'Ayyash ibn Hammud/Mahmud, a descendant of 'Abbas ibn Mirdas – the famous poet who fought with the Prophet at the battle of Hunayn in the year 8/630. 'Ayyash entered al-Andalus with Musa ibn Nusayr. The first member of the family mentioned in the sources is Abu Ishaq ibn al-Hajj (d. 616/1219), who lived under the Almohads. The most famous is the Sufi Abu l-Barakat al-Balafiqi (d. 771/1370), who served the Nasrids as a judge.

6. Banu l-Ghafiqi (Qays). Ibn al-Khatib stresses that the al-Ghafiqi affiliation (nisba) borne by this family was not geographical but tribal, and that its ancestor was al-Ghafiq ibn al-Shahid ibn 'Akk ibn 'Adnan.[31] Only two members of the family are known, 'Abd Allah ibn Ahmad ibn Muhammad ibn Sa'id ibn Ayyub ibn al-Hasan ibn al-Munakhkhil ibn Zayd al-Ghafiqi (d. 731/1330) and Muhammad ibn Ahmad ibn Zayd al-Ghafiqi (d. 762/1360), both active in Nasrid times.[32]

7. Banu l-Hajj al-Numayri (Mudar). This family's ancestor was Thawaba ibn Hamza al-Numayri, who settled in the area of Guadix. Its most famous member is Abu Ishaq Ibrahim ibn 'Abd Allah (d. c. 785/1383), a jurist and a poet who served the Nasrids as a secretary and a judge.[33] Abu Ishaq had family links with other important Nasrid families, such as the Banu Arqam,[34] the Banu 'Asim al-Qaysi[35] and the Banu Juzayy.[36]

8. Banu l-Hasan (al-Bunnahi) al-Judhami (Yemen).[37] The most famous member is the jurist Abu l-Hasan 'Ali al-Bunnahi (d. 794/1391), already mentioned, who served the Nasrids as a judge and in other capacities. Al-Bunnahi is the author of a history of the judges of al-Andalus, in which he gives information about his family indicating that members of the family served the Umayyads and the 'Amirids, amassing great wealth and properties, which were subsequently lost at the end of the Almohad period. Al-Bunnahi had a close and, for a time, friendly relationship with Ibn al-Khatib, but he was eventually put in charge of the trial against the author of the *Ihata* that led to the latter's death. The enmity between the two has left traces in a number of writings, and in one of them Ibn al-Khatib severely criticises al-Bunnahi for his obsession with proving the nobility and antiquity of his lineage.

9. Banu Khaldun al-Hadrami (Yemen, but not Qahtan), to which belonged the famous historian Ibn Khaldun (d. 808/1406).[38] The family's ancestor was 'Uthman ibn Bakr ibn Khalid, called Khaldun, a Yemeni Arab among the conquerors who shared kinship with the Prophet's Companion Wa'il ibn Hujr and who settled first in Carmona and then in Seville.

10. Banu l-Mallahi al-Ghafiqi ('Adnan). The family's ancestor was Marwan al-Dakhil, who entered al-Andalus during the conquest. The most famous member of the family is 'Abd al-Wahid ibn Ibrahim ibn Mufarrij ibn Ahmad ibn 'Abd al-Wahid ibn Hurayt ibn Ja'far ibn Sa'id ibn Muhammad ibn Haql/ Jafl ibn al-Khiyar ibn Marwan al-Dakhil al-Ghafiqi al-Mallahi al-Gharnati (d. 619/1222), author of a *Kitab al-shajara fi al-ansab* and a *Ta'rikh fi a'lam Ilbira wa-ansabihim wa-anba'ihim*, one of the sources used by Ibn al-Khatib.[39]

11. Banu Sa'id al-'Ansi (Yemen). The ancestor who settled in al-Andalus (Cordoba) was a Yemeni called 'Abd Allah ibn Sa'd ibn al-Hasan. This 'Abd Allah had the following *nasab*: ibn 'Uthman ibn al-Husayn ibn 'Abd Allah ibn Sa'id ibn 'Ammar ibn Yasir ibn Malik ibn Kinana ibn Qays ibn al-Husayb ibn Ludim ibn Tha'laba ibn 'Awf ibn Haritha ibn 'Amir ibn Yahya ibn Anas ibn Malik ibn Adad ibn Zayd al-Ansi (Yemen, Madhhij). He was, therefore, a descendant of 'Ammar ibn Yasir, who died in 37/657 at the battle of Siffin and was a follower of 'Ali against Mu'awiya. 'Abd Allah ibn Sa'd arrived in al-Andalus as a soldier in the regiment (*jund*) of Damascus, which was settled in Granada.[40] Nothing further is known of the family, however, until the sixth/twelfth century, when the Banu Sa'id of Alcalá la Real appear, serving the Almoravids, then the Almohads and, in the seventh/thirteenth century, the Hafsids. To this family belonged the famous man of letters Ibn Sa'id al-Maghribi,[41] who had family links to the historian and genealogist al-Mallahi.

Apart from these Granadan families, Ibn al-Khatib also mentions that the ancestors of two prominent Andalusis belonged to the families of Arab conquerors. The first is the famous traveller Ibn Jubayr al-Kinani (Mudar,

d. 614/1217), whose ancestor 'Abd al-Salam ibn Jubayr al-Kinani entered al-Andalus with Balj ibn Bishr. The second is 'Abd al-Rahman ibn Muhammad ibn 'Abd Allah al-Ma'afiri (Yemen, d. 518/1124), a descendant of 'Uqba ibn Nu'aym, who belonged to the *jund* of Damascus settled in Granada.

As regards the Nasrids or Banu Nasr, they presented themselves as descendants of Sa'd ibn 'Ubada al-Khazraji[42] through Sa'd's son Qays, who had been governor of Egypt. The Khazraj – together with the Aws – were called *Anṣār* (Defenders) because of the help they gave to the Prophet Muhammad in Medina, and this Sa'd ibn 'Ubada al-Khazraji had been on the verge of becoming the Prophet's successor after his death.[43] Descendants of this leader of the Prophet's Ansar were known to have settled in the Iberian Peninsula,[44] and some Andalusi *nasabs* explicitly record this lineage,[45] to which I shall return.

All of the Granadan families mentioned by Ibn al-Khatib have an Arab ancestry; no Berber conqueror is mentioned. This fact can be taken as reflecting the pattern of settlement in the area: Ilbira/Granada became the abode of the *jund* of Damascus, which formed part of Balj ibn Bishr's troops. Nonetheless, the absence of any descendant of the Zirid Berbers who had settled in the area as rulers of the Taifa kingdom of Granada is striking. Manuela Marín has recently dealt with the Arab predominance in the area of Granada in a study analysing the ethnic affiliation of seventy-four religious scholars active during the Umayyad period.[46] This overwhelming presence of Arabs singles out the area of Granada (together with some other areas such as Seville and Beja), as in the rest of al-Andalus both Arab and Berber settlements are recorded. Ibn al-Khatib did find it worthwhile to indicate that a descendant of the famous Masmuda Berber Yahya ibn Yahya (d. 234/848) – whose transmission of Malik's *Muwatta'* became canonical in the Islamic West – had been connected with Granada,[47] but what was relevant for him was Yahya's Maliki pedigree, not his Berber ethnicity.

Ibn al-Khatib's strong concern to stress an ancestry going back to the conquest period is not paralleled in his biographical dictionary of Granada with a similar concern with ancestors active under the Umayyads of al-Andalus. Ibn al-Khatib records in his *Ihata* twelve biographies of Granadan scholars from the Umayyad period,[48] but he does not claim their ancestry for notable families in his own times. The only partial exception is the case of 'Abd al-Malik ibn Habib al-Sulami (d. 238/852), perhaps the most renowned Umayyad-era scholar from Granada, who was related to the Banu l-Balafiqi (no. 5 above). In some of these cases, the ancestry was not prestigious or was linked to an unpleasant past; for example, the poet Abu l-Makhshi al-Tamimi had had his tongue cut out because of his lampoons of the Umayyads.[49] In the case of Asbat ibn Ja'far,[50] Asbat was the ancestor of Sa'id ibn Sulayman ibn Judi, a famous Arab rebel during the amirate of the Umayyad 'Abd Allah (r. 275–300/888–912), but in spite of the fact that Ibn al-Khatib states that many villages in his times still bore Asbat's name, no scholarly Granadan family claimed his ancestry. Was this so because descent from Asbat ibn Ja'far could have been seen as threatening to the Nasrids of Ibn al-Khatib's own day?

Ibn al-Khatib also records in his *Ihata* the biographies of non-scholars from the Umayyad period who had some connection with Granada. Some of these figures are Arabs of the period of the conquest, such as a son of Musa ibn Nusayr (the Arab commander of the conquering army), Yusuf al-Fihri (a descendant of 'Uqba ibn Nafi' and a governor of al-Andalus) and his supporter al-Sumayl. Eight of the fourteen historical figures are members of the Umayyad family[51] and three are rebels against the Umayyads (Sawwar ibn Hamdun, Sa'id ibn Sulayman ibn Judi and 'Umar ibn Hafsun). Again, none of these figures appear as ancestors of Nasrid families.[52]

RULERS, ANCESTORS AND HISTORY WRITING

Al-Andalus as a political entity had a beginning and an end. The beginning was the Muslim conquest that began in 93/711, and the end was the fall of Granada into Christian hands in 897/1492. Many rulers came and went during these eight centuries of Muslim power in the Iberian Peninsula. Among the conquerors, the Arab Fihri family[53] (members of the tribe of Quraysh) had a prominent role, especially during the times preceding the arrival of 'Abd al-Rahman I in the year 138/756 – an arrival determined by the fact that 'Abd al-Rahman I's Umayyad relatives had been defeated and massacred by the 'Abbasids. From 138/756 until the abolition of the Umayyad caliphate in 422/1031, the Umayyads of al-Andalus tried in different ways to maintain and increase their legitimacy to rule: by claiming the inheritance of their ancestors; by performing *jihād* against the Christians; by weakening and destroying hostile local rulers, while installing and supporting loyal allies in their place; and by developing a complex religious policy in which the links between Cordoba and Medina were stressed.[54] Later on, during the fifth/eleventh century, local rulers with different ethnic backgrounds and different claims to legitimacy emerged.[55]

None of the genealogical claims made by these rulers in their legitimising efforts involved the pre-Islamic history of the Iberian Peninsula,[56] with the exception of the failed attempt in the second half of the third/ninth century by the non-Arab convert (*muwallad*) rebel Ibn Hafsun, whose Visigothic ancestry is probably to be linked to his conversion to Christianity.[57] The claims made by the rulers of al-Andalus involved Arab ethnicity, even in those cases when rulers were known to be of Berber origin, such as the Aftasids, Taifa rulers of Badajoz, who adopted a Himyari genealogy. This was also the genealogy claimed by the Almoravids, Berber Sanhaja who became rulers of al-Andalus after defeating the Christians in the battle of Zallaqa (479/1087). For their part, the Mu'minids,

Zanata Berbers who succeeded the Almoravids as rulers of the Islamic West and leaders of the Almohad movement, claimed to be northern Arabs, and specifically Qaysis.[58] The Qaysi genealogy was needed for the Mu'minids' self-proclamation as caliphs, a title the Mu'minids felt was legitimate to adopt as successors to a messianic figure, the Mahdi Ibn Tumart. Although he was presented as a descendant of the Prophet's family, Ibn Tumart was a Berber from the Masmuda, a tribal group with a long history of producing prophets and messianic figures.

Opponents to the Almohads made use of different genealogies in their claims to rule. Ibn al-Ahmar was eventually successful; his descendants – the Nasrids of Granada – adopted an Ansari genealogy. This genealogy linked them to Prophetic times through the family's alleged ancestor Sa'd ibn 'Ubada al-Khazraji. This Sa'd had been left out of those entitled to the caliphate, and, as a consequence, southern Arabs or Yemenis were proclaimed destined to be viziers (*wuzarā'*) and not amirs (*umarā'*), which in principle eliminated the possibility of an Ansari caliphate.[59] In al-Andalus, the Ansari genealogy had a long tradition of being adopted by non-Arabs as a way to indicate their allegiance to Islam outside Arab ethnicity: One could claim to be an Ansari without belonging to the actual Ansari tribes of Aws or the Khazraj simply by virtue of being willing to defend Islam and its Prophet at any period in time.[60]

The writing of history dealing with al-Andalus – that concentrated on rulers and on their rights to rule – had neither the same beginning nor the same end as al-Andalus as a political entity and continued long after al-Andalus had been lost to the Christians.[61] It had begun mostly in connection with the need to legitimise the Umayyads of al-Andalus and, therefore, had a strong pro-Umayyad character, aiming – with more or less success – to obliterate the memory of the period when al-Andalus was nominally under the rule of the Umayyad caliph in Damascus, during which time the conquerors enjoyed a high degree of political autonomy.[62] It does not seem arbitrary that the material compiled by Ibn al-Khatib precisely traced back the ancestry of eleven families from Granada to that period of the conquest.

The conquest of al-Andalus, as already mentioned, had taken place under Umayyad rule, and Umayyad legitimacy was therefore implied in any account of that conquest. However, when discussing the lineages of Granadan families, Ibn al-Khatib does not focus on links with the Umayyads, such as those of patronage. Those were the links to which Ibn al-Qutiyya – writing in the first half of the fourth/tenth century under the first Umayyad caliph of Cordoba – paid attention in his *Ta'rikh*.[63] The Umayyads were part of the history of al-Andalus and much could be learned from them,[64] but for Ibn al-Khatib they were not the axis of Granadan identity.

Ibn al-Khatib's material focuses instead on the conquest and on those Muslims who were the first to enter the Iberian Peninsula, that is, the Arab conquerors, whose descendants continued to ensure the preservation of the Arabic language and Arabo-Islamic learning. Stress is put on the continuity of the presence of Arab tribal lineages in Granada, and thus Ibn al-Khatib mentions the Abshami, 'Absi ('Abd ibn Baghid), 'Amili, Ansari, 'Ansi, Asadi, Asbahi, Ashja'i (Ashja'a ibn Rayth), Awsi, Ayadi, Azdi, Bajili, Bakri, Balawi, Dabbi, Dawsi, Fahmi, Fazari, Fihri, Ghafiqi (Ghafiq ibn al-Shahid), Ghassani (Ghassan al-Azd), Hadrami, Hakami, Hamdani, Hijaji, Hilali (Hilal ibn 'Amir), Himmi, Himyari, Hudhali, Jazali, Judhami, Ju'fi, Juhan, Kala'i, Kalbi, Khath'ami, Khawlani, Khazraji, Khushani, Kilabi (Kilab ibn Rabi'a), Kinani, Kindi, Laythi, Ma'afiri, Madhhiji, Makhzumi, Mazini, Mazni, Muradi, Murri, Namari (Numayr ibn 'Amir), Qahtani, Qays (Qays 'Aylan), Quda'i, Qurashi, Qushayri, Ru'ayni, Sadafi, Sa'di, Saksaki, Sakuni, Salmani (Sulayman ibn Mansur), Saluli, Sha'bi, Sarihid, Sulami, Taghlibi, Ta'i', Tha'labi, Tamimi, Tanukhi, Thaqafi, Taymi, Tujibi, 'Udhri, Umawi, Ummi, 'Uqayli ('Uqayl ibn Ka'b), Ya'muri, Yahsubi and Zubaydi affiliations. These nisbas are not only documented by Ibn al-Khatib's pen but can also be shown to have been present both in the towns and in the countryside: In a document from 1226 referring to the village (qarya) of Falix (Almería), twelve out of the fifty men mentioned have Arabic nisbas (six Ghassani, three Qaysi, one Ghafiqi, one Hamdhani and one Judhami).[65] The issue is not the extent to which these Arab lineages had been preserved even seven centuries after the conquest, but rather the needs that they were then addressing. As a servant of the Nasrids and one whose writings were put at the service of the dynasty, Ibn al-Khatib was involved in the complex Nasrid attempt to foster political viability for the Nasrids' kingdom by claiming continuity with the early Islamic period of al-Andalus – a claim that aimed to counteract the Nasrids' rivals and enemies, both Christian and Maghribian, but which also served an internal audience.

The Nasrids were ruling a land that had been greatly diminished since the time of the Muslim conquest of the Iberian Peninsula, a land that was under constant threat by Christians who asserted their right to conquer Muslim territory because that land had belonged to them before the arrival of the Muslims, as the Mozarab (Arabised Christian) Sisnando proclaimed in a famous passage quoted by the last Zirid ruler of Granada:

He [Sisnando] said to me face to face: "Al-Andalus originally belonged to the Christians. Then they were defeated by the Arabs and driven to the most inhospitable region, Galicia. Now that they are strong and capable, the Christians desire to recover what they have lost by force. This can only be achieved by weakness and encroachment. In the long run, when it has neither men nor money, we'll be able to recover it without any difficulty."[66]

Stressing that those who lived in the Nasrid kingdom were direct descendants of the Arab conquerors of al-Andalus conveyed the message that the population of Nasrid Granada had nothing to do with that pre-Islamic past of the Iberian Peninsula claimed by the Christian enemy. The roots of the Nasrid population came from elsewhere, but they were entitled to live where their ancestors had settled because their rights to the land were those of conquest and of religion. The ancestors remembered are the *dākhilūn*, that is, those Arabs who entered al-Andalus as conquerors, bringing with them not only their religion, but also their language and culture. The native Hispano-Roman and Visigothic population had been so assimilated to Arab ethnicity that no pre-conquest genealogical memory survived and no kinship, therefore, could be established with the population of the neighbouring Christian polities. There were also no genealogical links with Berber neighbours across the Straits, such as the Zanata Banu Marin, who sometimes provided military help against Christian enemies but who also could become enemies in their attempts to become the new rulers of what was left of al-Andalus.

As indicated at the beginning, al-Andalus was considered to be an island surrounded by the sea and by Christians, an island that at the time of the Nasrids in the seventh/thirteenth and eighth/fourteenth centuries was inhabited by Arabs who took pride in their ancestry linking them to Arabia and Syria, and who would be witnesses to the Truth until the coming of the "hour": either the Last Hour, for those who hoped to be able to resist Christian pressure, or the hour to cross the Straits and to find a new life in Muslim lands. How the Mudéjars could adapt this picture – as far as genealogy is concerned – to their plight does not seem to have been envisaged by Ibn al-Khatib, who has nothing to say about those Muslims who chose or had to stay and live under Christian rule.[67] Umayyad restoration – as we have seen – was attempted during the Morisco rebellion, but when it failed, some Moriscos who wanted to stay in the Iberian Peninsula tried another way to find a place for themselves in the new society, a way that still involved the preservation of Arab ethnicity and the Arabic language, but also meant the abandonment of Islam.[68]

Notes

1. M. I. Fierro and S. Faghia, "Un nuevo texto de tradiciones escatológicas sobre al-Andalus", *Sharq al-Andalus*, vol. 7, 1990, pp. 99–111. For a general overview of eschatological expectations see my "Doctrinas y movimientos de tipo mesiánico en al-Andalus", in *Milenarismos y milenaristas en la Europa Medieval: IX Semana de Estudios Medievales (Nájera, del 3 al 7 de agosto de 1998)*, Nájera: Instituto de Estudios Riojanos, 1999, pp. 159–75.
2. For the new reading of the name – first proposed by Muhammad ben Cherifa – see Mª I. Calero Secall, "Los Banū l-Ḥasan al-Bunnāhī: Una familia de juristas

malagueños (ss. X–XV)", in C. Castillo, I. Cortés and J. P. Monferrer (eds), *Estudios árabes dedicados a D. Luis Seco de Lucena (en el XXV aniversario de su muerte)*, Granada: Universidad de Granada, 1999, pp. 53–76.

3. Calero Secall, "La peste en Málaga, según el malagueño al-Nubahi", in *Homenaje al Prof. Jacinto Bosch Vilá*, vol. 1, Granada: Universidad de Granada, 1991, pp. 57–72, at p. 59.

4. Fierro and Faghia, "Un nuevo texto de tradiciones escatológicas", numbers 7–12; in a similar vein, see the eschatological traditions collected in an eighth-/fourteenth-century text, *Dhikr bilad al-Andalus*, ed. and trans. L. Molina, Madrid: CSIC, 1983, pp. 10–11 (for the Arabic text); pp. 22–3 (for the Spanish translation).

5. J. N. Lincoln, "Aljamiado prophecies", *Publications of the Modern Language Association of America*, vol. 52, 1937, pp. 631–44; L. López Baralt, "El oráculo de Mahoma sobre la Andalucía musulmana de los últimos tiempos", *Hispanic Review*, vol. 52, 1984, pp. 41–57; L. P. Harvey, "A Morisco collection of apocryphal hadiths on the virtues of al-Andalus", *Al-Masaq*, vol. 2, 1989, pp. 25–39.

6. L. del Mármol y Carvajal, *Historia de la rebelión y castigo de los moriscos en el Reino de Granada*, vol. 1, 2nd reprint, Madrid: Imprenta de Sancha, 1797, pp. 251–3.

7. Mármol y Carvajal, *Historia*, vol. 1, p. 180.

8. M. Marín, "*'Ilm al-nuǧūm* e *'ilm al-ḥidṯān* en al-Andalus", in *Actas del XII Congreso de la UEA I (Málaga, 1984)*, Madrid: Union Europeenne d'Arabisants et d'Islamisants, 1986, pp. 509–35, esp. p. 521.

9. C. Pellat, "Ibn al-Zubayr", in P. Bearman, Th. Bianquis, C. E. Bosworth, E. van Donzel, and W. P. Heinrichs (eds), *Encyclopaedia of Islam*, 13 vols, 2nd edn. Leiden: E. J. Brill, 1960–2005. Online edition.

10. Fierro, "Los Banū 'Āṣim al-Ṯaqafi, antepasados de Ibn al-Zubayr", *Al-Qanṭara*, vol. 7, 1986, pp. 53–84, esp. pp. 54–8.

11. Ibn Harith al-Khushani, *Akhbar al-fuqaha' wa-l-muhaddithin*, eds M. L. Avila and L. Molina, Madrid: CSIC and ICMA, 1992, biography number 73, p. 73. For the use of the term *muwālī* see Fierro, "*Mawālī* and *muwalladūn* in al-Andalus (second/eighth–fourth/tenth centuries)", in M. Bernards and J. Nawas (eds), *Patronate and Patronage in Early and Classical Islam*, Leiden: E. J. Brill, 2005, pp. 195–245, n. 15.

12. Fierro, "Los Banū 'Āṣim", pp. 59–72.

13. Ibn al-Khatib, *al-Ihata fi akhbar Gharnata*, vol. 1, ed. M. 'A. A. 'Inan, Cairo: Maktabat al-Khanji, 1973–7, pp. 188–93.

14. Fierro, "Los Banū 'Āṣim", pp. 72–5.

15. The chronology could be stretched to the first half of the sixth/twelfth century if we take as trustworthy the genealogical information about the member of the family mentioned as living under the Almoravids: See n. 12 above.

16. See, for example, al-Marrakushi (d. 702/1289), *al-Dhayl wa-l-takmila*, vol. 1, Beirut: Dar al-Thaqafa wa-l-Tawzih, 1973–84, pt. 1, 39–45, no. 31; al-Dhahabi (d. 748/1348), *Tadhkirat al-huffaz*, vol. 4, ed. 'A. R. Y. al-Mu'allimi, Hyderabad: Matba'at Da'irat al-Ma'arif al-Nizamiyya, 1968–70, pp. 1,484–5, no. 1,169.

17. I take Ibn al-Khatib's information from Marín, "Ibn al-Ḥaṭīb, historiador de la época omeya en al-Andalus", *Revue de la Faculté de Lettres Université Sidi Mohamed Ben Abdellah*, vol. 2, no. 2, 1987, pp. 7–23. Ibn al-Khatib himself claimed an ancestor who had entered al-Andalus at the time of the conquest; see E. Molina López, *Ibn al-Jatib*, Granada: Editorial Comares, 2001, pp. 33–9.

18. María Jesús Rubiera, "El Dū l-wizāratayn Ibn al-Ḥakīm de Ronda", *Al-Andalus*, vol. 34, 1969, pp. 105–21. A genealogical tree of the Banu l-Hakim is included in *Biblioteca de al-Andalus*, vol. 3, *De Ibn al-Dabbag a Ibn Kurz*, eds J. Lirola and J. M. Puerta, Almería: Fundación Ibn Tufayl, 2004, pp. 245–55, no. 528; see also pp. 255–9, no. 529, and pp. 259–61, no. 530, all by F. N. Velázquez Basanta.

19. Jesús Rubiera, "Los Banu Escallola, una dinastía granadina que no fue", *Andalucía Islámica Textos y Estudios*, vols 2–3, 1981–2, pp. 85–94.

20. This family has been studied by Velázquez Basanta, "De Ibn Ḥayyān a Ibn al-Jaṭīb: Los Banū Aḍḥà al-Hamdānī, una familia árabe de Elvira", in Frédéric Bauden (ed.), *Ultra mare: Mélanges de langue arabe et d'islamologie offerts à Aubert Martin*, Louvain: Peeters, 2004, pp. 213–47.

21. See the entry by J. Lirola Delgado and A. Rodríguez Figueroa devoted to this member of the Banu Adha who became ruler of the post-Almoravid Taifa kingdom of Granada in *Enciclopedia de al-Andalus: Diccionario de autores y obras andalusíes*, vol. 1, eds Lirola and Puerta, Granada: El Legado Andalusí, 2003, pp. 408–12, no. 218.

22. On Yemeni settlements in al-Andalus, see the study by M. F. al-Wasif, "La inmigración de árabes yemeníes a al-Andalus desde la conquista islámica (92/711) hasta fines del s. II/VIII", *Anaquel de Estudios Árabes*, vol. 1, 1990, pp. 203–19.

23. Various members of the family have entries in *Biblioteca de al-Andalus*, vol. 4, *De Ibn al-Labbana a Ibn al-Ruyuli*, eds Lirola and Puerta, Almería: Fundación Ibn Tufayl, 2006; see pp. 138–9, no. 784; p. 140, no. 785; pp. 140–3, no. 786; and pp. 143–4, no. 787, with a genealogical tree on p. 141. The author of all entries is V. C. Navarro Oltra.

24. For *aḥādīth* transmitted by Bakr ibn Bakkar, see al-Tujibi (d. 730/1329), *Barnamaj*, ed. 'A. H. Mansur, Tunis: al-Dar al-'Arabiyya li-l-Kitab, 1981, p. 216.

25. Fierro, "The Introduction of Ḥadīth in Al-Andalus (2nd/8th–3rd/9th centuries)", *Der Islam*, vol. 66, 1989, pp. 68–93.

26. *Biblioteca de al-Andalus*, vol. 4, no. 786.

27. J. T. Monroe, *The Shu'ūbiyya in al-Andalus*, Berkeley – Los Angeles: University of California Press, 1970, pp. 30–62.

28. See on them J. M. Fórneas, "Los Banū 'Aṭiyya de Granada", *Miscelánea de Estudios Árabes y Hebraicos*, vol. 25, 1976, pp. 69–80; vol. 26, 1977, pp. 27–60; and vols 27–28, 1978–9, pp. 65–77.

29. *Enciclopedia de al-Andalus*, pp. 515–17, no. 267 (R. El Hour).

30. On them, see C. de la Puente, "La familia de Abū Isḥāq Ibn al-Ḥāŷŷ de Velefique", in Marín and J. Zanón (eds), *Estudios onomástico-biográficos de al-Andalus: V*, Madrid: CSIC, 1992, pp. 309–48, as well as her entries on members of the family in *Enciclopedia de al-Andalus*, pp. 97–101, no. 46, and in *Biblioteca de al-Andalus*, vol. 3, *De Ibn al-Dabbag a Ibn Kurz*, pp. 332–5, no. 573; pp. 335–6, no. 574; and pp. 336–8, no. 575, with a genealogical tree on p. 333.

31. Ibn al-Khatib, *al-Ihata*, vol. 3, pp. 411–12. The *nisba* al-Ghafiqi in al-Andalus has been analysed by H. de Felipe, "Gafiqíes en al-Andalus: Datos para la evolución de una *nisba*", in Marín and de Felipe (eds), *Estudios onomástico-biográficos de al-Andalus: VII*, Madrid: CSIC, 1995, pp. 533–50.

32. *Enciclopedia de al-Andalus*, pp. 172–3, no. 95 (A. Rodríguez Figueroa).

33. *Biblioteca de al-Andalus*, vol. 3, *De Ibn al-Dabbag a Ibn Kurz*, pp. 341–51, no. 579

(Lirola Delgado and A. C. López López), with a genealogical tree on p. 342.

34. On the Banu Arqam, see *Enciclopedia de al-Andalus*, pp. 477–82, nos 247–9 (the last person mentioned, d. 657/1259, wrote a genealogical treatise on the Arabs).

35. L. Seco de Lucena, "Los Banū 'Āṣim, intelectuales y políticos granadinos del siglo XV", *Miscelánea de Estudios Árabes y Hebraicos*, vol. 2, 1953, pp. 5–14.

36. C. del Moral and Velázquez Basanta, "Los Banu Yuzayy: Una familia de juristas e intelectuales granadinos del siglo XIV. I: Abu l-Qasim Muhammad Ben Yuzayy", *Miscelánea de Estudios Árabes y Hebraicos*, vol. 45, 1996, pp. 161–201.

37. Calero Secall, "Los Banū l-Ḥasan al-Bunnāhī", and her entry in *Enciclopedia de al-Andalus*, pp. 131–6, no. 66, with a genealogical tree on p. 133.

38. *Biblioteca de al-Andalus*, vol. 3, *De Ibn al-Dabbag a Ibn Kurz*, pp. 578–97, no. 676 (M. A. Manzano Rodríguez), with a genealogical tree of the Banu Khaldun on pp. 580–1.

39. Ibn al-Khatib, *Ihata*, vol. 3, pp. 176–7.

40. Ibn al-Khatib, *Ihata*, vol. 4, pp. 152–8.

41. G. Potiron, "Un polygraphe andalou du XIIIᵉ siècle", *Arabica*, vol. 13, 1966, pp. 142–67; M. H. al-'Iyadi, *Ibn Sa'id al-Andalusī: Hayatuhu wa-turathuhu al-fikri wa-l-adabi*, Cairo: Maktabat al-Anjilu al-Misriyya, 1972; R. Arié, "Un lettré andalou en Ifriqiya et en Orient au XIIIᵉ siècle: Ibn Sa'id", in Rachel Arié (ed.), *L'Occident musulman au Bas-Moyen Age*, Paris: De Boccard, 1992, pp. 47–72; W. Hoenerbach, "Los Banū Sa'īd de Alcalá la Real y sus allegados: Su poesía según la antología *al-Mugrib*", *Homenaje al Prof. Jacinto Bosch Vilá*, vol. 2, Granada: Universidad de Granada, 1991, 739–73, continued in *Revista del Centro de Estudios Históricos de Granada y su Reino*, vol. 3, 1989, pp. 81–102; *Biblioteca de al-Andalus*, vol. 5, *De Ibn Sa'ada a Ibn Wuhayb*, eds Lirola and Puerta, Almería: Fundación Ibn Tufayl, 2007, pp. 132–3, no. 1,062; pp. 133–4, no. 1,063; pp. 134–5, no. 1,064; pp. 135–6, no. 1,065; pp. 136–7, no. 1,066; pp. 137–66, no. 1,67; pp. 166–8, no. 1,068; pp. 168–70, no. 1,069; p. 170, no. 1,070; pp. 171–5, no. 1,071; pp. 175–6, no. 1,072; and pp. 176–7, no. 1,073. Numbers 1,065–70 and 1,072–3 are written by P. Cano Ávila, number 1,071 by C. del Moral and the rest by "Documentación". A genealogical tree can be found on pp. 138–9.

42. F. Vidal Castro, "Frontera, genealogía y religión en la gestación y nacimiento del reino nazarí de Granada. En torno a Ibn al-Ahmar", in F. Toro Ceballos and J. Rodríguez Molina (eds), *III Estudios de Frontera: Convivencia, defensa y comunicación en la Frontera; En memoria de Don Juan de Mata Carriazo y Arroquia. Congreso celebrado en Alcalá La Real, del 18 al 20 de noviembre de 1999*, Jaén: Diputación Provincial de Jaén, 2000, pp. 793–810.

43. It is unclear to what extent Sa'd ibn 'Ubada's failed attempt to succeed the Prophet as leader of the Muslim community could have added to the religious legitimisation of the Nasrids. In order to clarify this point, Sa'd ibn 'Ubada's portrayal in Nasrid times needs to be studied. 'Ali ibn Muhammad al-Judhami al-Bunnahi (d. 794/1391) included in one of his works a biography of Sa'd ibn 'Ubada and his son Qays: See E. Lafuente Alcántara, *Inscripciones árabes de Granada precedidas de una reseña histórica y de la genealogía detallada de los reyes alahmares*, Granada: Universidad de Granada, 2000 [1859], p. 61. See now on this issue María Jesús Rubiera, "El califato nazarí", *Al-Qanṭara*, vol. 29, 2008, pp. 293–305, at pp. 296–300.

44. E. Terés, "Linajes árabes en al-Andalus según la 'Yamhara' de Ibn Ḥazm", *Al-Andalus*, vol. 22, 1957, pp. 55–111 and 337–76, esp. pp. 339–40. The areas of settlement of these descendants of Sa'd ibn 'Ubada were Corbalán (Zaragoza) and Ronda, as well as Medina Sidonia. Scholars with the *nisba* al-Ansari recorded in the biographical dictionaries come mostly from the eastern regions of al-Andalus (in some cases their origins lie in the area of Zaragoza) and from Almería, Granada and Málaga.

45. See examples in *Biblioteca de al-Andalus*, vol. 3, *De Ibn al-Dabbag a Ibn Kurz*, nos 452 (V. C. Navarro Oltra), 631 (p. 489ᵃ) (B. Boloix Gallardo), 648, 649, 650 (V. C. Navarro Oltra), and *Enciclopedia de al-Andalus*, vol. 1, no. 166 (C. de la Puente). Mª L. Ávila has dealt with three Ansari families from al-Andalus in "Tres familias ansaries de época almohade", *Al-Qanṭara*, vol. 30, 2009, pp. 361–401.

46. Marín, "Los ulemas de Ilbira: saberes islámicos, linajes árabes", *Miscelánea de Estudios Árabes y Hebraicos*, vol. 57, 2008, pp. 169–203.

47. The person in question is Yahya ibn 'Abd Allah ibn Yahya: Ibn al-Khatib, *Ihata*, vol. 4, p. 373.

48. They have been studied by Marín, "Ibn al-Ḥaṭīb, historiador", pp. 8–14.

49. Terés, "El poeta Abū-l-Majšī y Ḥassāna la Tamimiyya", *Al-Andalus*, vol. 26, 1961, pp. 229–44.

50. Ibn al-Khatib, *Ihata*, vol. 1, p. 418.

51. For an example, see Velázquez Basanta, "Al-Ḥakam I visto por Ibn al-Jaṭīb", *Qurtuba*, vol. 3, no. 3, 1998, pp. 171–9.

52. Apart from the studies already mentioned, the following deal with important families in Granada: L. Seco de Lucena, "Acerca de algunas familias ilustres arábigo-granadinas: Notas para el estudio de Granada bajo la dominación musulmana", *Miscelánea de Estudios Árabes y Hebraicos*, vol. 1, 1952, pp. 33–7; Seco de Lucena, *Los Abencerrajes: Leyenda e Historia*, Granada: F. Román, 1960; Seco de Lucena, "Alamines y Venegas, cortesanos de los nasríes", *Miscelánea de Estudios Árabes y Hebraicos*, vol. 10, 1961, pp. 127–42; Seco de Lucena, "Nuevas noticias sobre los Mufarriy", in *Études Lévi-Provençal*, vol. 1, Paris: Maisonneuve et Larose, 1962, pp. 299–305; M. S. Carrasco Urgoiti, "Apuntes sobre el mito de los Abencerrajes y sus versiones literarias", *Miscelánea de Estudios Árabes y Hebraicos*, vol. 47, 1998, pp. 65–88; Ávila, "Los Banū Manẓūr al-Qaysī", in L. Molina (ed.), *Estudios onomástico-biográficos de al-Andalus: IV*, Madrid: CSIC, 1990, pp. 23–8; J. Bosch Vilá, "Los Banū Simāk de Málaga y Granada: Una familia de cadíes", *Miscelánea de Estudios Árabes y Hebraicos*, vol. 11, 1962, pp. 21–37; R. G. Peinado Santaella, "Los Banu l-Qabšanī: Un linaje de la aristocracia nazarí", *Historia, Instituciones, Documentos*, vol. 20, no. 20, 1993, pp. 313–53; M. Charouiti Hasnaoui, "Una familia de juristas en los siglos XIV y XV: Los Banū 'Āṣim de Granada", in Marín (ed.), *Estudios onomástico-biográficos de al-Andalus: VI*, Madrid: CSIC, 1994, pp. 173–85; Mª D. Rodríguez Gómez, "Los Banū Būnuh: Una familia de juristas de Almuñécar", in *Homenaje al profesor José María Fórneas Besteiro*, vol. 1, Granada: Universidad de Granada, 1995, pp. 607–14; Mª J. Viguera, "Componentes y estructuras de la población", in M. J. Viguera (ed.), *Historia de España Menéndez Pidal*, vol. 8, nos 3–4, *El reino nazarí de Granada (1232–1492)*, Madrid: Espasa Calpe, 2000, pp. 19–70, esp. pp. 20–1.

53. K. Sato, "Early Settlers (*ahl al-balad*) in Eighth-century Al-Andalus and Ifriqiya:

Analysis of the Fihr Family", *The Toyo Gokuho*, vol. 77, 1996, pp. 51–76 (in Japanese).

54. G. Martínez-Gros, *L'idéologie omeyyade: La construction de la légitimité du Califat de Cordoue (X^e–XIe siècles)*, Madrid: Casa de Velázquez, 1992; J. Safran, *The Second Umayyad Caliphate: The Articulation of Caliphal Legitimacy in Al-Andalus*, Cambridge, MA: Harvard University Press, 2000; and Fierro, "La política religiosa de 'Abd al-Rahman III", *Al-Qanṭara*, vol. 25, 2004, pp. 119–56.

55. F. Clément, "Origines ethno-culturelles et pouvoir dans l'Espagne musulmane des Taifas V^e/XIe siècle", *Mélanges de la Casa de Velázquez: Antiquité et Moyen Age*, vol. 29, no. 1, 1993, pp. 192–206 and Clément, *Pouvoir et légitimité en Espagne musulmane à l'époque des Taifas (V^e/XIe siècle): L'imam fictif*, Paris: L'Harmattan, 1997.

56. See on this point G. Martínez-Gros, *Identité andalouse*, Arles, France: Sindbad, 1997 and A. Christys, "The *History* of Ibn Habib and Ethnogenesis in Al-Andalus", in R. Corradini, M. Diesenberger and H. Reimitz (eds), *The Construction of Communities in the Early Middle Ages: Texts, Resources and Artefacts, The Transformation of the Roman World*, vol. 12, Leiden: E. J. Brill, 2003, pp. 323–48. The reverse is also true, as the Christian conquest of al-Andalus was not accompanied by any revindication of genealogical proximity with the local population, a point made by M. Barceló, "La *spurcitia paganorum* que había en Coria antes de la conquista cristiana en junio de 1142 d.C.", in Barceló and J. Martínez Gázquez (eds), *Musulmanes y cristianos en Hispania durante las conquistas de los siglos XII y XIII*, Barcelona: Universitat Autònome de Barcelona, 2005, pp. 63–70, esp. p. 70.

57. Fierro, "Genealogies of Power in al-Andalus: Politics, Religion and Ethnicity during the Second/Eighth–Fifth/Eleventh Centuries", *Annales Islamologiques*, vol. 42, 2008, pp. 29–56.

58. Fierro, "Las genealogías de 'Abd al-Mu'min, primer califa almohade", *Al-Qanṭara*, vol. 24, 2003, pp. 77–108.

59. G. Lecomte, "Sur une relation de la *saqīfa* attribuée à Ibn Qutayba", *Studia Islamica*, vol. 31, 1970, pp. 171–83. For the use of the *saqīfa* episode by the Nasrids, see Rubiera, "El califato nazarí".

60. Fierro, "The Anṣārīs, Nāṣir al-Dīn and the Naṣrids in al-Andalus", *Jerusalem Studies in Arabic and Islam*, vol. 32, 2006, pp. 232–47.

61. Al-Maqqari (d. 1041/1632) compiled his famous literary and historical work on al-Andalus more than a century after the loss of al-Andalus: See R. Elger, "*Adab* and Historical Memory: The Andalusi Poet/Politician Ibn al-Khaṭīb as Presented in Ahmad al-Maqqarī (986/1577–1041/1632), *Nafḥ aṭ-ṭīb*", *Die Welt des Islams*, vol. 42, 2002, pp. 289–306.

62. See on this issue Fierro, "El conde Casio, los Banu Qasi y los linajes godos en al-Andalus", *Studia Historica, Historia Medieval*, vol. 27, 2009, pp. 181–9.

63. Fierro, "Familias en el *Ta'rīj iftitāḥ al-Andalus* de Ibn al-Qūṭiyya", in *Estudios onomástico-biográficos de al-Andalus: IV*, pp. 41–70.

64. Marín, "Ibn al-Ḥaṭīb, historiador", p. 21 notes that Ibn al-Khatib in his historical work *A'lam* compared certain episodes of Umayyad history with events that he had witnessed. For example, Ibn al-Khatib made use of an Umayyad precedent – that of the pledge of obedience (*bay'a*) paid to Hisham II, the minor son of al-Hakam

II who succeeded him to the Cordoban caliphate – to support a similar claim to succession on the part of a Nasrid sultan who was also a minor. See on this the study by Ávila, "La proclamación (bay'a) de Hisam II. Año 976 d.C.", Al-Qanṭara, vol. 1, 1980, pp. 79–114. Ibn al-Khatib's interest in the destiny of previous rulers is also shown when he comments that he had met a descendant of the Banu l-Hajjaj of Seville – who had ruled the town in the second half of the third/ninth century – who was amīr al-'aṭṭārīn (leader of the perfumists) in Málaga.

65. Viguera, "Componentes y estructuras de la población", p. 21, where the point is made that this apparent sign of Granadan Arabness really indicates socio-cultural values. See also Mª L. Lugo Acevedo, ed., El libro de las luces: Leyenda aljamiada sobre la genealogía de Mahoma; Estudio y edición crítica, Madrid: Trivium and SIAL, 2008, p. 52, for the continuing interest in genealogical lore among the Moriscos.

66. The Tibyān: Memoirs of 'Abd Allāh b. Buluggīn, Last Zīrid Amīr of Granada, trans. A. T. Tibi, Leiden: E. J. Brill, 1986, p. 90.

67. See on this point L. Jones, "Retratos de la emigración: La (re)conquista y la emigración de los ulemas a Granada, según la Iḥāṭa de Ibn al-Jaṭīb", in A. Echevarría (ed.), Estudios onomástico-biográficos de al-Andalus: XV, Biografías Mudéjares o la experiencia de ser minoría: Biografías islámicas en la España cristiana, Madrid: CSIC, 2008, pp. 21–58.

68. I am referring to the sophisticated and complex vision for Morisco survival planned by the forgers of the Lead Books found in Granada, for which see now M. García-Arenal, "El entorno de los Plomos: Historiografía y linaje", Al-Qanṭara, vol. 24, 2003, pp. 295–326 (extended version in M. Barrios and García-Arenal, eds, Los Plomos del Sacromonte: Invención y tesoro, Granada/Valencia: Publications de la Universidad de Valencia, Editorial Universidad de Granada, and Prensas Universitarias de Zaragoza, pp. 557–82); García-Arenal and F. Rodríguez Mediano, "Médico, traductor, inventor: Miguel de Luna, cristiano arábigo de Granada", Chronica Nova, vol. 32, 2006, pp. 187–231; and García-Arenal and Rodríguez Mediano, "Jerónimo Román de la Higuera and the Plomos of the Sacromonte", in K. Ingram (ed.), Conversos and Moriscos in Late Medieval Spain and Beyond, Leiden: E. J. Brill, 2009, pp. 243–68.

CHAPTER 6

Embarrassing Cousins: Genealogical Conundrums in the Central Sahara

JUDITH SCHEELE

Anybody looking for history (*ta'rīkh*) in the Central Sahara will soon be supplied with large quantities of *tawārīkh*: more or less historic documents looking suspiciously like genealogies. Sometimes, these *tawārīkh* are written documents, carefully preserved by their owners; in most cases, however, reference is made to documents that are strikingly elusive, supposedly kept in private or in public archives elsewhere, and that matter mainly because of their existence, or rather, because this existence can be publicly claimed as beyond doubt. These *tawārīkh* are important, even today, because they are much more than accounts of past events. Through their form, as written Arabic documents, and their content, which inevitably refers to names and figures known from Islamic history, they bear witness to the participation of individual families in universal history.

The Central Sahara has long been an area marked by an inherent dependency on outside connections, an economic and political dependency that is reflected in local notions of identity and social order. People are who they are because of their ability to publicly attach themselves to larger historical geographies of belonging that are coextensive with the putative universal scheme of Islamic history: Genealogies are but one way of establishing such connections beyond doubt, while written *tawārīkh*, where recognised as valid, act as a physical proof of the legitimacy of such claims. Drawing on unexplored local archives and long-term fieldwork in southern Algeria and northern Mali, this chapter will first describe the universalising aspirations of local genealogical writings and how they express and renegotiate local hierarchies. It will then analyse the contemporary popularity of genealogical writings in the area, and the embarrassment that results when various contrasting views of relatedness and identity meet within family settings in southern Algeria that grudgingly, in many cases, continue to be shaped by trans-Saharan mobility.[1]

GENEALOGIES, MOBILITY AND THE ORDER OF THE WORLD

The Central Sahara has long been a place marked by movement and regional connections, to the point where it can be argued that such connections are an essential prerequisite for the establishment of any kind of Saharan settlement.[2] When studying the area, we therefore need to rethink our most basic assumptions about the temporal and conceptual precedence of place over movement. This is valid not only from the point of view of socio-economic dependency on regional exchange, trade and outside investment, but it also applies to local notions of identity, social order and history. In a region where nobody ever claims to be indigenous, people's identities are bound up with the kind and range of outside connections that they can claim. Such claims are more than historical: They talk not only about origins, but about family connections, and hence, theoretically at least, they indicate contemporary range and potential future movement. "Shurafā'", as people put it, referring to people claiming descent from the Prophet Muhammad, "have cousins everywhere": Hence they are potentially welcome wherever they go and they can easily fit into local hierarchies, as their own ta'rīkh is taken to encompass all others.

Conversely, slaves or people of servile origin have no relatives, even if they come from far away: On capture, they forfeit their own kin identity, are re-baptised, and become attached to their master's lineage in a subordinate way. Publicly valued, wide-ranging outside connections and high status are thus intimately bound up. Ultimately, however, such distinctions hinge on local recognition: Slaves may be noble at home, and sharifian genealogies are ultimately all validated by public consensus (ijmā').[3] Despite the promise of a universal and stable social order that is inherent in genealogical patternings of the world – as everybody has a father or at least a mother, everybody also has a known position in the overall scheme – this promise can never be fulfilled, and debates over the authenticity of claimed genealogical connections remain vivid.

Hence, perhaps, the fact that across the region and with very few exceptions, history tends to be subsumed in genealogy, which in turn is taken to hold the key to the present, or rather, to what the present ought to be. It is the case that local history reads mostly like a long list of names that are attached to one or several known figures and places of the Islamic revelation. These names describe both family connections and a long journey west, thereby inscribing the local through a string of marked places, people and settlements into the universal geography of Islam.[4] Hierarchy and order are established implicitly, and often in terms of quantity: Although, of course, all people who matter have a genealogy, some have less than others, because they have been amiss in their moral obligation to remember. In the early twentieth century, the Malian Arab scholar Shaykh Bay described as follows one such set of people who, according to him, had forgotten their origins and who indeed never succeeded in establishing any history proper:

As to the beginnings of the *sūdān* [the original "black" inhabitants of northern Mali] and the details of their circumstances in this land, only God knows them, praise be upon Him. They are dead and with them died their stories (*akhbāruhum*), and all that is left are the ruins [of their buildings]. ... They were people whom fate has obliterated, and not people who write and produce history (*yu'arrikh*) and remember their affairs (*yahfaẓ akhbārahum*). They were like animals, all that was important to them was eating and drinking. ... And this is all that is known about them, and we [who] research into the ancient histories (*tawārīkh*) of the Arabs, as to these base people, there is no benefit for us in knowing about them.[5]

Clearly, the written word, as an important mnemonic device and as a marker of "civilisation", is crucial here.

More generally, there is an assumption that, although written genealogies similarly need to be validated by public recognition, and claims that other people's genealogies are forgeries are the stuff of everyday conversations, proper genealogy ought to have been written down somewhere. Mostly, people claim that this is certainly the case, but that the document has been "lost" or "stolen", or is kept in a larger and perhaps more prestigious collection. After all, the most prestigious genealogies recount stories of wide-ranging movement and list prodigious numbers of cousins scattered through vast areas; no wonder, then, that the relevant document may be elsewhere. Conversely, employees of the Malian national manuscript centre in Timbuktu complain about the large number of requests made to them for certificates that would prove prestigious descent to local and regional families: "Usually, it's all made up," the librarian says with a knowing smile. "But if people are keen, we can always accommodate them ..."

This local predilection for genealogies has, if anything, increased with the spread of literacy and new means of communication, although the genealogies themselves have often changed their physical appearance: Narrative lists of people and places have made room for more "scientific", tree-like drawings. In Kidal in northern Mali, near the Algerian border, Muhammad al-Amin Fall, a scholar from Mauritania long settled in this Tamacheq-speaking area, is currently busy compiling the genealogy of the most influential (Tamacheq-speaking) family there, the Ifoghas, who claim sharifian status.[6] His work is often dismissed as propaganda, both by European scholars[7] and by locals, but he is not daunted in his vast aspirations: In Arabic, he has compiled forty-seven densely covered pages of genealogies. All of these in fact refer to one gigantic family tree, numbered throughout. Rather than groups or families, these list individual names that for the initiated stand for larger social formations while for everybody else they remain utterly obscure. Further, they are written in classical Arabic, a language with which only few inhabitants of contemporary Kidal are familiar. Also striking is their redundancy: Just six of these genealogies are clearly ascribed to various fractions of the Ifoghas; the other forty-one only seem to matter because of an underlying aspiration to completeness. Hence, these diagrams cannot stand alone, but they rather provide props for more detailed expositions, or textual reminders of shared identity for internal consumption. Yet everybody locally seems to agree that these genealogies are clearly political: a way to prove the Ifoghas' sharifian descent and thus to justify their claims to local leadership. We thus seem to be dealing with a paradox: incomprehensible propaganda, perhaps akin to the absent but nonetheless crucial *tawārīkh* mentioned above. Muhammad al-Amin's project, then, takes most of its meaning from its claim to total encompassment: from the hierarchy it implies through omission, and from its open reference, through the Arabic script and repeated names, to the qur'anic revelation. What matters, at the end, is not to understand but to *have* a *ta'rīkh*, and to ideally have one that looks right and provides an unquestionable link with universal history and knowledge.

This penchant for genealogical models is in no way limited to people who are locally classified as "whites".[8] In Gao, just down the road from Kidal, Younoussa Hamara Touré uses his training as a French-speaking sociologist to compile a vast selection of his family's genealogies as a preliminary framework for research into local history. Younoussa defines himself as Arma, that is to say, as belonging to Songhay-speakers settled throughout the Niger bend. They claim to descend from members of the Moroccan army who conquered Timbuktu in the sixteenth century and have since achieved considerable political clout in the area. For his compilation, Younoussa is drawing on Arabic and French colonial sources, but his main focus is on oral history, mostly as collected among his own family. He has filled several dozen spreadsheets, one automatically linked to the rest, all carefully colour-coded according to the reliability of the information received. These sheets attempt to establish universal generations out of the diverse genealogical lore that he has recorded – an undertaking that he relates to have been "extremely difficult", as "local accounts hardly ever match at all". Younoussa's scheme links all major and minor Songhay settlements in the Niger bend to one another in a clear pattern of precedence, before connecting them to Moroccan and eastern origins. In this way, these settlements and their inhabitants are first ranked and then inscribed into universal history. Notionally, at least, his genealogies are part of the same scheme as Muhammad al-Amin's and the two could be connected, although this may mean having to trace genealogies back to their very origins, potentially leading to squabbles over precedence and the respective moral worth and authenticity of the connections claimed. Like Muhammad al-Amin, Younoussa is striving for completeness – the extent where the final point of his preliminary endeavour retreats with every step he takes towards it: By their universalising nature, genealogical schemes are always open-ended. Nonetheless, it is obvious that Younoussa's and Muhammad al-Amin's histories will only ever mention a very small fraction of society in northern Mali: Like beads on a string, genealogical narratives only pick out those who were contained in the storyline before it started to unfold. As a result, hierarchy and questions of status are once more implicit in the very structure of their undertaking.

CONTEMPORARY GENEALOGICAL QUANDARIES

The above reliance on genealogical accounts as a key to local identity and order is not merely reductive; it makes such claims inherently vulnerable and porous. If local status is a function of outside connections, it necessarily relies on other people, fictive or real. Yet other people, especially those living far away, are difficult to control and may well attempt to impose their own reading on the events. This is especially true as, at present, genealogical schemes are not the primary way in which people in the Central Sahara talk about belonging and social order. Since independence in the 1960s, national identity has become an important factor of distinction, especially in Algeria, where it came backed up by a powerful state apparatus, prestige and oil wealth. As a result, from a southern Algerian point of view, connections still matter, but the sources of power, prestige and legitimacy have partly shifted, from Islamic models to the centres of state revenue and influence. Trans-border genealogies have often been pruned accordingly, or at least, southern "cousins" tend to be referred to with embarrassment rather than pride. In northern Mali, genealogical pretensions to connections with the north are still voiced but often treated with suspicion. "Algerian ties" may potentially indicate links to illegal trans-border trade and "terrorism". More importantly, with the civil strife that broke out in Mali in the 1990s, pitting "black" against "white", many families have thought it wise to redefine their allegiances and to underplay their Arab connections, while on an individual level, people may decide to completely drop out of the category of "white" and redefine themselves as "black".[9]

Replacement, however, is never total. Rather, people try to accommodate genealogical visions of the world with new, more restrictive, realities, while even such modern items of identification as passports are ultimately subjected to the logic of genealogy. It is common knowledge that in northern Mali Algerian nationality is easily obtained by any "white" as long as just two Algerian nationals swear to his or her descent. Passports, meanwhile, are frequently rejected by Algerian police and officials, unless their owners can draw on powerful connections in Algeria itself and on a good reputation in the border area. People who lack such recognition are easily condemned as *"algériens Taiwan"*, that is, "fake Algerians", and may have to stand by and watch helplessly as their passports are destroyed by police officers. *Ijmāʿ* and wide-ranging ties on either side of the border hence remain as important as ever.

Questions of identity papers and the boundaries of the national community are increasingly important in southern Algeria, where the presence of northern Malian "cousins" grows steadily. Since the droughts of the 1970s and 1980s and the general insecurity of the 1990s, many northern Malians were forced to leave Mali and try their luck elsewhere, further south or in the Maghrib, and especially in Algeria.[10] Although they were publicly portrayed as foreign refugees and certainly looked the part in the national and international media – poor, disorientated and starving – many among them, especially Arabic-speakers, were in fact familiar with southern Algeria through long-standing exchange and trade relations and considered themselves cousins or at worst in-laws rather than foreigners.

Thus, the Nuaji: an Arabic-speaking group from the Tilemsi in northern Mali, who claim descent from a saint buried near Tamantit in the Algerian Touat. On arrival in Algeria, rather than settling in one of the various Red Cross refugee camps near the border – camps readily described as "shameful" and reserved for the "rabble" – they chose to "remember" and travelled straight to their ancestor's tomb, settling there. So far, this is not surprising: Their ancestor's tomb happens to be situated near a national road and within easy reach of all of the public conveniences that make life in Algeria quite desirable for northern Malians. What is remarkable, however, is not only that they were allowed to stay, but that, some years later, the local council decided to rebuild their shacks and to connect them to the local electricity and water networks, thereby publicly legalising their settlement.[11]

Today, non-Malian residents in Tamantit explain this with a resigned shrug: "After all," they say, "the Nuaji had come to settle with their grandfather: They said that if we wouldn't let them stay, they would leave and take their grandfather with them – just imagine the fuss!" It is difficult to ascertain to what extent this was true, or what other, less publicly avowable factors may also have played a part in this decision. Nonetheless, this is how it is portrayed today, in a way that makes sense to all. The Nuaji are by no means an exception: Hardly any settlement in the Touat would be complete without a Sahelian quarter, inhabited by cousins, in-laws or clients. *Zawāyā* (religious settlements and at times also Sufi centres, many of which were central to the organisation of trans-Saharan trade) have played a particularly important role here, and a large number of Sahelians, many of whom had paid allegiance to them for generations, are now settled on their land.[12] This willingness to facilitate settlement does not mean, however, that the Nuaji (or equivalent) and their Algerian "cousins" have manifested much family feeling in other contexts. Throughout southern Algeria, Sahelians are generally described as Berber "Tuareg", a term that bluntly denies any genealogical proximity and that has come to serve as pejorative shorthand for "white Malian settler, uncouth, immoral, uncivilised, dirty, involved in illegal trans-border trade and generally beyond the pale of good society". Consequently, Hassaniya, the Arabic dialect spoken throughout the western Sahel, is described as the "Arabic of the Tuareg", while the long veil, worn by most Sahelian women, has come to stand for a sign of their "Berber culture" – read: lax religious precepts and general troublesomeness.[13]

This rejection needs to be understood within the broader Algerian context, where northern Algerian cultural expression remains dominant, and where its espousal is a clear sign of upward social mobility for southerners, especially for women: hence the rejection of the long Saharan veil in favour of northern (or rather, international) Islamic garb. Most civil servants in the south are recruited in the north, and northern opinions of the south readily echo the description that southern Algerians like to give of their Malian "cousins", although here, "backwardness" rather than "immorality" is the key term. Yet, on the ground, relations are more complex: Sahelian women especially are a never-ending source of fascination, particularly for Algerian girls, as they are seen to represent a thoroughly despicable but nonetheless alluring ideal of femininity, independence and freedom. Sahelian "immorality" is closely connected to involvement in illegal trans-border trafficking and other illicit occupations that propose an alternative and perhaps rather more tangible model of upward social mobility and wealth.[14] Further, most southerners remember their own mothers and grandmothers as clad in long colourful veils, and perhaps even reciting poetry or genealogies in Hassaniya or Tamacheq. Rather than being foreign, these newly recovered "cousins" are all too close to the bone, bearing witness, not least through their shared genealogies, to the uncomfortable proximity of "the country of the Blacks" (bilād al-sūdān, the phrase generally used for the Sahel). Not surprisingly, then, most local artisanal fairs displaying "Saharan traditions" are staffed by Sahelian refugees, admired by large groups of giggling local girls in modern hijabs and baseball caps.

THE PROBLEM OF PAPERS

This uneasy relationship with southern cousins has deeper roots than mere struggles over state resources and ambitions to upward social mobility unhampered by poor relations. Southern Algeria remains marked by local hierarchies and status distinctions that have been little alleviated by the advent of a supposedly radically egalitarian nation-state and several agricultural revolutions.[15] By now, access to state resources may be essential to possessing high status; in many cases, however, such access is used in order to confirm and reinforce past status distinctions, and especially in order to bolster the claims of influential regional religious families. Yet these are the families that perhaps most rely on their genealogical ties as an integral part of their religious legitimacy, despite their publicly pronounced support for official Algerian Islam that claims to be suspicious of inherited *baraka* (divine blessing).[16] The path to be trodden is thus a narrow one, and southern interference is less than welcome. This is especially true as genealogies are known and recited but also often written down, and as written papers their circulation is difficult to control. Although such written proofs of unpleasant ties can easily be declared to be forgeries, this has become more difficult as state and public interest in the manuscript heritage of southern Algeria has soared recently.[17] As a result, the possession of manuscripts has become a key element of religious legitimacy, making it difficult to question the validity of any single one of them, at least publicly. This is especially true as many southern manuscript owners are painfully aware that their own collections may bear just too many proofs of connectedness, not merely to their southern cousins, but also to religious notions and practices that are now generally deemed to be beyond the pale.

This surplus of connectivity and the problems it may lead to are perhaps best illustrated in the example of the Kunta. The Kunta are a large religious federation, members of which can be found in today's Algeria, Mali, Mauritania, Niger and Morocco. In all of these places and beyond, the Kunta have accumulated and maintained considerable religious prestige, which is both proven and expressed by their far-ranging family connections and genealogical records. The Kunta have been the object of considerable scholarship. Kunta study centres have been established with private funds in Mauritania and Mali and throughout northern Mali, and although their prestige has suffered recently, they are still recognised as among the greatest regional scholars.[18] In Mali, the Kunta own a large collection of manuscripts in Timbuktu, another in Gao, and many smaller collections scattered throughout northern Mali. In Algeria, their headquarters in Zaouiat Kounta, seventy kilometres south-west of Adrar, boasts an equally large collection of "papers". These, however, the Algerian Kunta are careful to hide from their southern cousins, or at least this is what one of the Malian Kunta claims:

> I was curious about Zaouiat Kounta, I had heard so much about it, and especially I wanted to see their manuscripts, so I went out there and spoke to them. They were very cagey, very worried, especially when they saw that I was used to reading manuscripts and that I had some of my own ... and they never let me see theirs. It was later that I understood why: They were afraid I would find my own name in one of their papers, and that I had come to claim my inheritance![19]

Written *tawārīkh* then, the pride of their owners and the most conspicuous signs of their universal legitimacy, can easily become liabilities. The worry here is not so much about property, I think: By no stretch of the imagination could the Malian Kunta really claim property rights in Zaouiat Kounta, and, perhaps more to the point, Kunta who had come and asked to settle had indeed been granted land as "cousins", without having to show any papers. Rather, problems arise from struggles over religious legitimacy and the use and abuse of the flow of *baraka* that is necessarily shared by all Kunta.

Many Malian Kunta families who settled as refugees in the Sahelian quarter of Adrar are widely known for the services that they offer to Algerian middle-class families. Some Kunta men produce amulets that are highly priced, while some Kunta women specialise in the curing of nervous disorders, especially as seen in young girls and in barren women. Others excel in clairvoyance, which is much sought after among the Adrari middle classes. Strolling around the Sahelian quarters of Adrar, it is thus a rather common occurrence to encounter Algerian ladies who claim to have no knowledge whatsoever of this part of town furtively picking their way through rubbish heaps, children and feral goats.

Algerian Kunta are very careful to stay aloof from their Malian cousins. The first time I visited the main Sahelian quarter of Adrar, I went with a Kunta friend of mine, who was very careful to point out the various religious short-comings of the people we encountered as well as their loose morals and their dangerous penchant for "sorcery". "Do not tell them your name," he whispered, "and be careful of what you eat or leave behind – one never knows ..." The problem here is not so much that the more "rational" Algerian Kunta (or other Algerians, for that matter) do not believe in such "superstitions", because they do (after all, these are but another manifestation of the potency of their own *baraka*), but rather that, more familiar with the broader Algerian context, they think that such use of their shared inheritance is illicit, or at least hardly suitable for public consumption.

Tellingly, the only real clash I witnessed between the two sets of "cousins" was on an inherently public and state-centred occasion. In 2006, the first national centre for manuscripts was opened with great pomp in Adrar; in early 2007, all manuscript owners in the region were convened for a first meeting. The importance of this meeting clearly lay beyond the actual business to be dealt with (of which there was little): Rather, the meeting was taken as defining who was officially recognised as a manuscript owner and hence a religious authority, endorsed by peers and by state officials. Among the crowd, dressed in care-fully ironed white robes and modern suits, one group of shaykhs stood out by their colourful garb, unkempt beards and wild hairstyles: the Malian Kunta, visibly shunned by all, but with their pockets bulging with Islamic manuscripts, including numerous *tawārīkh* proving their legitimacy. As soon as they spotted me, they beckoned me to come over, showing me their genealogical records and various other documents. Within minutes, another shaykh, soberly dressed in white, pulled me away: "Don't you waste your time with them," he whispered. "Them and their scraps of paper – they have nothing to do with us, they are mere sorcerers." Yet there was no denying that these "sorcerers" were his own cousins, nourished by the same *baraka* as himself; that they owned as many and as valuable manuscripts as anybody else, if not more; and that their "scraps of paper" may contain the *ta'rīkh* that made them one and that underpinned their shared legitimacy. With this new state-backed emphasis on the written word, the public validity of shared *tawārīkh* no longer depended uniquely on local recognition, but also on more rigid official appraisal; and the Algerian and Malian Kunta can appear as direct rivals, despite or rather because of their mutual dependency. What was actually at stake here was less the overall validity of a genealogical vision of the world than debates over the authenticity and scope of the legitimising connections that both parties claimed for themselves – in other words, who could encompass the other within their own dense network of prestigious ties, thereby implicitly defining their local identity and status.

CONCLUSION

In the Central Sahara, outside connections and notions of range are central to local identities and social hierarchies. One common way of talking about such connections is in terms of genealogies that, region-wide, have come to subsume most historical writings. Yet such genealogies are not merely accounts of the past; rather, they establish a socio-spatial order that is taken to indicate future possibilities as much as past mobility. Hence, genealogical writings are closely bound up with notions of status and have lost none of their past popularity, but rather continue to be seen as the true key to social order. This is shown through recent attempts by local scholars to extend known genealogical schemes to include their own families – attempts that remain incomprehensible to the lay person, as by definition they refer to a larger, putatively universal whole without which they cannot make sense.

Yet this inherent dependency on reference to outside connections bears within it its own dangers: Wide-ranging connectedness may be desirable but, as it necessarily involves other people, it can easily backfire. Universal measures of moral worth do not admit any doubt, but can be claimed by all; written records indicate permanence and historic and spiritual continuity, but they may also recall things that one would rather forget, especially if they fall into the wrong hands. This becomes especially true when new powerful sources of political influence, wealth and legitimacy make their appearance, such as (in Algeria in particular) the nation-state. This has led to a re-centring of older patterns of connections, often to the detriment of southern ties that now necessarily cross national borders. Southern "cousins" have thereby become "refugees" whose closeness to Algerian families has become a source of anxiety rather than pride. Nonetheless, they remain closely bound up with southern Algerian society, if only as a living reminder of what Algeria ought not to be; and, as the example of the Nuaji shows, they cannot be rejected out of hand. However, as seen in the example of the Kunta, such private arrangements fail if larger issues of legitimacy and state recognition are brought into play. In such cases, all that remains of a long history of regional connectivity and cultural intimacy is the bitter taste of mutual embarrassment.

NOTES

1. This article is based on sixteen months of fieldwork in southern Algeria and northern Mali carried out in 2007–8 on local manuscript archives, and on archival research in Aix-en-Provence, Paris and Bamako, financed by Magdalen College, Oxford, and by the British Academy (Grant no. SG-47632). It was written up during a post-doctoral fellowship held at All Souls College, Oxford. My greatest obligations are of course to my hosts and informants in Algeria and Mali.

2. P. Pascon, *La maison d'Iligh*, Rabat: Paul Pascon, 1984; A. Bensaad, "Eau, urbanisation et mutations sociales dans le Bas-Sahara", in M. Côte (ed.), *La ville et le désert, le bas Sahara algérien*, Paris: Karthala, 2005, pp. 95–119; and J. Scheele, "Traders, Saints and Irrigation: Reflections on Saharan Connectivity", *Journal of African History*, vol. 51, no. 3, 2010, pp. 281–300.

3. H. Touati, "En relisant les *Nawāzil* Mazouna, marabouts et chorfa au Maghreb central au XVe siècle", *Studia Islamica*, vol. 69, 1989, pp. 70–94, and "Prestige ancestral et système symbolique šarifien dans le Maghreb central du XVIIe siècle", *Arabica*, vol. 39, 1992, pp. 1–24. Also, D. Powers, *Law, Society and Culture in the Maghrib, 1300-1500*, Cambridge: Cambridge University Press, 2002.

4. For examples of such historical writings, see the large number of relevant genealogies kept in the de Gironcourt collection at the Institut de France in Paris and at the Centre de documentation et de recherches Ahmed Baba (CEDRAB) in Timbuktu. See also B. Hall, "Mapping the River in Black and White: Trajectories of Race in the Niger Bend, Northern Mali", PhD dissertation, University of Illinois, 2005.

5. Shaykh Bay (written c. 1910), Manuscript no. 2407/97 of the de Gironcourt Collection, held at the Institut de France in Paris. Shaykh Bay was a Kunta scholar settled among the Tuareg Ifoghas near Kidal. His influence extended throughout what is today north-east Mali, north-west Niger and southern Algeria, especially the Hoggar mountains; see P. Marty, *Études sur l'islam et les tribus du Soudan*, vol. 1, *Les Kounta de l'Est, les Bérabichs, les Iguellad*, Paris: E. Leroux, 1920, pp. 119–37; G. de Gironcourt, *Missions de Gironcourt en Afrique occidentale 1908–1909 et 1911–1912: Documents scientifiques*, Paris: Société de Géographie, 1920, pp. 147–9; various reports kept in the Malian National Archives in Bamako (ANM), Fonds anciens, box 1D305.

6. The Ifoghas are by now the leading family in and around Kidal, a position that they owe mainly to French intervention during the colonial period; see P. Boilley, *Les Touaregs Kel Adagh. Dépendances et révoltes: Du Soudan français au Mali contemporain*, Paris: Karthala, 1999. The term "Ifoghas" is rather recent; see Charles Grémont, *Les Touaregs Iwellemmedan (1647-1896): Un ensemble politique de la boucle du Niger*, Paris: Karthala, 2010. Historically, it seems to refer to religious scholars more generally; see, for example, Shaykh Bay's use of the term, MS no. 2407/92, and H. Claudot-Hawad, "Adrar des Ifoghas", *Encyclopédie Berbère*, vol. 2, 1985, pp. 556–8.

7. See, for instance, B. Lecocq, *Disputed Desert: Decolonisation, Competing Nationalisms and Tuareg Rebellions in Mali*, Leiden: E. J. Brill, 2010.

8. That is, Arabic- and Tamacheq-speakers of free descent. Distinctions by colour are common in the area, but tend to refer to descent and lifestyle rather than appearance: see Hall, "The question of 'race' in the pre-colonial southern Sahara", *Journal of North African Studies*, vol. 10, nos 3–4, 2005, pp. 339–68. For a linguistic analysis of similar categories in neighbouring Mauritania, see C. Taine-Cheikh, "La Mauritanie en noir et blanc: Petite promenade linguistique en hassāniyya", *Revue du Monde musulman et de la Méditerranée*, vol. 54, 1989, pp. 90–105.

9. On the conflicts of the 1990s, see G. Klute, "Hostilités et alliances: Archéologie de la dissidence des Touaregs au Mali", *Cahiers d'études africaines*, vol. 137, 1995, pp. 55–71; and Boilley, "Aux origines des conflits dans les zones touarègues et maures", *Relations internationales et stratégiques*, vol. 23, 1996, pp. 100–7. For background, see Grémont, A. Marty, Rh. ag Moussa and Y. H. Touré, *Les liens sociaux au Nord-Mali: Entre fleuve et dunes*, Paris: Karthala, 2004.

10. On the droughts of the 1970s and 1980s and their impacts on local society, see E. ag Foni, *L'impact socio-économique de la sécheresse dans le cercle de Kidal*, Bremen: BORDA, 1979; Ch. ag Baye and R. Bellil, "Une société touarègue en crise: Les Kel Adrar du Mali", *Awal*, vol. 2, 1986, pp. 49–84; E. ag Ahar, "L'initiation d'un ashamur", *REMMM*, vol. 57, 1990, pp. 141–52; A. Giuffrida, "Clerics, Rebels and Refugees: Mobility Strategies and Networks among the Kel Antessar", *Journal of North African Studies*, vol. 10, nos 3–4, 2005, pp. 529–43.

11. This and the following paragraph are based on field research and interviews conducted in Tamantit in autumn 2008.

12. This is the case, for instance, in Aoulef Cheurfa and Akabli in the Tidikelt (where Sahelian settlement dates to the nineteenth century; see Chardenet, "Akabli", n. d. [early 1900s], kept at the French Centre d'archives d'outre-mer [CAOM] in Aix-en-Provence, box 22H50). For the example of another set of "Nuaji" in Morocco, see A. M. di Tolla, "Les Nouaji, 'Touaregs' du Tafilalet", *Cahiers de l'IREMAM*, nos 7–8, 1996, pp. 215–22.

13. This negative perception of "Berber culture" mainly derives from demonised accounts of political events in Kabylia, a Berber-speaking area in north-eastern Algeria, in the 1980s and 2000s.

14. On trans-border trafficking, see E. Grégoire, "Sahara nigérien: Terre d'échanges", *Autrepart*, vol. 6, 1998, pp. 91–104 and Scheele, "Tribus, Etats et fraude: La région frontalière algéro-malienne", *Études Rurales*, vol. 184, 2009, pp. 79–94.

15. J.-C. Granier, "Rente foncière et régulation économique dans le Gourara algérien", *Revue Tiers-Monde*, vol. 83, 1980, pp. 649–64, and Y. Guillermou, "Survie et ordre

social au Sahara: Les oasis du Touat-Gourara-Tidikelt en Algérie", *Cahiers des Sciences Humaines*, vol. 29, 1993, pp. 121–38.

16. Although this suspicion is easily accommodated at times; see S. Hadj Ali, "Algérie: le premier séminaire national des zaouias", *Maghreb, Machrek, Monde Arabe*, vol. 135, 1992, pp. 53–62 and Scheele, "Recycling *baraka*: Knowledge, Politics and Religion in Contemporary Algeria", *Comparative Studies in Society and History*, vol. 49, no. 2, 2007, pp. 304–28.

17. This interest is reflected in numerous recent publications, mainly for a popular audience; for instance, S. Bouterfa, *Les manuscrits du Touat*, Algiers: Barzakh, 2005, and A. Abdelhamid, *Manuscrits et bibliothèques musulmanes en Algérie*, Méolans-Revel, France: Atelier Perrousseaux, 2006. Several (often polemical) articles have appeared in the national press; see, for instance, "La sauvegarde des manuscrits du Sud algériens en débat", *El Moudjahid*, 29 October, 2005; "D'Alger à Tamanrasset, un mois pour le patrimoine et les attentes", *La Tribune*, 19 April, 2007; "Algérie: Pillage des manuscrits. De hauts responsables impliqués", *Infosoir*, 8 May, 2007; "Un anthropologue algérien accuse", *Infosoir*, 8 May, 2007.

18. See especially Marty, *Études*; F. Bibed, "Les Kunta à travers quelques extraits de l'ouvrage Al-Tarâ'if wa al-talâ'id de 1756 à 1826", PhD dissertation, Université d'Aix-Marseille I, 1997; A. Batran, *The Qadiriyya Brotherhood in West Africa and the Western Sahara: The Life and Times of Shaykh al-Mukhtar al-Kunti, 1729–1811*, Rabat: Institut des études africaines, 2001; M. S. Hutiyya, *Tuwat wa-l-Azawad*, Algiers: Dar al-Kitab al-'Arabi, 2007.

19. Interviewed in Tit in the Tidikelt in March 2008.

PART THREE

Genealogy as a Source for Writing History

CHAPTER 7

Was Marwan ibn al-Hakam the First "Real" Muslim?

FRED M. DONNER[*]

Marwan ibn al-Hakam ibn Abi l-'As, a leading member of the Umayyad family during the first/seventh century and himself briefly *amīr al-mu'minīn* ("commander of the Believers") from 64 until 65 AH (684–5 CE), is – like most members of the Umayyad clan – not very favourably remembered by the Islamic historical tradition. The main obstacle standing in the way of achieving a sound assessment of Marwan (or, for that matter, of almost any other figure of his time) is the virtual absence of documentary evidence about him.[1] This forces us to rely on reports found in later narrative sources, in which the surviving historical facts may be unrecoverable or may be totally obscured by masses of partisan invective and later embellishment, added for polemical purposes. This is especially true for figures like Marwan, who were deeply involved in the intense political rivalries that afflicted the early community of Believers, including the infighting that took place within the ruling circles of the new Umayyad regime. While the many reports about the events of their day may provide a fair idea of what the various parties were fighting about, the barrage of charges and counter-charges in these reports often leave the historian completely unable to decide just what the position of any of the main actors was on a particular issue, or even what their actions may have been. Above all, it is difficult to discern what we may call the moral qualities of the protagonists, since the accounts about them usually aim primarily to establish or to undermine precisely these moral qualities. This is because political legitimacy in the early Islamic tradition was felt to be rooted, in large measure, in the perceived virtue of the claimant: The basic attitude was that only a God-fearing, righteous person could plausibly claim authority to lead the community of Believers.

The figure of Marwan does not fare very well in the moralistic universe of these narrative sources. Among the many negative reports about Marwan, some accuse him of having been the first to delay the *khuṭba* (sermon) during the Friday prayer, a tampering with established ritual that was not generally approved.[2] He is sometimes depicted as ill-tempered, as, for example, when he became angry at the highly esteemed Companion of the Prophet and conquest hero Sa'd ibn Abi Waqqas when the latter suggested to Marwan that he order the people of Syria to stop cursing 'Ali during prayers.[3] Other accounts accuse him of having been a shameless libertine.[4]

Marwan was very close to the third *amīr al-mu'minīn*, 'Uthman ibn 'Affan, himself a highly controversial figure in Islamic historiography, and this probably did not help his reputation. This personal closeness between the two was based on close kinship. Marwan and 'Uthman are often described as first cousins, since 'Uthman's father, 'Affan ibn Abi l-'As, was the brother of Marwan's father, al-Hakam ibn Abi l-'As. But their relationship was actually closer than that, because they had the same mother, Amina bint 'Alqama ibn Safwan of the Kinana tribe, who was married for a time to 'Uthman's father, 'Affan, and then, after being divorced from him, to his brother al-Hakam, Marwan's father.[5] The fact that 'Uthman and Marwan were half-brothers on their mother's side is often obscured by the patrilineal bias of the Islamic sources, which tend to give a person's ancestry only in the male line; however, recent research shows that links on the maternal side often played a very important role in the creation of social networks of real political significance.[6] Marwan served as scribe for his older half-brother/cousin[7] and may have been put in charge of the finances of Medina by 'Uthman.[8] Some reports note that people disliked 'Uthman's closeness to Marwan and the influence that the latter had on him, and claim that many questionable or unfortunate things that happened in 'Uthman's reign were actually Marwan's doing.[9] It seems a bit strange, however, that the older half-brother should have been so much under the influence of his younger sibling – one would rather expect the influence to go in the other direction – and it may be that this account represents an attempt by later Islamic tradition to salvage 'Uthman's reputation as one of the so-called "rightly guided" (*rāshidūn*) caliphs, by making Marwan at least by implication the fall guy for the unhappy events at the end of 'Uthman's twelve-year reign (13–25/644–56). When insurgents besieged 'Uthman in Medina during the First Civil War, Marwan apparently was one of the main figures attempting to defend him. It is said that he was severely wounded and was almost killed on the *yawm al-dār*, the day when the aged 'Uthman was finally killed in his house.[10]

Many reports offer blanket condemnations of Marwan (or, more commonly, of his father or whole family) but do so in general terms without any specific charge being laid – a feature that arouses one's suspicion that we are dealing mainly with polemic, rather than historical fact, in such accounts. Often these accounts are cast in the form of supposed sayings of the Prophet Muhammad, in which he clairvoyantly predicts evil things associated with Marwan or simply condemns him (or his father, or family) as evil.[11] In one report, for example, the Prophet and a few Companions pass by Marwan's father al-Hakam, upon which the Prophet gratuitously says, "Woe unto my community in the loins/offspring of this one" (*waylun li-ummatī fī ṣulbi hādhā*).[12] In another report of this kind, the Prophet curses al-Hakam three times and then says, "This one will oppose the book of God and the *sunna* of His apostle."[13] In another, the Prophet reports that in a dream he saw "the Banu l-Hakam or the Banu Abi l-'As jumping on my pulpit as apes jump".[14]

One account describes al-Hakam asking permission to enter the Prophet's house, whereupon Muhammad says,

> Let the viper in, or son of a snake, the curse of God upon him and on whoever issues from his loins – except for the Believers, and they are few. They [that is, his unbelieving descendants] honour the earthly life, and they abase the hereafter and [are] people of deceit and treachery, and they are exalted in the world but have no share in the hereafter.[15]

Another report implies that the Banu Marwan are not people of *al-dīn*, proper religion.[16] A supposed hadith of the Prophet, attributed to Ibn 'Abbas, closes with the Prophet declaring, "The banner of *iblīs* (the devil) is with the Banu Umayya until the Hour; they are our enemies, their party (*shī'a*) is enemy to our party."[17] There is even an exercise in creative exegesis, in which the Prophet claims that he, 'Ali, al-Hasan, al-Husayn and the Banu Umayya are referred to in the Qur'an – the former four being identified with the sun, the moon and the daylight, whereas the Umayyads are identified with the night.[18]

The most striking of these "generic" condemnations has the supposed anti-Marwan sentiments of the Prophet actually conveyed by another Umayyad, Mu'awiya ibn Abi Sufyan. Marwan reportedly comes to him to make a request and during his visit announces that he is "the father of ten, the uncle of ten, and the brother of ten". After he leaves, Mu'awiya tells 'Abd Allah ibn 'Abbas – who happened to be present – "I heard the Prophet say, 'When the Banu l-Hakam reach thirty [in number], they will take the wealth of God among themselves by turns, and they will make slaves of the worshippers of God, and they will corrupt the book of God.'"[19] After relating one of several variations of this account, Ibn 'Asakir notes that one of its transmitters ('Atiyya) was "among the extremist Shi'a" (*min ghulāt al-shī'a*).[20]

It seems likely, indeed, that many of these anti-Marwan and generally anti-Umayyad reports were first coined by Shi'i sympathisers with 'Ali and his family, who appear to have been important in forging the historiographical theme of *fitna* or debates over political legitimacy within the early Muslim community.[21]

An interesting example of this tendency is found in the report that al-Hasan and al-Husayn, sons of 'Ali and themselves eventually included in the line of Shi'i imams or divinely guided leaders, prayed the "prayer of the imams" (*ṣalāt al-a'imma*) behind Marwan, presumably implying that he had once acknowledged the leadership of 'Ali but had subsequently repudiated it.[22]

On the other hand, the traditional sources also contain some accounts that are either neutral or non-judgemental, or that shed a more positive light on Marwan. Some short reports have Marwan declaring, "I recited (or: read – *qara'tu*) the book of God over forty years; then I came to the bloodshed I am involved in now, and this is the state of affairs" (*qara'tu kitāb Allāh mundhu arba'īn sana, thumma aṣbaḥtu fīmā anā fīhi min hurāq al-dimā'i, wa-hādha al-sha'n*).[23] If nothing else, this report suggests how long Marwan claimed to have recited the Qur'an when the bloody events of Marj Rahit (64/684) decided his claim to the office of *amīr al-mu'minīn* on behalf of the Umayyad family.

Marwan is also reported to have led the pilgrimage (in AH 43, 45, 55 or 57 depending on the account).[24] These reports may be taken as an indication that Marwan was not merely governor of Medina (which he was on and off several times under Mu'awiya in the 40s and 50s) but that he was also considered to be someone who was sufficiently religiously upright to lead this important ritual for the community of Believers. Other reports describe how Marwan's signet ring was inscribed with pious phrases: *al-'izza li-llāh*, "Power belongs to God", according to one report, or following another, *āmantu bi-l-'azīz al-raḥīm*, "I believe in the Powerful and Merciful One."[25] These observations implicitly advance the idea that Marwan was a person of pious disposition. Even more striking is another tradition, related by al-Mada'ini (d. c. 235/850 or earlier), stating that Marwan was one of the best readers of the Qur'an (or, possibly, one who recited the Qur'an most frequently?) (*kāna min aqra' al-nās li-l-qur'ān*).[26] Finally, we can note a report in which 'Ubayd Allah ibn Ziyad, the Umayyads' governor in Iraq, makes an appeal to the Banu Umayya to back Marwan's claim to be *amīr al-mu'minīn*; in making his case he says, "[Marwan] has age (i.e. maturity), religious knowledge and merit" (*la-hu sinnan wa-fiqhan wa-faḍlan*).[27] He is, in short, being presented as a claimant with strong credentials in terms of both experience and virtue.

The contradictory nature of the surviving literary reports about Marwan raises the question of how to evaluate them. Both sets of reports – those that present Marwan as impious or sinful and those that portray him in a morally positive light – can be suspected of having polemical intent and hence of being exaggerated or even completely fabricated, one way or the other; and there is no plausible basis, on the face of the accounts themselves, on which to decide which group of accounts is more trustworthy. As noted above, this kind of dilemma affects reports about most of the key political figures of early Islamic history. In this case, however, it may be possible to solve the conundrum that this poses for the historian by examining the onomastic and genealogical record – that is, the information that survives about peoples' names and the names of their children.

Onomastic evidence has, to be sure, certain drawbacks. Most obviously, it can only provide very limited information about someone – the kind reflected in the names themselves – whereas narrative reports can convey information of almost infinite variety. Even this limited information, however, can sometimes be of considerable significance. Richard Bulliet, who can be said to have pioneered the use of onomastic evidence in the study of Islamic history, was able to use the shift from non-Muslim Persian names to Muslim names in an individual's long patronymic as the key for estimating when a family in Iran embraced Islam. This determination for hundreds of different families then provided the basis on which he was able to estimate the rate at which Iranians converted to Islam.[28] Nonetheless, the restricted range of information actually contained in names usually imposes severe limits on what can be deduced from them.

A second possible problem with onomastic evidence is that it comes to us through literary transmission, just like the narratives whose very unreliability (or, at least, indeterminacy) has led us to search for other kinds of evidence in the first place. Yet there is good reason to think that the record of family names is less likely to be subjected to gross distortion in the course of transmission than are narrative reports, at least for several generations after the death of a person, for the simple reason that people are likely to know the proper names of at least their own relatives and immediate ancestors, and probably of other people who played a significant role in their lives. Falsification of names, then, is harder to get away with and, in any case, would not really have much polemical utility. We can assume, then, that most personal names in the genealogical record are probably fairly accurate at least for three or four generations. In looking at the onomasticon of a whole family, of course, various individuals may have been left out of a genealogy – especially those who died young and, in a patriarchal society, many daughters – but the names that are recorded are likely to be reliable.

When we examine the onomasticon of the families who played a prominent role in the early Believers' movement, some interesting patterns emerge. The clans of Quraysh, hailing from Arabia, naturally tended to rely heavily on traditional Arabian names, such as 'Ali, al-Hasan, Khalid, Mu'awiya, Yazid, Marwan, and so on. Such names have no intrinsic Islamic content. The old Arabian theophoric names, such as 'Abd Yaghuth (servant of the god Yaghuth) were naturally dropped after the rise of Islam, as their honouring of pagan deities became anathema. In their place, probably, we see a scattering of monotheistic theophoric names, such as 'Abd Allah or 'Ubayd Allah.

Most interesting, however, is the gradual appearance in the community of Believers of names that can be considered Islamic: not only monotheistic theophoric names, but theophoric names linked to one of the names of God found in the Qur'an (such as 'Abd al-Rahman or 'Abd al-Karim), or names that refer to figures (usually prophets) mentioned in the qur'anic text, or the name "Muhammad" itself. It would seem fair to assume that Believers who were deeply pious may more frequently name their children after qur'anic prophets or after the Prophet Muhammad himself, or use theophoric names evoking one of God's qur'anic names.

When we examine the genealogies of leading families of the early Believers' movement, a striking fact emerges: Marwan ibn al-Hakam is one of the very first to have given a large number of his sons "Islamic" names. Most genealogies list sixteen or seventeen children of Marwan, borne to him by five different wives and one concubine.[29] Of these, twelve or thirteen were sons (it is possible that he had more daughters of whom the genealogists made no mention). Of these sons, five had names that can be considered traditional Arabian or specifically family names (such as names of close relatives of Marwan) – that is, non-Islamic names. They include Mu'awiya ibn Marwan (borne to him by his wife 'A'isha bint Mu'awiya ibn al-Mughira ibn Abi l-'As, daughter of one of his first cousins); Bishr (by his wife Qutayya bint Bishr of the Kilab tribe); Aban and 'Uthman (by his wife Umm Aban, daughter of his cousin and half-brother 'Uthman ibn 'Affan); and 'Umar (or 'Amr), borne to him by his wife Zaynab bint 'Umar of the Makhzum clan of Quraysh.

On the other hand, Marwan seems to have given seven (or eight) of his sons names that can be considered Islamic. The best known of these is of course 'Abd al-Malik, borne to Marwan by his wife 'A'isha, followed closely in fame by 'Abd al-'Aziz ibn Marwan, borne to Marwan by his wife Layla bint Zabban of the Kalb tribe. Four sons of his wife Umm Aban, daughter of 'Uthman, bore Islamic names: 'Ubayd Allah, 'Abd Allah (who died young), Ayyub and Dawud. An *umm walad* (slave woman who bore her owner a child) apparently named Zaynab also bore him a son named Muhammad. Ibn Sa'd also lists a son named 'Abd al-Rahman, said to be the son of Marwan's wife Qutayya bint Bishr, who died young, but he is – perhaps for this reason – not listed in the other sources. This list of seven sons – or eight, if we include 'Abd al-Rahman – given Islamic names is striking; there is, moreover, a hint that Marwan may have had yet another son, named al-Qasim, because al-Baladhuri notes that Marwan's agnomen (*kunya*) was at first Abu l-Qasim and then became Abu 'Abd al-Malik, suggesting that an otherwise forgotten first son al-Qasim may have died young (in infancy?).[30] Al-Qasim is not, of course, a qur'anic name, but it was well known that the Prophet's *kunya* was Abu l-Qasim, so this bit of evidence, if true, suggests that Marwan may have wished to acquire for himself the same *kunya* as the Prophet by naming his first son al-Qasim.

All considered, the record of names that Marwan gave his children strongly suggests that he was profoundly impressed with the message in the Qur'an and delivered by the Prophet Muhammad of the need to honour God and His prophets, including Muhammad himself. This evidence does not, of course, mean that we can simply dismiss all narrative reports that are critical of Marwan, or that we should unquestioningly embrace those reports that depict him as a model of piety. It does, however, mean that we must take seriously the possibility that Marwan was, in fact, deeply religious and that he was someone dedicated to advancing the goals of the Believers' movement, as he understood it. Few figures at this early stage in the history of the Believers' movement exhibit such a striking pattern of giving "Islamic" names to their children; indeed, the only close parallel is with 'Ali ibn Abi Talib, among whose many sons one finds, in addition to the well-known al-Hasan and al-Husayn and other sons with traditional Arabian names, two Muhammads, an 'Ubayd Allah, an 'Abd Allah, and possibly a Yahya and a second 'Abd Allah.[31]

Given the strongly negative overtone found in most traditions about Marwan, the title of this article may seem intentionally provocative. It is not, however, entirely facetious. The question of who is "really" a Muslim was one that vexed Muslim theologians and jurists for centuries – mainly, however, because they were actually trying to decide not only who was a Muslim, but who was a "good" (observant, properly pious) Muslim. That is, they were speculating on just which requirements of piety and behaviour would secure for someone the eternal reward of paradise. This was – and remains to this day – a question about which it has proven impossible for Muslims to reach complete consensus; it was particularly difficult in the first century AH because the question was intimately tied to rivalry among the competing claimants to leadership of the community (for example, between the Khawarij, the Shi'a and others).

For our purposes, however, we can settle on a much simpler definition of a "real Muslim", a definition that is relevant to the seventh-century Believers' movement and the context of inter-monotheist controversy out of which Islam first emerged as a distinct religious confession. As I have argued elsewhere, it seems likely that Muhammad first founded a community of Believers (*mu'minūn*) dedicated to strict monotheism and rigorous observance of a pious way of life in accordance with God's revealed law. This early community of Believers apparently included not only those who followed the Qur'an, but also some righteous Jews and Christians who also qualified as Believers, since they were monotheists living by the law found in their scriptures, the Torah and Gospels, which are honoured by the Qur'an.[32] It was only a generation or two after the death of Muhammad, at about the end of the seventh century CE, that the Arabian leaders of the Believers' movement began clearly to distinguish themselves from their erstwhile Christian and Jewish associates in the Believers' movement, using the qur'anic term "Muslim" as their new term of self-designation. In this historical context, a Muslim is someone who recognises Muhammad as God's prophet and the Qur'an as God's revealed word. For acknowledgement of the Qur'an as scripture and for Muhammad as prophet were the criteria that came to separate Muslims of whatever kind and of whatever merit decisively from Christians, Jews, Zoroastrians and others, both theologically and, therefore, sociologically. "Islam" as it has been recognised for centuries can be most simply defined in this way: as a community of Believers in God, in the Qur'an and in the Prophet Muhammad.

As we have seen, Marwan ibn al-Hakam, more than any other figure of his generation, drew on names of qur'anic prophets when naming no less than a half-dozen of his own sons; and he named another son Muhammad, after the prophet whom he had known and followed in his own youth. Given the fact that the naming of a child is a matter of considerable gravity for anyone, it is therefore fair to conclude that the values reflected in these names must have been something of great importance to Marwan. He was the first, it seems, to grasp fully, and to affirm publicly through the names he gave his children, the importance of emphasising to one and all that the Qur'an was God's word, and Muhammad was God's prophet. At the end of his life, moreover, Marwan was in a position to advance his views as the official doctrine of the state. It is therefore not far-fetched to suggest that Marwan may have played a key role in persuading the early community of Believers that it needed to sharpen its communal self-definition so as to make clear that it was not merely a monotheist community, but that it was also one that embraced a particular reverence for the Qur'an as God's word and for Muhammad as God's prophet. This shift, which essentially defined Islam as a separate religious confession and caused it to crystallise from the matrix of the Believers' movement, was a process that was carried out mainly by his successors, starting with his son 'Abd al-Malik; but it seems likely that it began with Marwan. If it did, Marwan has as good a claim as anyone after the Prophet himself to be called "the first real Muslim", architect of the basic conceptual framework that we recognise even today as Islam.

NOTES

* This paper was presented in November 2010 at the annual meeting of the Middle East Studies Association in San Diego, CA. I am grateful to the graduate students in my "Early Islamic Lunch" seminar held in the winter of 2010, for their helpful comments on the draft of this paper: Mehmetcan Akpinar, Sulaiman Ali Hasan, Anthony R. Heffron, Pascal Held, Joshua Mabra, Daniel Mahoney, Rana Mikati, Elizabeth Urban and Liran Yadgar. They are, of course, in no way responsible for any of its shortcomings.

1. There are fragments of silk *ṭirāz* fabric bearing the inscription "['Abd] Allah Marwan, *amīr al-mu'[min]īn*"; see A. Grohmann, *Arabische Paläeographie*, vol. 2, Vienna:

Österreichische Akademie der Wissenschaften, 1971, p. 81. It is not clear whether these fragments refer to Marwan ibn al-Hakam or to his grandson, Marwan (II) ibn Muhammad, the last Umayyad *amir al-mu'minin* (r. 127–32/744–9); arguments in favour of both have been proposed in the scholarship.

2. Ibn 'Asakir, *Ta'rikh madinat Dimashq*, vol. 57, ed. 'U. ibn Gharama al-'Amrawi, n.p.: Dar al-Fikr, 1997, pp. 250–1 (hereafter, *TMD* 57). See the report transmitted on the authority of Rawh ibn 'Ubada – Daw (?) ibn Qays – 'Iyad ibn 'Abd Allah ibn Sa'd ibn Abi Sarh – Abu Sa'id al-Khudri.

3. *TMD* 57, p. 248, lines 6–13 (… Ibn Abi Khaythama – Ibrahim ibn al-Mundhir – Ya'qub ibn Ja'far ibn Abi Kathir – Muhajir ibn Mismar – 'A'isha bint Sa'd).

4. *TMD* 57, p. 248, lines 14–20 (… Ibn Ishaq – Salih ibn Kaysan – 'Ubayd Allah ibn 'Abd Allah).

5. Muhammad ibn Sa'd, *Kitab al-Tabaqat al-kabir*, vol. 5, ed. K. V. Zetterstéen, Leiden: E. J. Brill, 1905, p. 24 (hereafter, Ibn Sa'd 5); *TMD* 57, p. 235, lines 17–25, and p. 232, lines 9–14.

6. See A. Q. Ahmed, *The Religious Elite of the Early Islamic Hijaz: Five Prosopographical Case Studies*, Oxford: Linacre College, Unit for Prosopographical Research, 2011; also published as vol. 14 of *Prosopographica et Genealogica*. I am grateful to Dr Ahmed for making an advance copy of this important work available to me.

7. See note 5 for references.

8. *TMD* 57, pp. 240–1 says that 'Uthman made Marwan governor of Medina, but as 'Uthman himself was in Medina no governor was needed, so this report is probably a mistake for Mu'awiya's time, when Marwan was appointed governor of Medina. Ibn Sa'd 5, p. 24, line 25 (*qalu*) merely says that 'Uthman appointed Marwan as his scribe and to oversee the taxes/finances (*amwal*).

9. Ibn Sa'd 5, pp. 24–5; *TMD* 57, pp. 257–8 (… Abu 'Umar ibn Hayyuwayh – Ahma ibn Ma'ruf – al-Husayn ibn Fahm – Muhammad ibn Sa'd).

10. *TMD* 57, p. 258; Ibn Sa'd 5, p. 25 (… al-Waqidi).

11. For example, *TMD* 57, p. 269, lines 3–9 (… Suwayd ibn Sa'id – Yahya ibn Sa'id al-Qattan – Arta'a ibn al-Mundhir – Damra ibn Habib): The Prophet refuses to perform the ceremony of *tahnik* (rubbing the infant's palate with a date-pit to bring blessing upon the child) on the infant Marwan because "he will give birth to tyrants and will oppose me in my community".

12. *TMD* 57, p. 267 bottom (… Mu'adh ibn Khalid – Ibrahim ibn Muhammad ibn Abi Salih – Nafi' ibn Jubayr ibn Mut'im – his father).

13. *TMD* 57, p. 267 middle (… Muhammad ibn Sadran – al-Mu'tamir ibn Sulayman – his father – Hanash – 'Ata' – Ibn 'Umar). The reference to "the *sunna* of God's apostle" in particular suggests that this report is from long after the time of the Prophet, probably from the second/eighth century. See F. M. Donner, *Narratives of Islamic Origins: The Beginnings of Islamic Historical Writing*, Princeton, NJ: Darwin Press, 1998, pp. 44–5.

14. *TMD* 57, p. 265 bottom (… al-Zanji – al-'Ala' ibn 'Abd al-Rahman – his father – Abu Hurayra). Compare *TMD* 57, p. 266 middle.

15. *TMD* 57, p. 268 (two accounts); Ahmad ibn Jabir al-Baladhuri, *Ansab al-ashraf*, vol. 5, ed. S. D. Goitein, Jerusalem: Hebrew University Press, 1936, p. 126.

16. *TMD* 57, p. 249 middle–bottom and p. 250 top.

17. *TMD* 57, p. 273 (... Musa ibn Idris – his father – Jarir – Layth – Mujahid – Ibn 'Abbas).

18. Ibid.

19. *Ittakhadhū māl allāh baynahum duwalan, wa-'ibād Allāh khawalan, wa-kitāb Allāh daghalan. TMD* 57, p. 252 top (... Ibn Lahi'a – Abi Qabil – Ibn Mawhib), and several variants on pp. 252, 253.

20. *TMD* 57, p. 253 middle (... Salih ibn 'Umar – Mutarrif – 'Atiyya – Abu Sa'id).

21. Donner, *Narratives of Islamic Origins*, pp. 184–90.

22. *TMD* 57, p. 248 (... al-Rabi' – al-Shafi'i – Hatim ibn Isma'il – Ja'far ibn Muhammad – his father).

23. *TMD* 57, p. 264 middle (... al-Harith ibn Miskin – Ibn Wahb – Malik).

24. *TMD* 57, pp. 241–2 contains several such reports.

25. *TMD* 57, pp. 264–5 (... al-Asma'i – 'Adi ibn 'Umara – his father – Harb ibn Ziyad, and ... Ishaq ibn Ibrahim ibn Sinan – Abu 'Abd al-Rahman 'Abd Allah ibn Abi Madh'ur – "a man of knowledge").

26. Al-Baladhuri, *Ansab al-ashraf*, vol. 5, p. 125.

27. Al-Baladhuri, *Ansab al-ashraf*, vol. 5, p. 144.

28. R. Bulliet, *Conversion to Islam in the Medieval Period: An Essay in Quantitative History*, Cambridge, MA: Harvard University Press, 1979.

29. The genealogical information that follows is extracted from Mus'ab al-Zubayri, *Nasab Quraysh*, ed. E. Lévi-Provençal, Cairo: Dar al-Ma'arif, 1953, pp. 160–1; Ibn Sa'd 5, p. 24; and W. Caskel, *Ğamharat an-nasab: Das genealogische Werk des Hišam Ibn Muḥammad al-Kalbī*, vol. 1, Leiden: E. J. Brill, 1966, Table 10.

30. Al-Baladhuri, *Ansab al-ashraf*, vol. 5, p. 125.

31. Compare al-Zubayri, *Nasab Quraysh*, pp. 40–5, who does not know the two 'Abd Allahs; Ibn Sa'd, vol. 3, pp. 11–12 lists one 'Abd Allah (and many daughters not known to al-Zubayri); Caskel/Ibn al-Kalbi, vol. 1, Table 5 lists two 'Abd Allahs. Ahmed's *The Religious Elite of the Early Islamic Hijaz* (Chapter 5), based on far more extensive research than that conducted here, refers to the two Muhammads, 'Ubayd Allah, and one 'Abd Allah, but not a second 'Abd Allah or a Yahya.

32. Donner, *Muhammad and the Believers: At the Origins of Islam*, Cambridge, MA: Harvard University Press, 2010; Donner, "From Believers to Muslims: Confessional self-Identity in the Early Islamic Community", *Al-Abhath*, vols 50–1, 2002–3, pp. 9–53.

CHAPTER 8

Genealogy and Ethnogenesis in al-Mas'udi's Muruj al-dhahab

SARAH BOWEN SAVANT[*]

In the tenth century, the litterateur and historian al-Mas'udi (d. 345/956) composed one of the most eclectic accounts of the origins of the Persians surviving today. He begins his discussion of the subject in his *Muruj al-dhahab wa-ma'adin al-jawhar* with the statement that "the people have disagreed with one another regarding the Persians (*al-Furs*) and their genealogies (*ansābihim*)", and then proceeds to place on apparently equal footing a number of theories, including some that are evidently pre-Islamic in origin and some arising after the emergence of Islam. He positions his discussion of the Persians' genealogy amidst sections on Iranian history, both ancient and Sasanian (224–651 CE), but makes virtually no effort to reconcile the contradictions in his material. Some years later, he draws on this material again in his *Kitab al-Tanbih wa-l-ishraf*. What, then, is al-Mas'udi doing in the *Muruj*? Why does he bring together such evidently disparate statements – and is there anything that he seeks to show through this?

In what follows, I review this section of the *Muruj* and then consider al-Mas'udi's arrangement of the evidence and his likely sources and motives. Al-Mas'udi presents a remarkable picture of Islamisation in progress, including traces of negotiations over Iranians' sense of history. But I think we also have in his book a subtle but persuasive strategy for opposing Iranians' growing cultural confidence and autonomy.

DESCENT FROM PROPHETS: POSSIBILITIES

Al-Mas'udi sets the tone for his account by gathering together several theories that start from biblical and Muslim prophetic history. The first of these had a certain currency among Muslims: the Persians' eponymous ancestor, Faris, was the son of a Yasur ibn Shem ibn Noah. The "Nabat", likewise, descended from another son of Yasur named Nabit. This genealogy presents the Persians as "brothers" to the Aramaic-speaking population of 'Iraq (as opposed to the Nabateans of Petra). Al-Mas'udi attributes it to Hisham ibn Muhammad al-Kalbi (d. 204/819 or 206/821), his father (d. 146/763) and other Arab savants. Most likely it was inspired by biblical genealogy, for, as Charles Pellat hypothesised, the Arabic name Yasur can be read as a cognate of Asshur, a son of Shem named in Genesis 10: 22 and 1 Chronicles 1: 17.[1]

Al-Mas'udi also features a lineage that plays with the common root (*f-r-s*) for Persians on the one hand and horsemen on the other. Some persons, he reports, find the Persians to descend from a Hidram ibn Arpachshad ibn Shem ibn Noah. This Hidram – who is not listed among Shem's grandsons in Genesis[2] – was the father of "ten and some men" (*bid' at 'ashar rajulan*), each a courageous horseman (*fāris*), and "therefore, they were named 'Persians' (*al-Furs*) because of [their] horsemanship (*furūsiyya*)". In support, al-Mas'udi excerpts a poem by one Khattab ibn al-Mu'alla al-Farisi asserting the Persians' horsemanship:

> Because of us, the horsemen (*al-fawāris*) were called Persians (*Fursān*).
>> From us come noble youths
> And men of mature age whom running and charging has folded, as if [they]
>> were still] charging on the day of battle.[3]

The statement may define the Persians as a union of different lines from Hidram, much as the Children of Israel and the Arabs represented a union of the descendants of Isaac and Ishmael, respectively.

Another theory associates the Persians with a place that was well known in al-Mas'udi's day and afterwards for its natural beauty: Shi'b Bawwan in Fars, the province that was the historic home of the Achaemenid and Sasanian empires. This theory also makes something of the Asshur of Genesis and 1 Chronicles, as it claims that the Persians descended from Bawwan ibn Iran ibn Yasur ibn Shem ibn Noah. Shi'b Bawwan in the land of Fars, al-Mas'udi notes, is famous for its beauty and the plentitude of its forests, running waters and various birds. It is mentioned by poets, one of whom said:

> Shi'b Bawwan then Wadi al-Rahib,
>> It is there that you meet rest [after] misfortunes.

Al-Mas'udi has nothing more to say about this genealogy, although it seems to have remained a point of conjecture among scholars after him.[4]

Three other theories that he mentions at the start of his genealogy section more directly suggest that he drew on Jewish interlocutors, and perhaps Iranian

Jewish ones. The theories are presented noncommittally. The first depicts Persians as descendants of "Joseph ibn Jacob ibn Isaac ibn Abraham", and thus, implausibly, places them *among* the Children of Israel.[5] The second is prejudicial and relates to Lot. Al-Masʿudi tells his readers that "a group of people" claimed that the Persians (*Furs*) were among the descendants of Lot through "his two daughters Rabbatha and Zaʿirtha". He says that the "followers of the Torah" have "a long affair regarding that", but offers no further details.[6] The biblical story features Lot as a nephew of Abraham and two of Lot's daughters, each of whom tricks her father with alcohol to have sexual relations with her so that she may produce offspring. The elder daughter bears a son whom she calls Moʾab and who, Genesis states, "is the father of the Moabites to this day". The younger daughter bears a son whom she calls Benammi, and who is "the father of the Ammonites to this day".[7] In the Bible, neither daughter is named, nor is it the case that the Persians are mentioned. Still, the theory is more biblical than qurʾanic since in the Qurʾan the number of daughters is not specified (they are referred to in the plural form, *banāt*, rather than in the Arabic dual form, as two daughters), and there is no reference to alcohol, incest or offspring. The point of the theory is that Persians descend from degraded and incestuous relationships between Lot and his daughters. For this reason, Ignaz Goldziher, citing Ibn Badrun (d. 529/1134), believed that "Arab fanaticism represented them as being descended from Lot".[8]

Al-Masʿudi also notes that some persons held the opinion that all Persian peoples (*ajnās al-Furs*) and people of the districts of Ahwaz in Khuzistan descend from a figure by the name of ʿAylam (*ʿAylām*).[9] ʿAylam most likely refers to an eponymous founder of Elam, an ancient country encompassing the Persian plateau in the late third millennium BCE. It was reduced to the territory known as Susiana in the Achaemenid period (c. 700–330 BCE), corresponding with the later province of Khuzistan. It is this reduced Elam that is referred to in Achaemenid inscriptions and in the Bible and Apocrypha. The Bible, indeed, refers to a son of Shem by the name of Elam in Genesis 10: 22 and 1 Chronicles 1: 17.[10] In the preceding and following lines, al-Masʿudi alludes to his unnamed sources as Persians. It is possible that his sources may have been Jews, for whom the Bible connected the land of Elam (that is, Persia) and its people to Noah's line through Shem. Or maybe they were non-Jews who knew Jews. The continuity of the idea is by no means proven and would represent a remarkable feat of memory, but it is noteworthy that the first-century Jewish scholar Flavius Josephus (d. c. 100 CE) believed that the Persians descended from Shem's son Elam, as he wrote: "Elam left behind him the Elamites, the ancestors of the Persians."[11]

Al-Masʿudi throws his weight behind none of these genealogies, although he does present them as possibilities. His indifference is suggested by his reporting earlier in the *Muruj*, where he treats prophetic history and genealogy as the common past of Muslims. There, he cites "the Torah" regarding Noah's descendants, but makes no mention of Elam, nor does he repeat the Elam claim in a separate section dedicated to Persia's kings and their origins.

DESCENT FROM FIGURES ASSOCIATED WITH IRAN'S PRE-ISLAMIC PAST: IRANIANS ARE NOT AUTOCHTHONS

Al-Mas'udi gives us no reason to believe that Persians in his day were won over to prophetic history or genealogy; in fact, he admits that they do not believe that a flood occurred, a key element of prophetic history. Still, he tackles ideas that may challenge Persians' integration and generally raises doubts about theories that treat Iranians as autochthons. Regarding the legendary figure of Kayumart, he promotes the idea that Kayumart was Iran's first king rather than the founder of the human race, a role ascribed to him in Zoroastrian cosmogony, although perhaps accepted by non-Zoroastrian Iranians as well. He does this before his treatment of genealogy, when he narrates the chronology of Persia's ancient kings, beginning with Kayumart. He allows only that a minority of Persians believe Kayumart to have been the father of the human race (*aṣl al-nasl*).[12] He notes with disapproval that Zoroastrians saw him as the founder of the human race (*mabda' al-nasl*), thought that he and his wife grew from a rhubarb plant (*al-rībās*) and that he dwelled in Istakhr in Fars, relayed stories about Iblis and Kayumart and believed other things that are "too shameful to cite".[13] Some people, al-Mas'udi continues, believe that Kayumart was Adam's eldest son; others regard him to be one of Noah's descendants, named Immim ibn Lud (Lawid) ibn Aram ibn Shem ibn Noah. That is because "Immim was the first one of Noah's descendants who settled in Persia, and Kayumart [also] had settled in Persia."[14] Al-Mas'udi then takes the liberty to refer to Kayumart as Kayumart ibn Lud.[15] This idea was known before al-Mas'udi's day and had been promoted by some of his predecessors.[16]

Al-Mas'udi also shows that the lineage of the mythical Persian king Afridun (Faridun) was not, as some Iranians held, *sui generis*. He does this in a variety of ways in his section on genealogy. He admits that there is no doubt among Persians that they descend from Afridun and his son, Iraj. But what, he seems to ask, do we really know about Afridun's progeny? A story about Afridun's descendant Manushihr casts doubt on received wisdom: While some say that the Sasanians descend from Manushihr and that Manushihr was a grandson of Afridun (through Iraj), he may in reality have been the son of a man by the name of Manushkharnar ibn Manush[khurank] ibn Wirak. Manushkharnar (Manushihr's father) went to Persia, where he married a Persian queen, a daughter of Iraj named Kudak, who bore Manushihr, whose descendants multiplied, "conquering and ruling the earth". The other kings were in awe of Manushihr's descendants "on account of their courage and horsemanship". With their rise, the ancient Persians "became extinct like past nations and the original Arabs (al-'arab al-'āriba)".[17]

Al-Mas'udi enlightens his readers with a theory about this mysterious line: Wirak was the very same person as Abraham's son Isaac, and therefore the Persians descend from him. He admits that this idea does not originate with the Persians themselves but rather with Arabs, specifically with learned men from Nizar ibn Ma'add, that is, "northern" Arab tribes, who claimed a bond with Persians when they boasted against the "southern" Yemenis. Still, he says, most Persians "are led to this" and do not deny it. He provides poetic attestations by the Qurashi Ishaq ibn Suwayd al-'Adawi (d. c. 131/749), Jarir ibn 'Atiyya (d. c. 110/728–9) and Bashshar ibn Burd (d. 167 or 168/784–5). He cites another poet referring to Isaac as "the one named Wirak":

> Our father is Wirak, and by him I vie for glory
>> When the boaster [, my opponent,] boasts of his birth.
> Our father, Wirak, was a servant and a messenger [of God],
>> Ennobled by the nobility of [his] message and generosity to pilgrims.
> So if the tribes' lords boast: who is like me
>> When my house is like the necklace's most precious charm?[18]

Al-Mas'udi has waded here into obscure onomastic territory. The name Wirak (Wizak) is attested in Middle Persian (Pazand) and reached the poet and al-Mas'udi through uncertain channels.[19] The variety of detailed reports regarding Manushihr's ancestors and their appearance in multiple sources, although with variations, suggest written records at odds with one another, possibly supported by oral transmission. Al-Tabari (d. 310/923) mentions a Wirak as a female or male ancestor of Manushihr (without reference to Isaac). He also mentions a view according to which Manushihr descended from Isaac (as "Manushihr ibn Manushkharnar ibn Ifriqis ibn Isaac ibn Abraham") but dismisses it as not representative of the Persians' own opinions. There is no genealogical link between Wirak and Manushkharnar.[20] After al-Mas'udi, these names continue to circulate.

Nevertheless, all this obscurity provides an opportunity for al-Mas'udi to link the Persians into prophetic history. Correspondingly, al-Mas'udi shows himself to be critical of two other genealogies that come from this grab bag of names. Some Persians, he says, claimed that Wirak was the son of an Irak ibn Burak and that this Burak was the final son produced from a line of seven women. Each of the women was born of a virgin birth (min ghayr al-dhakar), except the first, who was a daughter of Iraj ibn Afridun. Al-Mas'udi argues:

Reason rejects this and sense disallows it. The laws of nature and experience reject it, except for [that birth] by which God distinguished the Messiah, Jesus, son of Mary, so as to show His miracles and signs, and which departed from the laws of nature and from what we would mention as [normal] experiences.[21]

He then mentions another seven-woman genealogy that lists Afridun as Manushihr's ancestor: Afridun had incestuous relations with a daughter of Iraj, and then with the daughter of that union, and so on through a total of seven incestuous unions, resulting in Manushihr. Manushihr would then be both a son of Afridun and a descendant from Iraj and seven women.[22] However, al-Mas'udi appears to reject this theory, as he proceeds to refer synonymously to the descendants of Manushihr and Isaac. A chaotic time elapsed between the reign of Afridun and the reign of Manushihr, he says, but then "dominion passed from the descendants of Afridun to the descendants of Isaac". Al-Mas'udi notes that if everything he has reported about the Persians is relied upon, the total amount of time that passed between Kayumart and "the descendants of Isaac" is 1,922 years.[23] A supposition that al-Mas'udi is speaking of Manushihr and his Persian descendants as Isaac's descendants is confirmed upon reading al-Mas'udi's section on the Sasanian kings, where he mentions the span of time between Kayumart and the transfer of rule to Manushihr as being exactly 1,922 years.[24]

The Tanbih was the last of al-Mas'udi's works, and it was completed just before his death in 345/956, some ten years after he finished the edition of the Muruj that survives today.[25] It is noteworthy that in the Tanbih, when al-Mas'udi summarises the Muruj's contents, he repeats in detail ideas about Isaac but not the other theories – as if recognising the particular agenda of his own work. Curiously, he nonetheless undermines the theory by admitting that it arose after the appearance of Islam.[26]

AL-MAS'UDI'S ARRANGEMENT OF THE EVIDENCE

In the Muruj al-Mas'udi was evidently working with different sources and in different ways. His section on genealogy presents the fruits of a rather wide investigation into several sources, some oral.[27] It is written as a research summary and it is placed between sections that are organised chronologically and deal first with the Persians' most ancient history (including, very briefly, the Arsacids) and second with the Sasanians. Ancient and Sasanian history are of an altogether different character than this research into genealogy and also differ markedly from one another. Ancient history comprises accounts reported as if by an anthropologist. This is where, as mentioned above, al-Mas'udi cites opinions on Kayumart's origins but prefers to treat him as one of the world's first kings. Al-Mas'udi reports that Persians say they perceived a need for order and stability, so they selected a king, Kayumart, who they now claim was the world's first king. They also claim he was the first to prescribe silence during meals as the more salubrious way of eating. They do not agree on the length of his reign; some say he lived 1,000 years, others less. Al-Mas'udi follows this account with reports on other ancient kings, including Hushang, Tahmurath, Jamshid, al-Dahhak and Afridun; he mentions along the way Farasiyab, Zaww, conflict between "the Persians and the Turks", the killing of Siyawakhs and the story of Rustam. All of this, says al-Mas'udi, is "explained" (*mashrūḥ*) in the *Kitab al-Sakisaran*, which was translated to Arabic from the "ancient Persian language" (*al-fārisiyya al-ūlā*) by Ibn al-Muqaffa' (the great transmitter of Iran's pre-Islamic heritage, d. 139/756). Al-Mas'udi ends the section with the last of the Kayanids, emphasising his efforts to take due account of the different opinions on the Persians' earliest history. And so we are led to believe that he has presented the Persians' own views of their ancient history.[28]

When he moves to the Sasanians, after the section on the Persians' genealogies, he deals with the history of their kingship, the offices that supported it, the organisation of Sasanian society and its provincial government, and many other matters. The narrative becomes less fragmented, more internally coherent, and altogether longer. Al-Mas'udi quotes the first Sasanian king, Ardashir (r. 224–40 CE), explaining the structure of society and the necessity of social hierarchy, the importance of just kingship and the requirements for courtesans. His edicts are recalled, as are two of his letters. Al-Mas'udi is here likely working with sources in which he has some confidence and parts of which he has faithfully copied. There are convergences between his text and an earlier text (the *Kitab al-Taj*) attributed, falsely, to the litterateur al-Jahiz (d. 255/868–9). Al-Mas'udi cites "*al-Kar-namaj*" (Middle Persian, *Kar-namag*; New Persian, *Kar-nameh*) and refers, perhaps, to a circulating copy of the *'Ahd Ardashir* (as Ardashir's Testament, *'ahd*, "in the hands of the people").[29] Such reproductions, and claims to them, may be expected when the subject is closer to his own day and on a firmer epistemological footing.[30]

It is clear from his reporting on ancient and especially Sasanian history that al-Mas'udi was dealing with a body of onomastic material that could not easily be ignored and that took little notice of prophetic genealogy or history. These sections thus sharply contrast with the views he expresses in his section on the Persians' genealogy and, earlier in the *Muruj*, in his treatment of prophetic history. The onomastic record seems to have been poorly tended – there is little or no way of verifying the origins, antiquity or transmission of these names in al-Mas'udi's sources or, given manuscript inconsistencies, even in the *Muruj* itself. There are many inconsistencies. However, the names of Kayumart's successors in the text of Pellat's Arabic edition illustrate well enough that al-Mas'udi's sources for chronology made virtually no reference to the ideas he presents in his summary of theories:[31]

Awshanj [Hushang] ibn Farwak ibn Siyamuk ibn Yarniq ibn Kayumart

Tahmurath ibn Waywanjahan ibn Anqahadh ibn Awshanj[32]

Jam [Jamshid], brother to Tahmurath

al-Dahhak, also known as Biwarasb ibn Arwandasb ibn Zanjad ibn Barishand ibn Tah ibn Farwak ibn Siyamuk ibn Mashiyah ibn Kayumart

Afridun ibn Athfiyan ibn Jam

Manushihr ibn Iran (also known as Iraj) ibn Afridun

Sahm ibn Aban ibn Athfiyan ibn Nudhar ibn Manushihr

Farasiyab ibn Bashank ibn Zayy Arsan ibn Turak ibn Sabanyasb ibn Durushasb ibn Tuh ibn Dusrun ibn Tuj ibn Afridun

Zaww ibn Tahmsasf ibn Kamjahubar ibn Harasf ibn Waydanj ibn Raghgh ibn Manush ibn Nudhar ibn Manushihr

In his translation, Pellat mostly omits these genealogies, no doubt because of the variants scattered across manuscripts of the *Muruj* and the challenges of transliterating them into French. While several of the names appear in other sources, al-Tabari's *Ta'rikh* included, there is not a single, stable record against which to compare any of them for ideas about Iranian genealogy.

The genealogy of the Sasanians, beginning with Ardashir, is similarly uncon-nected to prophetic history. It is possible that al-Mas'udi's sources – or perhaps al-Mas'udi himself – were interested in whether or not the Sasanians descended from the Achaemenids; one genealogy, featuring Dara (Darius), suggests yes, and another suggests no:

Ardashir ibn Babak Shah ibn Sasan ibn Babak ibn Sasan ibn Bihafarid ibn Dara ibn Sasan ibn Bahman ibn Isfandiyar ibn Bistasf ibn Luhrasf
[Or:]
Ardashir ibn Babak ibn Sasan al-Asghar ibn Babak ibn Sasan ibn Babak ibn Mihramas ibn Sasan ibn Bahman ibn Isfandiyar ibn Bistasf ibn Luhrasf

Even though Manushihr is named in neither of these genealogies, al-Mas'udi concludes that whether or not these are correct, there is no doubt that Ardashir ultimately descends from Manushihr.[33] This may surprise, unless one remembers that in the preceding section treating the Persians' genealogies, al-Mas'udi has made much out of Manushihr and his connection to Abraham, Isaac and prophetic genealogy. Here, then, he has left Ardashir's genealogy as he has received it, having already connected an autochthonous vision back to prophetic genealogy.

AL-MAS'UDI'S SOURCES

But how does al-Mas'udi justify in the *Muruj* such linkages of the Persians to prophetic genealogy? Besides the works already mentioned, al-Mas'udi names in his introduction and within the *Muruj* several texts from the early Arabic tradition. These include a work by Abu 'Ubayda Ma'mar ibn al-Muthanna (d. c. 209/824–5) on *akhbār*, or reports, about the Persians, which al-Mas'udi says was based on the work of a man by the name of 'Umar, "known as Kisra" (*al-ma'rūf bi-kisrā*). Quoting Abu 'Ubayda's text amid his reporting on the Arsacids, al-Mas'udi says that the book treats ancient and more recent dynasties and the life and memorable words of their kings and their genealogies, and also contains descriptions of districts, canals and towns and the names of the great families and their titles, such as *Shahārija*.[34] He also mentions a historical work by the polymath Ibn Khurradadhbih (d. c. 300/911, particularly well known as a geographer), which features the biographies of the kings of Persia and other peoples (*al a'ajim wu-ghayrihā*), as well as Ibn Khurradadhbih's book "*fi al-masālik wa-l-mamālik*" ("on itineraries and kingdoms"). Also germane are Ibn Qutayba's *Kitab al-Ma'arif* and, more deeply, al-Tabari's *Ta'rikh*, as well as works by figures closely associated with the 'Abbasid court, including a book by Da'ud ibn al-Jarrah touching on Persian history (*fi al-ta'rīkh al-jāmi' li-kathīr min akhbār al-Furs wa-ghayrihā min al-umam*). There were also two books by Muhammad ibn Yahya al-Suli (d. 335/947) on the 'Abbasid caliphs, their court and their poetry.[35]

Al-Mas'udi may have used any of these as sources for genealogy. Yet I also suspect that he had more abundant and varied fragments of Iran's past to work with, and here I would like to introduce a new term and a theory to go with it. The term is "sourcebooks" and refers to collections of texts, some quite brief, which were bound into books that the Arabic tradition would recognise as *majmū'āt* ("collections"). These were not "books" in the conventional sense, but instead represented the result of different situations in which the need to organise and preserve small texts arose – for example, when a manuscript collector died and left a collection of disparate pieces to his heirs, who organised related materials together, or when a librarian or a manuscript seller put together topically related materials. For readers such as al-Mas'udi, these collections would have provided an invaluable resource, but, like modern course reading packs, they lacked identities of their own.

Al-Mas'udi tells us in the *Tanbih* that he in fact saw such a work in Istakhr in the year 303/915–16 – approximately thirty years before he composed the *Muruj* and more than forty years before the *Tanbih*.[36] This was a large, illustrated manuscript, in the possession of some of the Persians' notable families, which treated the Persians, the history of their kings, buildings and political thought and several areas of their knowledge (*'ulūm*, perhaps referring to Zoroastrian religious knowledge). He says that this book was written up from what was found in the libraries (*khazā'in*) of the kings of Persia and that it was translated under the auspices of the caliph Hisham ibn 'Abd al-Malik (r. 105–25/724–43). He also says that it contained details not provided by other works that he had consulted – which he names as the *Khuday-nama*, *A'in-nama* and *Gah-nama* – and that he has given a full accounting of this history in the seventh section of his *Muruj*. He does not quote the book directly in the *Tanbih*, but he does launch into a long description of the contents of Persian history in the *Muruj* (including genealogy as a topic), implying, it would seem, that he had used this source. It is not, however, clearly identified in the *Muruj*.

We have several clues that suggest that a variety of other types of collections about Iran's pre-Islamic heritage circulated at the time. Al-Mas'udi's contemporary, Hamza al-Isfahani (d. after 350/961), for example, reported having known multiple versions of the *Khuday-nama* as well as different works on Persian royal history. Among the sources he mentions is a collection of "more than twenty" copies of the *Khuday-nama* by the Zoroastrian priest Bahram.[37] Hamza also tells us that he will reveal information in the *Khuday-nama* not included in the translations of Ibn al-Muqaffa' and Ibn al-Jahm, and then proceeds to explain what he has "read in a book quoting from their book, the Avesta".[38] These two statements suggest that Hamza had at hand composite manuscripts. Another relevant example is the Pahlavi *Letter of Tansar*, translated by Ibn al-Muqaffa' and reportedly written by Ardashir's chief Zoroastrian priest to a ruler in the Caspian region. Al-Mas'udi mentions this letter and cites an Arabic translation in the *Tanbih*.[39] The thirteenth-century author Ibn Isfandiyar says that while working on a Persian-language history of his native Tabaristan, he came across a volume containing ten separate treatises, among them an Arabic version of the *Letter*, which he retranslated into the Persian of his own day and included in his book.[40]

Extant manuscripts from before the eleventh century are rare, but it is also possible to speculate about the existence of sourcebooks on the basis of the later manuscript tradition, in which it was common to bind together different books by the same author or books that struck a compiler as topically related. Two outstanding examples come to mind. The first is a manuscript in Istanbul (Köprülü 1608) that contains four works pertaining to Ardashir, including the *'Ahd Ardashir*, mentioned above. Of the three other works included in the volume, two lack titles. Mario Grignaschi, who worked on the manuscript in the 1960s, believed the third to be an ancient, mistitled Arab-Iranian anthology, and the manuscript itself to be a reproduction of a much earlier source.[41] The second example is a codex dated to 1322 and containing thirty short Pahlavi works, which may represent a sourcebook outside of the Arabic tradition.[42]

The diffusion of such sourcebooks would go a long way towards explaining why al-Mas'udi and other scholars who transmitted Iran's pre-Islamic heritage tend to refer to their sources in ambiguous ways. Sourcebooks would have contained antique contents but did not have nameable agents of transmission because their compilers, who typically knew Arabic but not Pahlavi, perceived themselves and were perceived by others as playing a very minor role in their creation. Nor did the compilers view themselves as interpreters of a tradition, as did those who anthologised pre-Islamic Arabic poetry. Their work was more hands-off. The above-mentioned work of 'Umar, "known as Kisra", may have been such a book; that is why it is so little remembered, whereas the memory of Abu 'Ubayda, who created something new out of it, lives on. When al-Tabari or al-Mas'udi employ phrases such as "the Persians say", they may be referring to oral sources, but given the material included – for example, lengthy genealogies of long-gone dynasties or quotations that recur throughout Arabic literature – they probably meant written sources and possibly sourcebooks. When Ibn Qutayba attributes his reports to the "siyar al-'Ajam", varieties of this phrase occurring elsewhere, recensions of the *Khuday-nama* are frequently understood.[43] However, he has not named Ibn al-Muqaffa' or another agent, and perhaps he had sourcebooks at hand.

CONCLUSION

By al-Mas'udi's day, Muslims generally believed that all of humanity had descended from Adam, but there apparently remained room for disagreement on how Persians fit into this picture. How were the Persians' pre-Islamic ideas to be reconciled with Muslim ones? As he was writing, a good number of works were being drafted by Iranians that offered solutions that al-Mas'udi, if he knew about them, may not have favoured. Among these were a prose *Shah-nama* commissioned in 346/957 by a Samanid dynasty ruler named Abu Mansur Tusi and two more *Shah-namas* created by authors with ties to Balkh. Right around the same time, the poet Daqiqi undertook to compose a poetic version. This was followed, in 400/1010, by Firdawsi's completion of the *Shah-nama* for Sultan Mahmud the Ghaznavid that is known around the world today.[44]

Al-Mas'udi was a key witness to the early stages of a tradition of Iranian Muslim historiography and had a wide variety of materials at his disposal, including "classic" works of the Arab-Islamic heritage as well as, perhaps, unauthored collections. As a non-Iranian who had travelled widely and who had seen the great variety of ways in which Islam was adapted to local contexts, he may have been alarmed by the possibility that Iranians could disconnect themselves from the wider community. It is likely that he felt a need to stabilise the genealogical record in such a way as to support ideas that linked the Persians to prophetic history. And so, far from conducting a neutral survey, al-Mas'udi dug up rare and curious genealogies that cast doubt on the Iranians' self-image as autochthons. He deliberately complicated the picture he knew many Iranians to share, the traces of which he could not help but record. Stories about ancient Iranian history had long and deep roots in Iran and required engagement. Al-Mas'udi's approach to genealogy reflects a negotiation: He passes on much of Sasanian-era historiography surviving in his day but adds a separate treatment of genealogy and comments on the Sasanian-era materials.

Al-Mas'udi was likely well aware of increasing claims by political elites to an antique Iranian heritage. But his were still early days, and I suspect that his concern was primarily ethnogenic, addressing broader questions of cultural affiliation that were not limited to political elites but rather were deeply related to the accelerating pace of conversion and the potential for Iranians to go their own way. By contrast, al-Biruni (d. after 442/1050), who wrote about genealogies two or three generations later, was more deeply informed about eastern Iran and, with a Ziyarid patron, more directly involved in the complex dynastic politics of his age, as Parvaneh Pourshariati has argued.[45]

The failure of al-Mas'udi's approach is suggested by the fact that neither political elites nor Iranians generally adopted the ethnogenic theories he advances. Few, if any, Iranians today reckon themselves to be children of Isaac, although the idea persisted in some quarters. The theories that al-Mas'udi proposed conflicted in too many ways with other ideas of greater antiquity among Iranians, and reconciling them proved too complicated a task. On the other hand, Muslim Iranians did come to accept the general framework of prophetic history and genealogy and to find a way to live with the ambiguity of its relationship to Iranian history. The long-term success of perspectives such as those of al-Mas'udi is suggested by Firdawsi's *Shah-nama*, which nests Iran's history within a broader, although unexplored, narrative framework, which begins with creation and continues after the Arab conquests, and in which Kayumart is Iran's first king.

NOTES

* I would like to thank Touraj Daryaee, John Hayes, Konrad Hirschler, Farid Panjwani, Parvaneh Pourshariati, Arash Zeini and particularly Wadad Kadi for their insightful and constructive comments on drafts of this chapter. On the diverse ways in which an Arab-centred history was revised in order to take greater account of Iranian perspectives, see my *The New Muslims of Post-Conquest Iran: Tradition, Memory, and Conversion*, Cambridge: Cambridge University Press, 2013. The first chapter deals broadly with genealogy and ethnogenesis and draws to some extent on al-Mas'udi's work.

1. Al-Mas'udi, *Muruj al-dhahab wa-ma'adin al-jawhar*, vol. 1, ed. C. Pellat, Beirut: al-Jami'a al-Lubnaniyya, 1965–79, paragraph 563. Hereafter, I generally cite the *Muruj*'s paragraphs, which match those in Pellat's French translation, *Les Prairies*

d'Or, Paris: Société asiatique, 1962–97. I have not been able to identify this genealogy in the two volumes prepared by W. Caskel and G. Strenziok dealing with
Ibn al-Kalbi: *Ǧamharat an-nasab: Das genealogische Werk des Hišam Ibn Muḥammad
al-Kalbī*, Leiden: E. J. Brill, 1966.

2. Genesis 10 and 1 Chronicles 1 do know a Hadoram as a son of Joktan, a son of Eber,
a son of Shelah, a son of Arpachshad, a son of Shem.

3. *Muruj*, para. 563.

4. *Muruj*, para. 564. See also "Bawwan" in Yaqut al-Hamawi, *Mu'jam al-buldan*, ed.
F. Wüstenfeld as *Jacut's geographisches Wörterbuch*, vol. 1, Leipzig: F. A. Brockhaus,
1866–73, pp. 751–4. Yaqut quotes several authorities relating to Shi'b Bawwan,
beginning with al-Mas'udi, whose reporting he reproduces, along with the poem
(although he quotes the genealogy as Bawwan ibn Iran ibn al-Aswad ibn Shem
ibn Noah). See also Ibn Khallikan (d. 626/1229), *Wafayat al-a'yan wa-anba' abna'
al-zaman*, vol. 4, ed. I. 'Abbas, Beirut: Dar al-Thaqafa, 1968–72, p. 55, where Ibn
Khallikan mentions Bawwan ibn Iran ibn al-Aswad ibn Shem ibn Noah.

5. *Muruj*, para. 563.

6. *Muruj*, para. 564.

7. Genesis 19: 1–38.

8. I. Goldziher, *Muslim Studies*, vol. 1, ed. S. M. Stern and trans. C. R. Barber and
Stern, London: Allen & Unwin, 1967–71, p. 135, n. 4. Ibn Badrun draws libe-
rally on the *Muruj* and al-Mas'udi's reporting on genealogy in his commentary on
a famous *qaṣīda*; see *Sharh qasidat Ibn 'Abdun*, Cairo: Matba'at al-Sa'ada, 1921, pp.
14ff.

9. *Muruj*, para. 565.

10. F. Vallat, "Elam", and R. Schmitt, "Achaemenid Dynasty", *Encyclopaedia Iranica*.
Elamites are referred to among the Children of Israel returning from Babylon in
Ezra 2: 7, 2: 31 and 8: 7 and in Nehemiah 7: 12 and 7: 34, and the Bible refers to
Elamites in the New Testament in Acts 2: 5–11, where the Elamites are mentioned
as one of the peoples through whom the Holy Spirit spoke on the day of Pentecost.
When the Bible is rendered into Arabic, Elam is written '*Aylām*.

11. Josephus, *Jewish Antiquities*, trans. W. Whiston, Ware, Hertfordshire: Wordsworth
Editions, 2006, p. 20.

12. *Muruj*, para. 530. There is minor variability in how al-Mas'udi's text renders many
Iranian names. I vocalise the name as Kayumart throughout, following Pellat's
index.

13. *Muruj*, para. 534. On Kayumart, see S. Shaked, "First Man, First King: Notes on
Semitic-Iranian Syncretism and Iranian Mythological Transformations", in Shaked,
D. Shulman and G. G. Stroumsa, eds, *Gilgul: Essays on Transformation, Revolution
and Permanence in the History of Religions Dedicated to R. J. Zwi Werblowsky*, Leiden:
E. J. Brill, 1987, pp. 238–56. See also T. Daryaee, "Gayōmard: King of Clay or
Mountain? The Epithet of the First Man in the Zoroastrian Tradition", in S. Adhami
(ed.), *Paitimāna: Essays in Iranian, Indo-European, and Indian Studies in Honor of
Hanns-Peter Schmidt*, Costa Mesa, CA: Mazda Publishers, 2003, pp. 339–49.

14. *Muruj*, para. 530. I have vocalised his name as Immim following Caskel, *Ǧamharat
an-nasab*, vol. 1, p. 40.

15. *Muruj*, para. 531. Also, in his general outline of prophetic history towards the
beginning of the *Muruj*, al-Mas'udi names Immim as one of Lud's children, reports

that "Immim ibn Lud ibn Aram settled the land of Persia (*nazala arḍ Fāris*)" and promises to discuss the genealogy in a later chapter. *Muruj*, para. 69.

16. The person of Immim is not included among Noah's descendants in Genesis 10 or 1 Chronicles. From an early date, however, Muslims identified Immim (perhaps vocalised Umaym as by Pellat) as a descendant of Shem. Immim appears to have been identified both as a father to Persia and, alternatively, as an ancestor to Wabar, who is mentioned alongside 'Ad and Thamud among the "original" Arabs. Ibn Qutayba (d. 276/889) traced "all the Persian peoples" to Immim ibn Lud ibn Aram ibn Shem ibn Noah. Ibn Qutayba, *al-Ma'arif*, ed. S. Okacha, Cairo: al-Hay'a al-Misriyya al-'Amma li-l-Kitab, 1992, p. 27. Also see J. Tkatsch, "Wabar", in P. Bearman, Th. Bianquis, C. E. Bosworth, E. van Donzel, and W. P. Heinrichs (eds), *Encyclopaedia of Islam*, 12 vols, 2nd edn. Leiden: E. J. Brill, 1960–2004. Online edition.

17. *Muruj*, paras 565–6. The vocalisation of Manushkharnar ibn Manushkhurank is uncertain.

18. *Muruj*, paras 566–9.

19. See "Wizak" in F. Justi, *Iranisches Namenbuch*, Marburg: N. G. Elwert, 1895, p. 374. Compare Ibn al-Balkhi, *Fars-nama*, eds G. le Strange and R. A. Nicholson, London: Luzac, 1921, p. 12.

20. Muhammad ibn Jarir al-Tabari, *Ta'rikh al-rusul wa-l-muluk*, vol. 1, ed. M. J. de Goeje, Leiden: E. J. Brill, 1879–1901, pp. 430–3.

21. *Muruj*, para. 570. I follow Pellat: "Les lois de la nature et de l'expérience la rejettent." See also s.v. "Manushihr" in the indexes, *Muruj*, vol. 7, p. 708.

22. Compare al-Tabari, *Ta'rikh*, vol. 1, pp. 431–2.

23. He adds that he has found likewise "in histories of this party in the land of Fars and in the country of Kirman". *Muruj*, para. 571.

24. *Muruj*, para. 657. See also al-Tabari, *Ta'rikh*, vol. 1, p. 433.

25. As T. Khalidi writes, the *Muruj* was written in 332 AH and it was revised between 332 and 336; in 345 al-Mas'udi revised and added to the 332–6 edition, but all extant manuscripts of the *Muruj* are of the 332–6 edition. A first edition of the *Tanbih*, al-Mas'udi's last work, was completed in 344, but the surviving edition, which is longer, was completed in 345. Khalidi argues that al-Mas'udi composed his works for different purposes; his surviving *Muruj* and *Tanbih* are not simple abridgements or restatements. Khalidi, "Mas'ūdī's Lost Works: A Reconstruction of Their Content", *Journal of the American Oriental Society*, vol. 94, no. 1, 1974, pp. 35–7.

26. *Kitab al-Tanbih wa-l-ishraf*, ed. M. J. de Goeje, Leiden: E. J. Brill, 1894, pp. 107–10; See also *Tanbih*, p. 85 and the discussion of Kayumart.

27. For a thorough overview of al-Mas'udi's sources for and treatment of Iranian history in the *Muruj* and *Tanbih*, see esp. M. Cooperson, "Mas'udi", *Encyclopaedia Iranica*; see also his pertinent characterisation of the *Muruj* and *Tanbih* as "supplements" to al-Mas'udi's now-lost *magnum opus*, *Akhbar al-zaman*.

28. *Muruj*, paras 530–62. On al-Mas'udi, the *Kitab Sakisaran* and Pahlavi texts translated into Arabic, see A. Christensen, *Les Kayanides*, Copenhagen: Andr. Fred. Høst & Søn, 1931, esp. pp. 142–4.

29. On the Sasanian-era sources, see C. G. Cereti, "Kār-nāmag ī Ardašīr ī Pābagān" and A. Sh. Shahbazi, "Historiography ii: Pre-Islamic period", both in *Encyclopaedia Iranica*.

30. *Muruj*, paras 576–663.

31. *Muruj*, paras 535–40. For some of these names, see Justi, *Iranisches Namenbuch*, esp. pp. 60–1 on "Baęwarāspa" and p. 126 on "Haoschyaṅha". Compare the *Muruj*, vol. 1, edition of M. Muhyi al-Din 'Abd al-Hamid, Beirut: al-Maktaba al-'Asriyya, 1988, vol. 1, pp. 222–6.

32. In his indexes, however, Pellat favours a manuscript variant he gives in his notes to para. 535: Tahmurath ibn Waywanjahan ibn [the biblical?] Arfakhshad ibn Awshanj; *Muruj*, vol. 7, p. 446, s.v. "Tahmurath".

33. *Muruj*, para. 576; also vol. 6, pp. 135–6, s.v. "Ardashir". See also G. Morrison, "The Sassanian Genealogy in Mas'ūdī", in S. M. Ahmad and A. Rahman (eds), *Al-Mas'ūdī: Millenary Commemoration Volume*, Aligarh: Indian Society for the History of Science and the Institute of Islamic Studies, Aligarh Muslim University, 1960.

34. The Arabic begins in para. 560 and reads: "*wa-qad dhakara Abū 'Ubayda Ma'mar ibn al-Muthannā al-Taymī 'an 'Umar Kisrā fi kitāb lahu fi akhbār al-Furs yaṣifu fihi …*" (following Pellat's vocalisation); see also paras 536 ('*Umar al-ma'rūf bi-Kisrā*), 538, 600 and 660.

35. *Muruj*, esp. paras 8–13 and 503. Curiously, al-Mas'udi does not mention (by name, at least) another work attributed to Ibn Khurradadhbih, a *Kitab Jamharat ansab al-Furs wa-l-nawaqil* (*The Book of the Principal Genealogies of the Persians and of the Transplanted Population*). On Ibn Khurradadhbih's works, including their citation by other scholars, see M. Hadj-Sadok, "Ibn <u>Kh</u>urradā<u>dh</u>bih", *Encyclopaedia of Islam*, 2nd edn. Al-Mas'udi clarifies that Da'ud was the grandfather of the 'Abbasid *wazīr* 'Ali ibn 'Isa (d. 334/946). Al-Suli, a contemporary of al-Mas'udi, was well aware of claims about the Persian–Isaac connection and recorded them; on this, see Savant, "Isaac as the Persians' Ishmael: Pride and the Pre-Islamic Past in Medieval Islam", *Comparative Islamic Studies*, vol. 2, no. 1, 2006, esp. pp. 9–13.

36. *Tanbih*, pp. 106–7. Al-Mas'udi's description has caught the attention of scholars interested in the history of Arabic illustrated books; for example, D. S. Rice, "The Oldest Illustrated Arabic Manuscript", *Bulletin of the School of Oriental and African Studies*, vol. 22, no. 1/3, 1959, p. 208 and J. M. Bloom, "The Introduction of Paper to the Islamic Lands and the Development of the Illustrated Manuscript", *Muqarnas*, vol. 17, 2000, p. 18.

37. *Kitab Ta'rikh sini muluk al-ard wa-l-anbiya'*, Berlin: Matba'at Kawiyani, 1921–2 [1340], pp. 9–10, 15, 19, 43–4. See also *The Annals of Hamzah al-Isfahani*, trans. U. M. Daudpota, Bombay: K. R. Cama Oriental Institute, 1932, pp. 63–4, 70, 75–6, 109.

38. Hamza, *Ta'rikh*, pp. 43–4. Compare A. Shahpur Shahbazi, "On the $X^w adāy$-nāmag", in D. Amin, M. Kasheff and A. Sh. Shahbazi (eds), *Iranica Varia: Papers in Honor of Professor Ehsan Yarshater*, Leiden: E. J. Brill, 1990, pp. 215–16.

39. *Tanbih*, p. 99; also see *Muruj*, para. 585. On al-Mas'udi and the *Letter of Tansar*, see Christensen, "Abarsam et Tansar", *Acta Orientalia*, vol. 10, 1932, pp. 46–7.

40. See M. Boyce's summary in *The Letter of Tansar*, Rome: Istituto Italiano per il Medio ed Estremo Oriente, 1968, pp. 1ff; for the volume, see Ibn Isfandiyar, *Tarikh-i Tabaristan*, vol. 1, ed. 'A. Iqbal, Tehran: Chapkhanah-i Majlis, 1941, pp. 12–41.

41. Grignaschi commented on folios 146^v to 167^r of Köprülü 1608 and provided relevant

translations to French in "Quelques spécimens de la littérature sassanide conservés dans les bibliothèques d'Istanbul", *Journal Asiatique*, vol. 254, 1966, pp. 1–142. He did not believe the copyist to have known Arabic. Far more attention has been paid to the ways in which Greek materials passed into Arabic. See especially D. Gutas, *Greek Thought, Arabic Culture: The Graeco-Arabic Translation Movement in Baghdad and Early 'Abbāsid Society (2nd–4th/8th–10th centuries)*, London – New York: Routledge, 1998.

42. See B. Utas, "The Pahlavi Treatise *Avdēh u sahīkēh ī Sakistān* or 'Wonders and Magnificence of Sistan'", *Acta Antiqua Academiae Scientiarum Hungaricae*, vol. 28, 1980, pp. 259–67.

43. Ibn Qutayba, *al-Ma'arif*, p. 12.

44. J. S. Meisami, *Persian Historiography to the End of the Twelfth Century*, Edinburgh: Edinburgh University Press, 1999, pp. 20–3, 37–45; V. Minorsky, "The Older Preface to the *Shāh-nāma*", in *Studi orientalistici in onore di Giorgio Levi della Vida*, vol. 2, Rome: Istituto per L'Oriente, 1956, pp. 159–79.

45. For Pourshariati's illuminating discussion of al-Biruni and dynastic claims regarding Parthian ancestry, see "The Parthians and the Production of the Canonical Shāh-nāmas: Of Pahlavī, Pahlavānī and the Pahlav", in H. Börm and J. Wiesehöfer (eds), *Commutatio et Contentio: Studies in the Late Roman, Sasanian, and Early Islamic Near East; In Memory of Zeev Rubin*, Düsseldorf: Wellem, 2010. Regarding dynastic claims to Iran's past more generally, see C. E. Bosworth, "The Heritage of Rulership in Early Islamic Iran and the Search for Dynastic Connections with the Past', *Iran*, vol. 11, 1973, pp. 51–62.

CHAPTER 9

Genealogical Prestige and Marriage Strategy among the Ahl al-Bayt: The Case of the al-Sadr Family in Recent Times

RAFFAELE MAURIELLO

"Because we are linked by blood and blood is memory without language."
Joyce Carol Oates, *I Lock My Door Upon Myself*

Historians have given little sustained attention to the customs of nobility within Islamic civilisation. The role of genealogy in shaping political, religious and social realities appears to have been overlooked particularly, or even ignored, in the case of the contemporary history of the Middle East. This, at least, is the case with the Family of the Prophet (Ahl al-Bayt). However, observed through the lens of genealogical prestige and marriage strategies, the role and behaviour of the descendants of the Family of the Prophet in recent times reveal customs of nobility that are close, or at least similar, to those witnessed in European history. Bearing in mind the vast literature on marriage policies among the European nobility,[1] this chapter argues that the socio-political categories developed in order to analyse the history of eminent families in European history, in particular for the late Middle Ages and for modern history, are relevant and useful in understanding the role of eminent families of the Ahl al-Bayt in contemporary Islamic societies.

The case study discussed here concerns the marriage strategy of a politically and religiously relevant 'Alid[2] branch of the Ahl al-Bayt, the al-Sadr. The choice of this family is based on its centrality to the Shi'i religious establishment,[3] as we have more data available on the marriages of its members than for other families of the Ahl al-Bayt. Reference will be made, moreover, to some 'Alid families that are linked to the al-Sadr by intermarriage or master–disciple bonds (the families of al-Sultani al-Tabataba'i, Khomeini, Khatami, Kalantar, al-Hakim, Bahr al-'Ulum, al-Khalkhali and al-Khu'i).

The quality of the data discussed will allow us to address a number of key issues concerning the marriage policy of the 'Alid Shi'i religious establishment – namely, what the predominant logic for marriage strategies is, whether it is linked to dynamics that are internal or external to the Family and whether these strategies help to explain the al-Sadr's resilience in maintaining their position of privilege over a span of several centuries. We will, further, identify the main types of marriage that we encounter, and, provided they are endogamic, we will see whether or not they follow the established pattern of first-cousin marriage.

My sources are mainly works of prosopography.[4] Prosopography is based on the investigation of a group of actors in history through the study of their lives and common background. It combines an investigation of the genealogies, interests and activities of the group with the study of detailed cases. In fact, given the previously mentioned disregard for the role of genealogy in contemporary history, this methodology has been significantly ignored as a tool for reconstructing the ideological and political history of Muslim societies during the last decades of the twentieth century. This is the case even of Shi'i Islam, where the production of prosopographical works, both printed[5] and online,[6] continues an uninterrupted tradition and plays a central role in Shi'i scholastic production.

The most interesting biographical and autobiographical sources related to contemporary history are normally biographies of single figures, in which there is the recurrent element of the individual subject being preceded by the biographies of two of his ancestors. These monographs are generally organised following the ancient practices of prosopography, insofar as they present the subject as part of a group and set him into lineages of family and mentor-masters. While they take their inspiration from the classical works on classes of individuals (*ṭabaqāt*), they differ from the latter in several regards. Most notably, there is a significant presence of women. This is a new development. Relevant in this respect is the case of *Waja' al-Sadr wa-min wara'i al-Sadr Umm Ja'far*,[7] which is a collection of the memoirs of Sayyida[8] Fatima al-Sadr. She is important for her family connections, as she is a daughter of Ayatollah al-'Uzma[9] Sayyid Sadr al-Din al-Sadr (1882–1954), a sister of Ayatollah Sayyid Musa al-Sadr (1928–78?),[10] the wife of Ayatollah al-'Uzma Sayyid Muhammad Baqir al-Sadr (1935–80),[11] and the mother-in-law of Sayyid Muqtada al-Sadr (1974?–)[12] and of Ayatollah al-'Uzma Sayyid Husayn al-Sadr (1952–). The memoirs, written down and edited by a close friend of Fatima, Amal al-Baqshi, arguably represent the first document from a female perspective on the 'Alids' lives, very different from the usual biographical genre in both style and voice.[13] Also relevant is the publication of single-figure biographies dedicated to women scholars known as *'ālimāt* (feminine plural of *'ālim*), including, as discussed below, Sayyida Amina al-Sadr (1937–80?).[14] Known as Bint al-Huda, she was the sister of Muhammad Baqir al-Sadr and the sister-in-law of Fatima al-Sadr.

I have cross-checked and integrated the literary (prosopographical) data with information provided by oral sources represented by members of the above-mentioned families. The interviews were largely conducted according to the criteria of the discipline of oral history; that is, they were recorded with the informed consent of the interviewees, who were informed of the use and purpose of the interviews.[15]

THE al-SADR FAMILY: AN OVERVIEW

The al-Sadr is a Musawi family. This means that its members claim descent from the seventh imam, Musa al-Kazim (d. 799). Throughout history, the *nisba* ("family name") of the 'Alid branch from which the al-Sadr claim descent has been subjected, as always happens, to several differentiations, a process known among anthropologists as lineage segmentation.[16] For the concerns of this chapter, going backward in time the al-Sadr family represents a branch of the Sharaf al-Din family, which in turn is a branch of the al-Musawi al-'Amili al-Juba'i family.

The al-Sadr are renowned in Shi'i communities and among other 'Alids. The members of this family have mainly settled in today's Lebanon in Jabal 'Amil, particularly the district of Sur (Tyre), and more recently in Beirut; in Iraq, in Kazimiyya, today a district of Baghdad, and in Najaf; and in Iran, in Qom and Tehran. We have several accounts of the prominent role that they have played throughout history. A record of this prominence is represented by the writings of Gertrude Bell (1868–1926, Oriental Secretary at the High Commission of Great Britain in Iraq). In the entry of 14 March 1920 in her collection of letters we read:

> It's a problem here how to get into touch with the Shiahs, not the tribal people in the country; we're on intimate terms with all of them, but the grimly devout citizens of the holy towns and more especially the leaders of religious opinion, the Mujtahids, who can loose and bind with a word by authority which rests on an intimate acquaintance with accumulated knowledge entirely irrelevant to human affairs and worthless in any branch of human activity … There's a group of these worthies in Kadhimain, the holy city, 8 miles from Bagdad, bitterly pan-Islamic, anti-British "et tout le bataclan." Chief among them are a family called Sadr, possibly more distinguished for religious learning than any other family in the whole Shiah world.[17]

What follows is a snapshot of eminent family members, gleaned from a bio-bibliographical dictionary:[18]

- Muhammad al-Sadr (c. 1883–1955 or 1956). He was one of the leaders of al-Istiqlal, the most important Arab nationalist party of his epoch in Iraq, and he was a long-serving president of the Iraqi Senate as well as one of the very few Shi'a to hold the position of prime minister in Iraq.
- Musa al-Sadr (1928–78?). In the 1960s and 1970s he led the Shi'i "renaissance" in Lebanon.
- Amina Bint al-Huda (1937–80?). She is considered an important Arab Islamic female writer.
- Muhammad Muhammad Sadiq al-Sadr (1943–99). He was the most important *marja'* living in Iraq – together with 'Ali Sistani – in the 1990s and established a movement, the Sadriyyin, which represented the fiercest opposition to the Anglo-American occupation of Iraq.
- Dr Rubab al-Sadr (1944–). She is the chairperson and director of the Imam Sadr Foundation, a Lebanese nongovernmental organisation affiliated to several international networks, such as the Economic and Social Council of the United Nations (ECOSOC) and the Lebanese Women League.
- Dr Muhammad al-Sadr (1951–). He was deputy foreign minister for Arabic and African affairs in the Islamic Republic of Iran under Muhammad Khatami's presidency.
- Husayn al-Sadr (1952–). He is an important *marja'* in Iraq.
- Muqtada al-Sadr (1974?–). He is one of the most important political leaders of post-Saddam Iraq.

MARRIAGE STRATEGY OF THE 'ALIDS:
THE CASE OF THE AL-SADR FAMILY

In the case of the al-Sadr, marriages give clear evidence of the centrality of the Family of the Prophet for the religious, political and social leadership of Shi'i communities in Lebanon, Iraq and Iran. I propose to take into account the cases reported in the table of marriages (see Table 9.1 at the end of this chapter).

With the marriages between Sayyida Fatima al-Sadr (1946–) and Sayyid Sadiq al-Sultani al-Tabataba'i (1943–), between Ayatollah al-'Uzma Sayyid Sadr al-Din al-Sadr (1882–1954) and a member of the Al Yasin family, and between the four sons of Ayatollah Sayyid Isma'il al-Sadr (1842–1920) and the daughters of Ayatollah Shaykh 'Abd al-Husayn Al Yasin, we have several cases of a man marrying a *bint khāla*, that is to say, the daughter of one's maternal aunt. We arguably find a similar case almost four centuries earlier in the marriage between Nur al-Din 'Ali al-Musawi al-'Amili al-Juba'i (1524 or 1525–90 or 1591) and a daughter of al-Shahid al-Thani (1506–58). Most probably, the latter is also related to the pattern of men marrying the widowed women within their families or the families' close entourages, a situation that we encounter with the marriage between the widow of Sayyid Sharif Sharaf al-Din (1881–1917) and Sharif's brother, Ayatollah 'Abd al-Husayn Sharaf al-Din (1873–1957).[19] Indeed, when we consider the data on the al-Sadr covering the last century, we notice a marked preference for intra-family endogamic marriages.[20] As we have just seen, a preferred marriage pattern is the one linked to the scheme *bint khāla*. Also popular is the *bint 'amm* scheme, that is, marriage to the daughter of a paternal uncle, traditionally practised among Middle Eastern populations.[21]

In order to explain intra-family endogamic marriages, we must first consider structural anthropology. While extension and dispersion are characteristics of kinship, and new marriages increase the number of ancestors and relatives, endogamy both limits this tendency and socially consolidates kinship and genealogy.[22] This is particularly the case with marriages between first cousins (*bint 'amm*, *bint khāla*, *ibn khāla* [son of a maternal aunt], and so forth). Moreover, should endogamic marriages among first cousins be repeated in successive generations, the number of collateral descendants would be effectively limited, thus favouring the closeness and exclusivity of kinship and genealogy. It is important to point out that we encounter marriages between first cousins among the very initiators of the 'Alid lineage, as demonstrated by the case of Zaynab (d. 682),[23] a daughter of Imam 'Ali ibn Abi Talib, and the case of Imam Muhammad al-Baqir (d. c. 735).[24] In the former case, the source explicitly mentions that Imam 'Ali ibn Abi Talib desired that his daughters marry their *ibn 'amms*, or paternal male cousins.[25]

Moreover, I suggest that, as proposed by Theodore P. Wright Jr for the *sāda* (pl. of *sayyid*) of India and Pakistan, we should take into account the hypothesis that endogamic marriages aim both to "maintain 'purity of blood' and to keep land within the family since daughters according to Shari'ah have a fixed share of inheritance which would be lost to the family if they married out".[26] It should be borne in mind that this share according to the Shi'i Ja'fari school of law is larger than it would be according to the Sunni schools.[27] Moreover, although the Ja'fari school maintains the 2:1 inheritance ratio established by the Qur'an for male/female shares, "unlike under Sunni law more distant male relatives on the paternal side had no special claims on inheritance and did not water down the rights of closer female heirs".[28]

A further relevant explanation for the 'Alids' preference for intra-family endogamic marriages and genealogy in general is related to their bid for political and social power. This bid involves, to a significant degree, ideas of *baraka* (the power to confer blessings), charisma and charismatic leadership.[29] Cases in point are Husayn al-Sadr (1945–) and Muqtada al-Sadr (1974?–), who both married daughters of Muhammad Baqir al-Sadr (1935–80), and the several marriage bonds between the al-Sadr and Khomeini families (in this respect, the link to the Khatami family also appears relevant[30]). These marriages allow us to touch upon some interesting and largely unanswered questions: What is the role of women in marriage strategies when they are daughters of a *marja'*? Do they bring with them properties, *khums* (a religious "tax" paid to a *marja'*) and/or *muqallidūn* (followers of a *marja'*)?

A secondary source reports that a son of Musa al-Sadr (1928–78?) married a granddaughter of Ruhollah Khomeini (1902–89), while a primary source refers to Muhammad Baqir al-Sadr as the first cousin on his father's side (*ibn 'amm*) of Muhammad Muhammad Sadiq al-Sadr (Muqtada's father).[31] Both pieces of information are contradicted by the large majority of my prosopographical and oral source data. However, we also know that several marriage bonds indeed link the al-Sadr and the Khomeini, and that three marriages occurred between Muhammad Baqir al-Sadr's daughters and Muhammad Muhammad Sadiq al-Sadr's sons, the most relevant concerning Muqtada al-Sadr. The key question is: Why is this marriage among first cousins and the overall links between Musa al-Sadr and Ruhollah Khomeini, on the one hand, and Muqtada al-Sadr and Muhammad Baqir al-Sadr, on the other, so important? My data seem to suggest that the importance of the overall links, real or fictitious, and the main reasons for the endogamic bonds between Musa al-Sadr and Ruhollah Khomeini and those between Muhammad Baqir al-Sadr and Muhammad Muhammad Sadiq al-Sadr are rooted in Muslim belief in the genealogical transmission of *baraka* and charismatic religious (and political) leadership.[32] The relation between endogamy within the Ahl al-Bayt and the genealogical transmission of *baraka* is at the core of Muqtada's bid for social prominence and political power in post-Saddam Iraq and provides the basis for the strong support he has received thus far[33] (and maybe also for the legitimisation to administer some of the foundations established by his father-in-law). This relation is even clearer when we consider that although he is still not a *mujtahid* (a scholar who has obtained a level of knowledge sufficient to formulate independent interpretations of the religious law), he is seen by many Iraqis as a religious leader, an indication of the social and political prominence that belonging to the Ahl al-Bayt can play "above" the rules of the Shi'i religious establishment, theoretically organised around principles of seniority in knowledge and teaching. It is interesting that 'Ammar al-Hakim (1971–), Muqtada's main rival in his bid for social prominence and political power within the Shi'i religious establishment in Iraq, has also been highlighting his 'Alid descent. 'Ammar is himself a member of the Ahl al-Bayt and his mother is a member of the al-Sadr.

My data indicates one further endogamic alliance between the al-Sadr and 'Alid families: This is with the Kalantar, a family related to Ayatollah al-'Uzma Ali Sistani (1930–) by marriage.[34]

Of course, another possible explanation for at least some intra-family endogamic marriages and for the large number of close-kin marriages could equally be a lack of suitable grooms for the women of the Family of the Prophet.

Another pattern we find in relation to the al-Sadr marriage strategy is one that we can call *"marja'-oriented-marriages"*, that is, alliances that were built through master–disciple relationships.[35] We are still within an endogamic policy, a policy pursued within the highest echelons of the religious establishment.[36] In this respect, an interview I conducted with Dr Sayyid Muhammad al-Sadr (1951–) is useful.[37] During this interview, Dr al-Sadr pointed out that his three sisters (Maryam, Tayyiba and Fatima) had all married 'ulama' (religious scholars) and that although one of the grooms was indeed a *sayyid* (and the son of a prominent *marja'* who resides in Qom), the other two were not 'Alids. He added that this occurred because his father, Ayatollah Sayyid Reza al-Sadr, had insisted that his daughters marry members of the religious establishment but had not required that they be *sayyids*, despite attaching value to *sayyid* descent.

The data analysed here also indicate that the al-Sadr have built marriage alliances with families of the Shi'i religious establishment that are non-'Alids, such as with al-Shahid al-Thani and his descendants[38] and with the Al Yasin family.[39] In the case of the al-Shahid al-Thani family, the sources refer to the descent of the wife of Sayyid Salih Sharaf al-Din (1710 or 1711–c. 1803), even though she was only the daughter of the grandson of a grandson of al-Shahid al-Thani. It is fairly clear that the wife brings prestige to her husband, if not material wealth.

These marriage alliances, moreover, show that the grooms of the women of the al-Sadr family can be chosen from among non-'Alids, but they must be men of high religious, political, social and/or economic status. The existence of "semimatrilinear ascriptions by blood" has been pointed out in quantitative studies on the role and presence of women in Muslim societies.[40] Similarly, the prestige of the women of the Family of the Prophet is evident in my data. In this respect, I should also mention an interview I conducted with a member of a long-established 'Alid family of Najaf: Ayatollah Sayyid Muhammad Sa'id al-Khalkhali (1959–).[41] During an interview in which we were discussing the role of *sāda* today, al-Khalkhali mentioned that marrying a *sayyida* was an "honour" that was normally reserved to a *sayyid*, and was a source of pride when conceded to a non-*sayyid*.

As for the role and presence of women in Muslim societies, an interview I conducted with Sayyid Fadil Bahr al-'Ulum is helpful. He, too, is a member of a long-established 'Alid family of Najaf.[42] Bahr al-'Ulum related the long-established preference of his family for the Kashif al-Ghita', a prestigious non-'Alid family of the Shi'i religious establishment of Iraq. He quoted his mother, who always insisted that the Bahr al-'Ulum could only marry members of this family. In this case, a strategy is acknowledged by an insider, as is the role of women in carrying it out.

In analysing Fadil Bahr al-'Ulum's information, I suggest a possible further role reserved for women. It can be argued that in the case of the 'Alids, women perform the critical role of memory collectors, transmitters and protectors of the family lineage and the privileges that it brings to them. The relevance of women who "surround a great man and then report on his words and deeds" in a society heavily reliant on orally transmitted information has been noted.[43] This role may even be enhanced by the fact that, as my biographical data about the al-Sadr suggest, family members who rise in prominence are frequently those who were still young when their fathers died,[44] therefore giving mothers an essential role as keepers of memory.

In conclusion, my data suggest that in recent times the al-Sadr family has followed a strategy of endogamy involving both the Family of the Prophet (Ahl al-Bayt) and non-'Alid members of the Shi'i religious establishment. There seems to be a preference for intra-family and inter-'Alid marriages, but marriages with non-'Alids occur when prominent members of the religious establishment or the wealthy[45] within the local elite are not *sayyids*.

My data indicates that the families with whom members of the al-Sadr family have established marriage bonds are very important for defining the social status of the al-Sadr. My interviews with members of the al-Sadr family suggest that their memory of genealogy is not only focused vertically, that is to say on the family's distant ancestors, but that it is equally nourished horizontally by bonds established with eminent families with whom they are allied. Moreover, it is precisely in the links created through their marriage alliances and in the (relevant oral) memory of these links that we find an explanation for the impressive resilience of the al-Sadr family (and the 'Alids in general). In this respect, the data about the al-Sadr also appear to suggest that male biological kinship alone provides an insufficient basis on which to build nobility. A significant number of the most religiously and politically important male members both of the al-Sadr family and of the 'Alid families allied with it appear to require the right sort of biological affiliation as the basis for an appropriate social affiliation. Their position is strengthened when they marry women who can provide children with the claim to social, religious and political prominence.

My data also suggests that 'Alid women attract much stronger disapproval than men do for marrying beneath their rank. On the other hand, as may be expected in a Muslim context, my sources do not believe it possible for the daughters of 'Alids to remain unmarried. Although we do find the case of Sayyida Amina al-Sadr (1937–80?), who did not get married, my interviews with women of the family clearly indicated that celibacy is still perceived in negative terms,[46] and this probably also explains why we encounter among the 'Alids marriage strategies that are less restrictive than expected.

Finally, contemporary prosopographical works, in particular the recent memoirs of 'Alid women – and, to a lesser extent, single-figure biographies dedicated to women scholars and oral sources internal to the Family of the Prophet – appear to be essential in providing elements that can be considered new or at least capable of offering more comprehensive perspectives on the dynamics internal to the lives of the Prophet's descendants and to the religious, political and social elites currently leading the Shi'i societies of the Middle East.

Table 9.1 Marriages involving Members of the al-Sadr Family

Bride	Groom
Daughter of Sayyid Husayn al-Musawi al-'Amili al-Juba'i (1500 or 1501–55 or 1556)[47]	Shaykh Zayn al-Din al-'Amili, known as al-Shahid al-Thani (1506–58)[48]
Daughter of al-Shahid al-Thani (*bint khāla*)	Sayyid Nur al-Din 'Ali al-Musawi al-'Amili al-Juba'i (1524 or 1525–90 or 1591)[49]
Daughter of Sayyid Muhammad Baqir al-Sabzivari (d. 1679)	Sayyid Muhammad Sharaf al-Din (1639 or 1640–1726 or 1727)[50]
Daughter of Shaykh (Muhammad ibn Hasan) al-Hurr al-'Amili (1623 or 1624–92 or 1693)	Sayyid Muhammad Sharaf al-Din[51]
Daughter of Shaykh 'Ali Muhyi al-Din al-'Amili, grandson of a grandson of al-Shahid al-Thani	Sayyid Salih Sharaf al-Din (1710 or 1711–c. 1803)[52]
Daughter of Ayatollah Shaykh Ja'far Kashif al-Ghita' (1743–1812)	Sayyid Sadr al-Din Muhammad Sharaf al-Din (1779–1847)[53]
Widow of Sayyid Sharif Sharaf al-Din (1881–1917), brother of 'Abd al-Husayn Sharaf al-Din	Ayatollah Sayyid 'Abd al-Husayn Sharaf al-Din (1873–1957)[54]
Female member of the Al Yasin family (*bint khāla*)	Ayatollah al-'Uzma Sayyid Sadr al-Din al-Sadr (1882–1954)[55]
Safiyya al-Tabataba'i al-Qummi, daughter of Ayatollah Sayyid Husayn al-Tabataba'i al-Qummi (1865–1947)	Ayatollah al-'Uzma Sayyid Sadr al-Din al-Sadr[56]
Female member of the Al Yasin family	Ayatollah Sayyid Isma'il al-Sadr (1842–1920)[57]
Four daughters of Ayatollah Shaykh 'Abd al-Husayn Al Yasin (d. 1932) (*bint khāla*)	Four sons of Ayatollah Sayyid Isma'il al-Sadr[58]
Only daughter of Ayatollah Sayyid Isma'il al-Sadr	Son of Ayatollah al-'Uzma Shaykh Muhammad Reza Al Yasin (d. 1950) (*ibn khāla*)[59]

Bride	Groom
Daughter of Ayatollah al-'Uzma Shaykh Muhammad Reza Al Yasin	Sayyid Muhammad Sadiq al-Sadr (1906–86)[60]
Parvin Khalili, daughter of Ayatollah Shaykh 'Aziz Allah Khalili (son of Mirza Husayn Khalili Tihrani)	Ayatollah Sayyid Musa al-Sadr (1928–78?)[61]
Granddaughter of Ayatollah al-'Uzma Sayyid Ruhollah Khomeini (1902–89)	Son of Sayyid Musa al-Sadr (according to a secondary source)[62]
Sayyida Fatima al-Sadr	Ayatollah al-'Uzma Sayyid Muhammad Baqir al-Sadr (1935–80) (*ibn 'amm*)[63]
Sayyida Amina al-Sadr (1937–80?)	Did not marry[64]
Sayyida Zahra' al-Sadr (1939 or 1940–)	Shaykh Iskandar Fayruzan[65]
Daughter of Sayyid Muhammad Ja'far al-Sadr	Ayatollah al-'Uzma Sayyid Muhammad Muhammad Sadiq al-Sadr (1943–99) (*ibn 'amm*)[66]
Sayyida Hanan al-Sadr	Sayyid Husayn al-Sadr (1945–)[67]
Sayyida Fatima al-Sadr (1946–)	Dr Sayyid Sadiq al-Sultani al-Tabataba'i (1943–) (*ibn khāla*), son of Ayatollah Sayyid Muhammad Baqir al-Sultani al-Tabataba'i (1919 or 1920–97 or 1998) and Sayyida Sadiqa al-Sadr (1924 or 1925–2004 or 2005)[68]
Zuhri Sadiqi (1950 or 1951–), daughter of Ayatollah Dr Shaykh 'Ali Akbar Sadiqi and Sayyida Mansura al-Sadr	Sayyid Muhammad Khatami (1943–)[69]
Sayyida Maram al-Sadr (*bint 'amm*)	Ayatollah al-'Uzma Sayyid Husayn al-Sadr (1952–)[70]
Dr Sayyida Fatima al-Sultani al-Tabataba'i (1954 or 1955–), daughter of Ayatollah Muhammad Baqir al-Sultani al-Tabataba'i and Sayyida Sadiqa al-Sadr	Sayyid Ahmad Khomeini, son of Ayatollah al-'Uzma Sayyid Ruhollah Khomeini (1902–89)[71]
Firishti A'rabi, daughter of Ayatollah Shaykh Muhammad Hasan A'rabifard and Sayyida Farida Khomeini	Sayyid Murtada al-Sultani al-Tabataba'i, son of Muhammad Baqir al-Sultani al-Tabataba'i and Sadiqa al-Sadr[72]
Layli Burujirdi, daughter of Shaykh Mahmud Burujirdi and Sayyida Zahra' Khomeini	Sayyid 'Abd al-Husayn al-Sultani al-Tabataba'i, son of Muhammad Baqir al-Sultani al-Tabataba'i and Sadiqa al-Sadr[73]
Sayyida Hawra' al-Sadr (1962–)	Shaykh Mahdi Fayruzan, son of Sayyida Zahra' al-Sadr and Shaykh Iskandar Fayruzan[74]

Bride	Groom
Sayyida 'Aliyya al-Sadr (1971 or 1972–)	Sayyid 'Abd al-'Aziz al-Hakim (1950–2009)[75]
Sayyida Maliha al-Sadr (1971–)	Sayyid Qusay Sharaf al-Din (1968–) (*ibn 'amma*)[76]
Sayyida Nubugh al-Sadr	Sayyid Mustafa al-Sadr (1964–99)[77]
Sayyida Hawra' al-Sadr, daughter of Sayyid Muhammad Baqir al-Sadr	Sayyid Mu'ammal al-Sadr (1971–99)[78]
Sayyida Asma' al-Sadr	Sayyid Muqtada al-Sadr (1974?–)[79]
Two daughters of Ayatollah al-'Uzma Sayyid Muhammad Muhammad Sadiq al-Sadr	Sayyid Dhiya' Kalantar and Sayyid Sultan Kalantar, sons of Ayatollah Sayyid Muhammad Kalantar[80]
Zahra' Ishraqi, daughter of Ayatollah Shaykh Shahab al-Din Ishraqi and Sayyida Sadiqa Khomeini	Dr Sayyid Muhammad Reza Khatami[81]
Sayyida Hawra' al-Sadr (1984 or 1985–)	Sayyid Yasir Khomeini[82]

NOTES

1. There is an endless bibliography on this issue. In writing this chapter, I particularly referred to A. Molho, *Marriage Alliance in Late Medieval Florence*, Cambridge, MA: Harvard University Press, 1994, in particular p. 13; J. J. Hurwich, "Marriage Strategy among the German Nobility, 1400–1699", *Journal of Interdisciplinary History*, vol. 29, no. 2, autumn 1998, pp. 169–95, in particular p. 190; P. H. Fleming, "The Politics of Marriage among Non-Catholic European Royalty", *Current Anthropology*, vol. 14, no. 3, June 1973, pp. 231–49, in particular pp. 232, 238 (while this article, originally written in 1967, is dated, it is of particular interest because of the wide range of families discussed and because on pp. 243–8 it contains comments on the paper by scholars plus a long reply by the author); J. Dewald, *The European Nobility, 1400–1800*, Cambridge: Cambridge University Press, 1996, p. 169; and G. Butaud and V. Piétri, *Les enjeux de la généalogie (XIIᵉ–XVIIIᵉ siècle): Pouvoir et identité*, Paris: Éditions Autrement, 2006, in particular p. 15.
2. More precisely, an 'Alid Husaynid Fatimid branch. For a perspective on this issue, see F. Daftary, *The Isma'ilis, Their History and Doctrines*, 2nd edn, Cambridge: Cambridge University Press, 2007, pp. 57–93.
3. I prefer this locution to the term "cleric" as, in my opinion, it reflects more properly the legal and social role of the 'ulama' in Muslim societies. Moreover, it should be borne in mind that there is not necessarily a "natural link", at least historically, between 'Alids and the 'ulama'.
4. For the concept of prosopography, see G. Beech, "Prosopography", in J. M. Powell (ed.), *Medieval Studies: An Introduction*, Syracuse, NY: Syracuse University Press, 1976, pp. 151–84 and L. Stone, "Prosopography", in *The Past and the Present Revisited*, revised edn, London: Routledge, 1987, pp. 45–73.

5. This is exemplified by the major contribution of Ayatollah al-'Uzma Sayyid Abu l-Qasim al-Khu'i to the field of *'ilm al-rijāl* (a biographical genre that examines the reliability of hadith transmitters): *Mu'jam rijal al-hadith wa-tafsil tabaqat al-ruwat*, in twenty-four volumes. This can be considered al-Khu'i's major literary work, at least for its extent and the time required for its completion. It is currently the main reference work for teaching *'ilm al-rijāl* in the *ḥawza 'ilmiyya* (traditional Shi'i seminary).

6. In this respect, see some websites linked to the al-Sadr family: www.imamsadr.net, http://imamsadr.ir, www.imam-moussa.com, www.revayatesadr.ir, www.alsader.org, www.mbsadr.com, www.husseinalsader.net, www.alsadronline.net (all still active when I last accessed them on 3 June 2011). Very interesting and characteristic is also a rich section of the website of the Imam Reza (A.S.) Network dedicated to the history of Hashimite prominent families (www.imamreza.net/arb/list.php?id=129), which was still active when accessed on 3 June 2011.

7. A. al-Baqshi, *Waja' al-Sadr*, Qom: Ijtihad, 1386 [SH/1427 AH/2007]. (Here and subsequently, dates in the solar hijri calendar are denoted by SH.)

8. In Shi'i religious literature, descendants of the Prophet carry the Arabic honorific "*sayyid*" (fem. *sayyida*), a word that currently in the Arab world is generally used as an equivalent of "Mr". On the other hand, leading 'ulama', particularly those who do not have 'Alid descent, are sometimes designated with the honorific "shaykh", a word generally used in the Arab world to designate tribal leaders.

9. Sometimes alteratively named *marja'*, this title refers to a religious scholar who is qualified to be followed in religious practice and matters of law by Shi'i believers.

10. On this figure, see F. Ajami, *The Vanished Imam: Musa Al Sadr and the Shia of Lebanon*, London: I. B. Tauris, 1986.

11. On this figure, see Ch. Mallat, *The Renewal of Islamic Law: Muhammad Baqer as-Sadr, Najaf and the Shi'i International*, Cambridge: Cambridge University Press, 1993.

12. On this figure, see P. Cockburn, *Muqtada Al-Sadr and the Fall of Iraq*, London: Faber and Faber, 2008.

13. It is interesting that, to the best of my knowledge, there is only one other work of this kind that is authored by an 'Alid woman: *Iqlim-i Khatirat* by Dr Sayyida Fatima al-Sultani al-Tabataba'i (1954 or 1955–), whose mother, Sayyida Sadiqa al-Sadr, was herself a member of the al-Sadr family. The book, published in Tehran by Pijuhishkadih-i Imam Khumayni–Mu'assasi-yi Tanzim va Nashr-i Athar-i Imam Khumayni in the spring of 2011, includes Fatima's memories related to the years from 1347 SH/1968–9 to 1357 SH/1978–9. In general, the pattern of "women narrating women" has appeared in the late nineteenth century and has been described as "exclusive", in that these works featured only women. See R. Roded, *Women in Islamic Biographical Collections: From Ibn Sa'd to Who's Who*, Boulder, CO: Lynne Rienner, 1994, p. 7. Several works have also appeared with men narrating (only) women's lives. Among them, Abu 'Abd al-Rahman al-Sulami (d. 412/1021), *Dhikr al-nisa' al-muta'abbidat al-sufiyyat*, a work that was first translated into English by a woman, Rkia E. Cornell, as *Early Sufi Women*, Louisville, KY: Fons Vitae, 1999, and then into Persian by another woman, Dr Maryam Hosseini, as *Nukhustin Zanan-i Sufi*, Tehran: Ilm, 1385 [SH/2006].

14. Such is the case of Shaykh M. R. al-Nu'mani, *al-Shahida Bint al-Huda, siratuha*

wa-masiratuha, Qom: Mu'assasa Isma'iliyan, 1378 [SH/1420 AH/2000], and 'A. K. Muhammad, *al-Shahida Bint al-Huda: al-Sira wa-l-masira*, Beirut: Dar al-Murtaza, 2004 [1425]. On Bint al-Huda, see J. Wiley, "'Alima Bint al-Huda, Women's Advocate", in S. L. Walbridge (ed.), *The Most Learned of the Shi'a: The Institution of the Marja' Taqlid*, Oxford: Oxford University Press, 2001, pp. 149–60, and Mallat, "Le féminisme islamique de Bint al-Houdâ", *Maghreb Machrek*, no. 116, 1987, pp. 45–58.

15. On oral history criteria, see the "General Principles" established by the Oral History Association (www.oralhistory.org, in particular the section "Principles and Best Practices"). For a definition of oral history sources, see J. Vansina, "Tradición oral, historia oral: Logros y perspectivas", *Historia, Antropología y Fuentes Orales*, no. 37, 2007, pp. 151–63. Some of the information provided by my oral sources falls more properly within the definition of oral traditions, that is, of "memorias colectivas del pasado". These are different from oral history proper in that they are "relatos transmitidos de boca en boca a futuras generaciones" (Vansina, p. 151). Other information I collected, including what I received from Sayyid Fadil Bahr al-'Ulum, should more correctly be considered "tradiciones superficiales informales" (Vansina, p. 157). The interviews took place from 2006 to 2010.

16. R. Fox, *Kinship and Marriage: An Anthropological Perspective*, Cambridge: Cambridge University Press, 1983, pp. 122–5.

17. G. Bell, *The Letters of Gertrude Bell*, vol. 2, ed. F. Bell, London: Ernest Benn, 1927, pp. 483–4.

18. The biographical information provided here is part of voluminous data I collected in a bio-bibliographical dictionary, covering about 160 figures, as part of my PhD thesis, "'Najafi' Shi'a Alids in Contemporary Islamic History through Prosopographic Sources", defended at the Dipartimento di Studi Orientali, Sapienza Università di Roma, in September 2009.

19. According to Rubab al-Sadr (27 May 2010) and Hawra' al-Sadr (April 2010), this marriage was requested by Sharif Sharaf al-Din himself in order to secure a safe future for his children.

20. This is demonstrated by the cases of Husayn al-Sadr, Husayn (ibn Muhammad al-Hadi) al-Sadr, Muhammad Baqir al-Sadr, Muhammad Muhammad Sadiq al-Sadr, Mustafa al-Sadr, Muqtada al-Sadr and Mu'ammal al-Sadr.

21. This element is proven by the cases of Husayn al-Sadr, Muhammad Baqir al-Sadr and Muhammad Muhammad Sadiq al-Sadr. On the relevance of this marriage pattern in Middle Eastern societies, see D. F. Eickelman, *The Middle East and Central Asia: An Anthropological Approach*, 4th edn, Upper Saddle River, NJ: Prentice-Hall, 2001, pp. 163–6.

22. J. Bestard, *Parentesco y modernidad*, Barcelona: Paidós, 1998, pp. 119–21.

23. Sayyid M. K. al-Qazvini, *Zindigani Hadhrat-i Zaynab az Viladat ta Shahadat*, trans. from Arabic by M. Iskandari, Tehran: Siyam, 2009 [1388 SH], pp. 55–7.

24. A. R. Lalani, *Early Shī'ī Thought: The Teachings of Imam Muḥammad al-Bāqir*, London: I. B. Tauris, 2004, p. 37.

25. Al-Qazvini, *Zindigani Hadhrat-i Zaynab*, p. 55.

26. Th. P. Wright Jr, "The Changing Role of the *Sādāt* in India and Pakistan", in B. Scarcia Amoretti and L. Bottini (eds), "The Role of the *Sādāt/Ašrāf* in Muslim

History and Civilization", special issue of *Oriente Moderno*, n.s., vol. 18 (79), no. 2, 1999, pp. 649–59, at p. 653. Although the reference to India and Pakistan may appear misleading, in fact, as I stated at the beginning of this chapter, my intention is to address the marriage policy of the Ahl al-Bayt in general; therefore, the case study of the 'Alid branch of the Family represented by the al-Sadr should be seen as a starting point for further investigations – and wider perspectives – on the Family of the Prophet in the entire Islamic ecumene.

27. N. J. Coulson, *Conflicts and Tensions in Islamic Jurisprudence*, Chicago: University of Chicago Press, 1969, pp. 31–3. For an analysis of these specificities within the framework of Iranian society, see N. R. Keddie and P. Paidar, "Sexuality and Shi'i Social Protest in Iran", in Keddie (ed.), *Women in the Middle East: Past and Present*, Princeton, NJ: Princeton University Press, 2007, pp. 297–323, particularly pp. 300–8.

28. E. J. Tucker, *Women, Family, and Gender in Islamic Law*, Cambridge: Cambridge University Press, 2008, p. 139.

29. For an interesting analysis of the link between *baraka* and charismatic leadership in a Muslim context, see F. F. Jacobsen, *Hadrami Arabs in Present-day Indonesia*, London: Routledge, 2009, pp. 95–113.

30. We have a direct link provided by the marriage of Zuhri Sadiqi, a daughter of Mansura al-Sadr, to Muhammad Khatami, and an indirect link provided by the marriage of Zahra' Ishraqi (a daughter of Sayyida Sadiqa Khomeini) to Muhammad Reza Khatami.

31. 'A. Ra'uf, *Marja'iyyat al-maydan Muhammad Muhammad Sadiq al-Sadr: Mashru'uhu al-taghyiri wa-waqa'i' al-ightiyal*, Damascus: al-Markaz al-'Iraqi li-l-I'lam wa-l-Dirasat, 1999, p. 74.

32. Anthropologists have hypothesised that in Middle Eastern societies the power of *baraka* "may, to some extent, be inherited" (Jacobsen, *Hadrami Arabs*, p. 107). Similarly – and with reference to the interrelation between purity of blood, mystical power and endogamic marriages within the Ahl al-Bayt – in the case of European royalty, "the belief in the mystical power of royalty, expressed in terms of purity of blood and symbolised in the belief in the healing power of a monarch's touch, has generally precluded marriage with nonroyal persons, even those from wealthy and powerful families" (Fleming, "The Politics of Marriage", p. 242).

33. The strength of this element was recognised by a large number of my interviewees, for example by Sayyid Jawad al-Khu'i (a grandson of the late Ayatollah Sayyid Abu l-Qasim al-Khu'i and a member of an important 'Alid family of Najaf), who affirmed that Muqtada's popular support in Iraq was due precisely to his claimed link with the role played by Muhammad Baqir al-Sadr (interview in al-Khu'i's house in Qom, March 2008).

34. "Blueblood Shia Cleric Comments on 'Backward' Sadrists and Sistani's Fears and Frustrations", confidential cable from US Embassy in Baghdad (31 January 2008); published online on 5 December 2010 and accessed 3 June 2011 at www.wikileaks. org, ref. 08BAGHDAD293.

35. As M. Litvak has shown, as early as the eighteenth century we have cases of this kind of marriage within the Shi'i religious establishment of Najaf and Karbala; Litvak, *Shi'i Scholars of Nineteenth-Century Iraq: The 'Ulama' of Najaf and Karbala'*, Cambridge: Cambridge University Press, 1998, p. 46.

36. Cases in point are Muhammad Sharaf al-Din (1639 or 1640–1726 or 1727), who married a daughter of Sayyid Muhammad Baqir al-Sabzivari and a daughter of Shaykh Muhammad al-Hurr al-'Amili (d. 1693); Sadr al-Din al-Sadr (1882–1954), who married a daughter of Sayyid Husayn al-Tabataba'i al-Qummi (1865–1947); Musa al-Sadr (1928–78?), who married a daughter of Shaykh 'Aziz Allah Khalil Tihrani; and Sadr al-Din Muhammad Sharaf al-Din (1779–1847), who married a daughter of Shaykh Ja'far Kashif al-Ghita' (1743–1812). Moreover, the last link was enhanced and kept through master–disciple relationships, such as the one between Sadr al-Din Muhammad Sharaf al-Din and the same Ja'far Kashif al-Ghita', and between Isma'il al-Sadr (1842–1920) and Shaykh Mahdi Kashif al-Ghita' (d. 1872). It is important to mention that the relevance of this marriage pattern in my data may prove to be partly misleading and caused by the specific orientation and purpose of most of my prosopographical sources. On the other hand, this pattern has been indicated as relevant in the religious establishment of Najaf and Karbala during the period from 1791 to 1904 (Litvak, *Shi'i Scholars of Nineteenth-Century Iraq*, pp. 158, 46).

37. Interview in his office at the Institute for Political and International Studies of the Iranian Ministry of Foreign Affairs (Tehran, 17 May 2011).

38. Three marriages: Husayn al-Musawi al-'Amili's daughter and al-Shahid al-Thani; 'Ali al-Musawi al-'Amili al-Juba'i and the widowed daughter of al-Shahid al-Thani; Salih Sharaf al-Din (1710 or 1711–c. 1803) and the daughter of Shaykh 'Ali ibn Muhyi al-Din, a grandson of a grandson of al-Shahid al-Thani.

39. Two marriages: one between Sayyid Haydar al-Sadr (1891–1937) and the daughter of Shaykh 'Abd al-Husayn Al Yasin, and the other between Sayyid Muhammad Sadiq al-Sadr (1906–86) and a daughter of Shaykh Muhammad Reza Al Yasin (d. 1950). Moreover, the tie with the Al Yasin was strengthened through master–disciple relationships, such as the one between Isma'il al-Sadr (1842–1920) and Shaykh 'Abd al-Husayn (d. 1932) and Muhammad Reza Al Yasin (d. 1950).

40. Roded writes that "although male kinship was of primary importance, female kinship was not ignored and in certain cases was crucial. ... Moreover, the semimatrilineal ascription by blood is paralleled to some extent by a similar phenomenon in the lineage of knowledge. The evidence we have strongly suggests that social prestige was transmitted through women as well as through men" (*Women in Islamic Biographical Collections*, p. 12).

41. Interview at the Imam Ali Foundation in London, April 2008. A son-in-law of Ayatollah al-Khu'i, al-Khalkhali is the official representative of Ayatollah Sayyid 'Ali Sistani in Great Britain.

42. London, 2006. Bahr al-'Ulum is the director of the Alsalam Foundation in London, an umbrella organisation that runs the Centre for Islamic Shi'a Studies (CISS), the Alulbayt School and the Iraqi Development Organization. Fadil is a Bahr al-'Ulum on both his father's and his mother's side.

43. Roded, *Women in Islamic Biographical Collections*, p. 11.

44. Cases of Muhammad Baqir al-Sadr, Amina Bint al-Huda and Muqtada al-Sadr.

45. Cases in point are the marriages between Zahra' al-Sadr and Iskandar Fayruzan, and between their son Mahdi and Hawra' al-Sadr.

46. Interview with Fatima bint Mahdi al-Sadr (1946–), Tehran, May 2010.

47. Throughout the table, the birth and death dates pertain to the immediately preceding named individual.

48. M. al-Amin al-'Amili, *A'yan al-Shi'a*, Beirut: Dar al-Ta'aruf li-l-Matbu'at, 1983, vol. 5, pp. 415–16, and vol. 6, p. 151.

49. Al-'Amili, *A'yan al-Shi'a*, vol. 8, p. 188; H. al-Kazimi al-'Amili al-Sadr, *Takmilat amal al-amil*, Beirut: Dar al-Adwa', 1986 [1407], pp. 289–90; al-'Amili, *A'yan al-Shi'a*, vol. 10, Beirut: Dar al-Adwa', 1986, pp. 6–7. On the problematic identification of Nur al-Din 'Ali ibn Husayn al-Musawi al-'Amili al-Juba'i, see M. Salati, "Presence and Role of the *Sādāt* in and from Ǧabal 'Āmil (14th–18th Centuries)", in Scarcia Amoretti and Bottini (eds), *The Role of the* Sādāt/Ašrāf *in Muslim History and Civilization*, pp. 597–627, at p. 617.

50. Al-'Amili, *A'yan al-Shi'a*, vol. 9, (1986 edn), pp. 59–60; al-'Amili al-Sadr, *Takmila*, pp. 335–7; 'A. H. Sharaf al-Din (with 'A. A. Sharaf al-Din), *Bughiyat al-raghibin fi silsilat Al Sharaf al-Din: Ta'rikh ajyal fi ta'rikh rijal; Kitab nasab wa-ta'rikh wa-tarajim*, vol. 1, Beirut: al-Dar al-Islamiyya, 1991 [1411], p. 624.

51. See the references in the immediately preceding note. This marriage took place after the death of Sharaf al-Din's first wife (see row above).

52. K. al-Husayni al-Ha'iri, "Tarjamat hayat al-Sayyid al-Shahid", in Ayatollah al-'Uzma Sayyid K. al-Husayni al-Ha'iri (ed.), *Mabahith al-usul: Taqrir li-abhath samaha Ayatollah al-'Uzma al-Shahid al-Sayyid Muhammad Baqir al-Sadr*, vol. 2, part 1, Qom: Markaz al-Nashr, 1987 [1407], pp. 11–168, at p. 16, and 'A. H. Sharaf al-Din, *Bughiyat al-raghibin*, vol. 1, p. 147.

53. Al-Ha'iri, "Tarjamat hayat al-Sayyid al-Shahid", pp. 16–20; al-Baqshi, *Waja' al-Sadr*, pp. 42–4. I also consulted two biographies available online: http://alsadrsite.com/sadraldeengrand.html (accessed on 8 December 2007) and http://alsadrsite.com/mosa.html, section on *al-sira* (biography) of Musa al-Sadr (accessed on 8 December 2007).

54. Several interviews with members of the al-Sadr and Sharaf al-Din families.

55. Al-Baqshi, *Waja' al-Sadr*, p. 53.

56. Al-Baqshi, *Waja' al-Sadr*, pp. 49–52, and H. E. Chehabi and M. Tafreshi, "Musa Sadr and Iran", in H. E. Chehabi (ed.), *Distant Relations: Iran and Lebanon in the Last 500 Years*, Oxford: Centre for Lebanese Studies and I. B. Tauris, 2006, p. 139. Al-Baqshi, *Waja' al-Sadr*, p. 53 reports that this marriage took place after the death of al-Sadr's first wife.

57. Al-Baqshi, *Waja' al-Sadr*, p. 48.

58. Al-Baqshi, *Waja' al-Sadr*, p. 48. One of these daughters, Batul Al Yasin, married Ayatollah Sayyid Haydar al-Sadr (1891–1937); see al-Ha'iri, "Tarjamat hayat al-Sayyid al-Shahid", pp. 26–30, and Wiley, "'Alima Bint al-Huda", p. 159, n. 14.

59. Al-Baqshi, *Waja' al-Sadr*, p. 48.

60. M. al-Asadi, *al-Sadr al-Thani, al-Shahid wa-l-Shahid*, London: Mu'assasat al-A'raf, 1999 [1420], and P. Cockburn, *Muqtada al-Sadr and the Fall of Iraq*, London: Faber and Faber, 2008, p. 100.

61. 'A. R. Abadari, *Imam Musa Sadr, Umid-i Mahruman*, Tehran: Javani-yi Rushd, 2001–2 [1381 SH], pp. 28–9. The father of 'Aziz Allah, Mirza Husayn Khalil Tihrani, was among the 'ulama' who shared the leadership of the Shi'i community following the death of Mirza-i Shirazi (d. 1895), and he was one of the three strongest supporters

of the Iranian constitutional movement in the early years of the twentieth century.

62. M. Lotfi, "Musa al Sadr: The Untold Story", *Asharq alawsat* (English edition), online, 31 May 2008 (www.asharq-e.com/news.asp?section=3&id=12930, accessed on 5 June 2011). This information was in fact denied by Hawra' al-Sadr in several interviews at her office in Tehran (April–June 2010).

63. Al-Ha'iri, "Tarjamat hayat al-Sayyid al-Shahid", p. 85, and F. Ajami, *The Vanished Imam: Musa al Sadr and the Shia of Lebanon*, Ithaca, NY: Cornell University Press, 1987, p. 25.

64. Al-Nu'mani, *al-Shahida Bint al-Huda*.

65. Several interviews with Hawra' al-Sadr in Tehran (April–June 2010). Fayruzan was a wealthy merchant of Qom.

66. Al-Asadi, *al-Sadr al-Thani*, p. 27.

67. Interview with Ghanim Jawad at the Khoei Foundation in London (10 April 2008).

68. Interview with Fatima al-Sadr (1946–) at the Mu'assasa-yi Farhangi Tahqiqati-yi Imam Musa Sadr in Tehran (11 May 2010). Sadiq Tabataba'i is a former speaker of the first (temporary) post-revolutionary government of the Islamic Republic of Iran.

69. Interview with Zuhri Sadiqi at the Bih Afarin-i Farda Foundation in Tehran (15 May 2011). Chehabi and Tafreshi ("Musa Sadr and Iran", pp. 143–4) mention that two nieces (the daughters of two sisters) of Musa al-Sadr married Muhammad Khatami and Ahmad Khomeini, but they do not mention the names of the two brides. Muhammad Khatami (1943–) is a former president of the Islamic Republic of Iran.

70. Answer to a small set of written questions I submitted to Husayn al-Sadr on 2 November 2007 through Ghanim Jawad.

71. S. Tabataba'i, *Khatirat-i siyasi-ijtima'i Duktur Sadiq Tabataba'i*, vol. 1, 2nd edn, Tehran: Mu'assasi-yi Tanzim va Nashr-i Athar-i Imam Khumayni–Chap va Nashr-i 'Uruj, 2008–9 [1388 SH], p. 10.

72. Ibid.

73. Ibid.

74. Interview with Hawra' al-Sadr and Mahdi Fayruzan (June 2010). Mahdi Fayruzan is a general director at Shahr-i Kitab, Iran's leading publishing house and book retailer.

75. Interviews at the Mu'assasa-yi Farhangi Tahqiqati-yi Imam Musa Sadr in Tehran (June 2010). 'Abd al-Aziz was a son of Sayyid Muhsin al-Hakim (1889–1970), the most important *marja'* in Iraq in the 1960s. A son of the couple, 'Ammar, is the leader of al-Majlis al-A'la al-Islami al-'Iraqi, one of the most important political and religious organisations in post-Saddam Iraq.

76. Personal communications by Rubab al-Sadr (oral) and Hawra' al-Sadr (written).

77. 'A. al-Zaydi Mayahi, *al-Safir al-khamis*, Beirut: Mumaththiliyyat al-Marja' al-Shahid al-Sayyid Muhammad al-Sadr fi Bayrut, 2001, pp. 243, 249; al-Baqshi, *Waja' al-Sadr*, p. 250; Cockburn, *Muqtada al-Sadr*, p. 103; and several interviews with Hawra' al-Sadr, Tehran, April–June 2010.

78. Ibid. Cockburn, who maintains that his information was provided by Ja'far al-Sadr, reports the years in which the marriages took place but does not specify who married whom. As for *Waja' al-Sadr*, this source does not mention the names of the brides, but it reports that the wife of Mustafa al-Sadr is known as "Umm Ahmad" while the wife of Mu'ammal is known as "Umm 'Ali".

79. M. al-Nuri al-Musawi, *al-Sayyid Muqtada al-Sadr: Sadr al-'Iraq al-thalith; Ahdafuhu, mawaqifuhu, mashru'uhu*, Beirut: Markaz Wali Allah li-l-Dirasat wa-l-Tawzi' wa-l-Irshad, 2004 [1425], p. 19, and several interviews with Hawra' al-Sadr (Tehran, April–June 2010).

80. Al-Asadi, *al-Sadr al-Thani*, p. 27, and "Blueblood Shia Cleric Comments" (cable). The names of the Kalantar were mentioned by one of my oral sources. This source also pointed out that Muhammad Kalantar had married a daughter of Sayyid 'Abd al-Mahdi al-Shirazi and that another daughter of al-Shirazi was the wife of Ayatollah al-'Uzma Sistani.

81. This information was confirmed by Hawra' al-Sadr during several interviews at her office in Tehran (April–June 2010). Muhammad Reza is Muhammad Khatami's younger brother and a former deputy speaker of parliament in the Islamic Republic of Iran.

82. Interview with Muhammad al-Sadr (1951–) at the Institute for Political and International Studies of the Iranian Ministry of Foreign Affairs (Tehran, 17 May 2011).

About the Contributors

Helena de Felipe is a senior lecturer in the Department of Modern Philology, Universidad de Alcalá, Spain. Her publications include *Identidad y onomástica de los bereberes de al-Andalus* (1997); co-edited with F. Rodríguez Mediano, *El Protectorado español en Marruecos: Gestión colonial e identidades* (2002); and, co-edited with L. Sánchez Ocón and M. Marín, *Ángel Cabrera: Ciencia y proyecto colonial en Marruecos* (2004). She is the author of several articles and books chapters on Berbers in the medieval period.

Fred M. Donner is a professor of near eastern history in the Oriental Institute and Department of Near Eastern Languages and Civilizations at the University of Chicago, and is the director of the university's Center for Middle Eastern Studies. His books include *The Early Islamic Conquests* (1981), *Narratives of Islamic Origins: The Beginnings of Islamic Historical Writing* (1998) and *Muhammad and the Believers: At the Origins of Islam* (2010), as well as volume 10, "The Conquest of Arabia", in the translation of *The History of al-Tabari* (1993). He is the editor of *The Expansion of the Early Islamic State* (2008) and *The Articulation of Early Islamic State Structures* (2012) and the author of numerous articles on early Islamic history, Islamic historiography and Qur'anic studies.

Maribel Fierro is a research professor at the Centre for Human and Social Sciences (CCHS) of the Consejo Superior de Investigaciones Científicas (CSIC) in Madrid. She has authored many articles on the history of the Islamic West (especially al-Andalus), Islamic law, heresy and the transmission of knowledge, and she has also edited and translated an early treatise by Ibn Waddah al-Qurtubi, *Kitab al-bida'* (1988), authored *Abd al-Rahman III: The First Cordoban Caliph* (2005) and, together with P. Cressier and L. Molina, edited *Los almohades: Problemas y perspectivas* (2005).

Raffaele Mauriello PhD is a researcher of the contemporary history and geopolitics of Shiʻa Islam and a translator of Arabic and Persian. His essays have appeared in journals such as *Iranian Review of Foreign Affairs, Outre-terre: Revue européenne de géopolitique*, and *Limes: Rivista italiana di geopolitica*. In 2013, he was awarded the World Prize for the Book of the Year by the Islamic Republic of Iran in the field of Islamic studies for his monograph *Descendants of the Family of the Prophet in Contemporary History: A Case Study, the Šīʻī Religious Establishment of al-Nağaf (Iraq)* (2011).

Kazuo Morimoto is an associate professor at the Institute for Advanced Studies on Asia, University of Tokyo. His publications in English include *Sayyids and Sharifs in Muslim Societies: The Living Links to the Prophet*, edited volume (2013). In Japanese, he has authored *Seinaru Kazoku: Muhanmado Ichizoku (The Holy Family of Islam: The Kinsfolk of Muhammad)* (2010) and he has edited *Perushiago ga Musunda Sekai: Mo Hitotsu no Yurashiashi (The World Tied by the Persian Language: A New Framework for Eurasian History)* (2009).

Zakaria Rhani is an assistant professor at the Institut Universitaire de la Recherche Scientifique, Université Mohamed V-Souisi (Rabat). He is the author of *Le pouvoir de guérir. Mythe, mystique et politique au Maroc* (forthcoming). He has also published numerous articles in Arabic, English and French in journals and in edited books.

Sarah Bowen Savant is an associate professor at the Institute for the Study of Muslim Civilisations, Aga Khan University, London. She has published articles on Persians and early Islamic historiography in journals and in edited volumes. She is the author of *The New Muslims of Post-Conquest Iran: Tradition, Memory, and Conversion* (2013).

Judith Scheele, a social anthropologist, is a postdoctoral research fellow at All Souls College, Oxford. Her doctorate focused on notions of knowledge, political legitimacy and community in Kabylia, Algeria. Her current research investigates trans-Saharan connections of all kinds, including legal and illegal trade, migration and scholarly links, with particular emphasis on southern Algeria, northern Mali, and, more recently, northern Chad. Her publications include *Village Matters: Knowledge, Politics and Community in Kabylia* (2009), *Smugglers and Saints of the Sahara: Regional Connectivity in the Twentieth Century* (2012) and various related book chapters and articles.

Zoltán Szombathy teaches at the Department of Arabic Studies, Eotvos Lorand University, Budapest. He has published numerous articles in both English and Hungarian, in addition to *The Roots of Arabic Genealogy: A Study in Historical Anthropology* (2003) and an edition of two manuscripts under the title *The History of Bidyini and Kaabu: Two Chronicles in Arabic from Guinea-Bissau* (2007).

Index